THE FABER LIBRARY   I

*by the same author*

The Complete Memoirs of George Sherston
Memoirs of a Fox-hunting Man
Sherston's Progress
Collected Poems 1908–56
Selected Poems
Siegfried's Journey 1916–20
The Old Century: And Seven More Years
The Weald of Youth

*edited by Rupert Hart-Davis*
War Poems of Siegfried Sassoon

# SIEGFRIED SASSOON

# Memoirs of
# an Infantry Officer

THE FABER LIBRARY

*faber and faber*

First published in 1930
by Faber and Faber Limited
3 Queen Square, London, WC1N 3AU

Faber Library edition first published in 1995

Photoset by Parker Typesetting Service, Leicester
Printed in England by Clays Ltd, St Ives plc

A CIP catalogue record for this book is
available from the British Library
ISBN 0-571-17651-8

2 4 6 8 10 9 7 5 3 1

# CONTENTS

# PART ONE
# AT THE ARMY SCHOOL

## I

I have said that Spring arrived late in 1916, and that up in the trenches opposite Mametz it seemed as though Winter would last for ever. I also stated that *as for me, I had more or less made up my mind to die* because *in the circumstances there didn't seem anything else to be done.* Well, we came back to Morlancourt after Easter, and on the same evening a message from the Orderly Room instructed me to proceed to the Fourth Army School next morning for a month's refresher-course. Perhaps Colonel Kinjack had heard that I'd been looking for trouble. Anyhow, my personal grievance against the Germans was interrupted for at least four weeks, and a motor-bus carried me away from all possibility of dying a murky death in the mine-craters.

Barton saw me off at the crossroads in the middle of the village. It was a fine day and he had recovered his good spirits. 'Lucky Kangaroo – to be hopping away for a holiday!' he exclaimed, as I climbed into the elderly bus. My servant Flook hoisted up my bulging valise, wiped his red face with his sleeve, and followed me to the roof. 'Mind and keep Mr. Sherston well polished up and punctual on parade, Flook!' said Barton. Flook grinned; and away we went. Looking back, I saw Barton's good-natured face, with the early sun shining on his glasses.

There were several of us on board (each Battalion in our Brigade was sending two officers) and we must have stopped at the next village to pick up a few more. But memory tries to misinform me that Flook and I were alone on that omnibus, with a fresh breeze in our faces and our minds 'making a separate peace' with the late April landscape. With sober satisfaction I watched a train moving out of a station with rumble and clank of wheels while we waited at the crossing gates. Children in a village street surprised me: I saw a little one fall, to be gathered, dusted, cuffed and cherished by its mother. Up in the line one somehow lost touch with such humanities.

The War was abundantly visible in supply-convoys, artillery horse-lines, in the dirty white tents of a Red Cross camp, or in troops going placidly to their billets. But everyone seemed to be off duty; spring had arrived and the fruit trees were in blossom; breezes ruffled the reedy pools and creeks along the Somme, and here and there a peaceful fisherman forgot that he was a soldier on active service. I had been in close contact with trench warfare, and here was a demonstration of its contrast with cosy civilian comfort. One has to find things out as one goes along, I thought; and I was wholeheartedly grateful for the green grass and a miller's wagon with four horses, and the spire of Amiens Cathedral rising above the congregated roofs of an undamaged city.

The Fourth Army School was at Flixécourt, a clean little town exactly halfway between Amiens and Abbeville. Between Flixécourt and the War (which for my locally experienced mind meant the Fricourt trenches) there were more than thirty English miles. Mentally, the distance became immeasurable during my first days at the School. Parades and lectures were all in the day's work, but they failed to convince me of their affinity with our long days and nights in the Front Line. For instance, although I was closely acquainted with the mine-craters in the Fricourt sector, I would have welcomed a few practical hints on how to patrol those God-forsaken cavities. But the Army school instructors were all in favour of Open Warfare, which was sure to come soon, they said. They had learnt all about it in peace-time; it was essential that we should be taught to 'think in terms of mobility'. So we solved tactical schemes in which the enemy was reported to have occupied some village several miles away, and with pencil and paper made arrangements for unflurried defence or blank-cartridged skirmishing in a land of field-day make-believe.

Sometimes a renowned big-game hunter gave us demonstrations of the art of sniping. He was genial and enthusiastic; but I was no good at rifle-shooting, and as far as I was concerned he would have been more profitably employed in reducing the numerical strength of the enemy. He was an expert on loopholes and telescopic-sights; but telescopic-sights were a luxury seldom enjoyed by an infantry battalion in the trenches.

The Commandant of the School was a tremendous worker and everyone liked him. His motto was 'always do your utmost', but I dare say that if he had been asked his private opinion he would have admitted that the School was in reality only a holiday for officers and N.C.O.s who needed a rest. It certainly seemed so to me when I awoke on the first morning and became conscious of my clean little room with its tiled floor and shuttered windows. I knew that the morning was fine; voices passed outside; sparrows chirped and starlings whistled; the bell in the church tower tolled and a clock struck the quarters. Flook entered with my Sam Browne belt and a jug of hot water. He remarked that we'd come to the right place, for once, and regretted that we weren't there for the duration. Wiping my face after a satisfactory shave, I stared out of the window; on the other side of the street a blossoming apple tree leant over an old garden wall, and I could see the friendly red roof of a dovecot. It was a luxury to be alone, with plenty of space for my portable property. There was a small table on which I could arrange my few books. Hardy's *Far from the Madding Crowd* was one of them. Also Lamb's *Essays* and *Mr. Sponge's Sporting Tour*. Books about England were all that I wanted. I decided to do plenty of solid reading at the Army School.

Near by was the Mess Room where fourteen of us had our meals. A jolly-faced Captain from the Ulster Division had undertaken the office of Mess President and everyone was talkative and friendly. With half an hour to spare after breakfast, I strolled up the hill and smoked my pipe under a quick-set hedge.

3

Loosening my belt, I looked at a chestnut tree in full leaf and listened to the perfect performance of a nightingale. Such things seemed miraculous after the desolation of the trenches. Never before had I been so intensely aware of what it meant to be young and healthy in fine weather at the outset of summer. The untroubled notes of the nightingale made the Army School seem like some fortunate colony which was, for the sake of appearances, pretending to assist the struggle from afar. It feels as if it's a place where I might get a chance to call my soul my own, I thought, as I went down the hill to my first parade. If only they don't chivvy us about too much, I added . . . It was not unlike the first day of a public school term, and my form-master (we were divided into classes of twenty-eight) was a youngish Major in the Oxford and Bucks Light Infantry. He was an even-tempered man, pleasant to obey, and specially likeable through a certain shyness of manner. I cannot remember that any of us caused him any annoyance, though he more than once asked me to try and be less absent-minded. Later in the year he was commanding a battalion, and I don't doubt that he did it excellently.

Every afternoon at half-past five the School assembled to listen to a lecture. Eyeing an audience of about 300 officers and N.C.O.s, I improved my knowledge of regimental badges, which seemed somehow to affect the personality of the wearer. A lion, a lamb, a dragon or an antelope, a crown, a harp, a tiger or a sphinx, these devices differentiated men in more ways than one. But the regimental names were probably the potent factor, and my meditations while waiting for the lecturer would lead me along pleasant associative lanes connected with the English counties – the difference between Durham and Devon for instance. There was food for thought also in the fact of sitting between a Connaught Ranger and a Seaforth Highlander, though both were likely to have been born in Middlesex. Queer, too, was the whole scene in that schoolroom, containing as it did a splendid sample of the Fourth Army which began the Somme Battle a couple of months afterwards. It was one of those peaceful war pictures which have vanished for ever and are rarely recovered even in imaginative retrospect.

My woolgatherings were cut short when the lecturer cleared his throat; the human significance of the audience was obliterated then, and its outlook on life became restricted to destruction and defence. A gas expert from G.H.Q. would inform us that 'gas was still in its infancy'. (Most of us were either dead or disabled before gas had had time to grow up.) An urbane Artillery General assured us that high explosive would be our best friend in future battles, and his ingratiating voice made us unmindful, for the moment, that explosives often arrived from the wrong direction. But the star turn in the schoolroom was a massive sandy-haired Highland Major whose subject was 'The Spirit of the Bayonet'. Though at that time undecorated, he was afterwards awarded the D.S.O. for lecturing. He took as his text a few leading points from the *Manual of Bayonet Training*.

'To attack with the bayonet effectively requires Good Direction, Strength and Quickness, during a state of wild excitement and probably physical exhaustion. The bayonet is essentially an offensive weapon. In a bayonet assault all ranks go forward to kill or be killed, and only those who have developed skill and strength by constant training will be able to kill. The spirit of the bayonet must be inculcated into all ranks, so that they go forward with the aggressive determination and confidence of superiority born of continual practice, without which a bayonet assault will not be effective.'

He spoke with homicidal eloquence, keeping the game alive with genial and well-judged jokes. He had a Sergeant to assist him. The Sergeant, a tall sinewy machine, had been trained to such a pitch of frightfulness that at a moment's warning he could divest himself of all semblance of humanity. With rifle and bayonet he illustrated the Major's ferocious aphorisms, including facial expression. When told to 'put on the killing face', he did so, combining it with an ultra-vindictive attitude. 'To instil fear into the opponent' was one of the Major's main maxims. Man, it

5

seemed, had been created to jab the life out of Germans. To hear the Major talk, one might have thought that he did it himself every day before breakfast. His final words were: 'Remember that every Boche you fellows kill is a point scored to our side; every Boche you kill brings victory one minute nearer and shortens the war by one minute. Kill them! Kill them! There's only one good Boche, and that's a dead one!'

Afterwards I went up the hill to my favourite sanctuary, a wood of hazels and beeches. The evening air smelt of wet mould and wet leaves; the trees were misty-green; the church bell was tolling in the town, and smoke rose from the roofs. Peace was there in the twilight of that prophetic foreign spring. But the lecturer's voice still battered on my brain. 'The bullet and the bayonet are brother and sister.' 'If you don't kill him, he'll kill you.' 'Stick him between the eyes, in the throat, in the chest.' 'Don't waste good steel. Six inches are enough. What's the use of a foot of steel sticking out at the back of a man's neck? Three inches will do for him; when he coughs, go and look for another.'

## II

Whatever my private feelings may have been after the Major's lecture, the next morning saw me practising bayonet-fighting. It was all in the day's work; short points, long points, parries, jabs, plus the always-to-be-remembered importance of 'a quick withdrawal'. Capering over the obstacles of the assault course and prodding sacks of straw was healthy exercise; the admirable sergeant-instructor was polite and unformidable, and as I didn't want him to think me a dud officer, I did my best to become proficient. Obviously it would have been both futile and inexpedient to moralize about bayonet-fighting at an Army School.

There is a sense of recovered happiness in the glimpse I catch of myself coming out of my cottage door with a rifle slung on my shoulder. There was nothing wrong with life on those fine mornings when the air smelt so fresh and my body was young and vigorous, and I hurried down the white road, along the empty street, and up the hill to our training ground. I was like a boy going to early school, except that no bell was ringing, and instead of Thucydides or Virgil, I carried a gun. Forgetting, for the moment, that I was at the Front to be shot at, I could almost congratulate myself on having a holiday in France without paying for it.

I also remember how I went one afternoon to have a hot bath in the Jute Mill. The water was poured into a dyeing vat. Remembering that I had a bath may not be of much interest to anyone, but it was a good bath, and it is my own story that I am trying to tell, and as such it must be received; those who expect a universalization of the Great War must look for it elsewhere. Here they will only find an attempt to show its effect on a somewhat solitary-minded young man.

At that time I was comfortably aware that the British Expeditionary Force in France was a prosperous concern. I have already remarked that the officers and N.C.O.s at the School epitomized a resolute mass of undamaged material; equally impressive was the equine abundance which I observed one afternoon when we were on our way to a 'demonstration' at the Army Bombing School. Hundreds of light and heavy draught horses were drawn up along a road for an inspection by the Commander-in-Chief (a bodily presence which the infantry mind could not easily imagine). The horses, attached to their appropriate vehicles and shining in their summer coats, looked a picture of sleekness and strength. They were of all sorts and sizes but their power and compactness was uniform. The horsehood of England was there with every buckle of its harness brightened. There weren't many mules among them, for mules were mostly with the Artillery, and this was a slap-up Army Service Corps parade, obviously the climax of several weeks' preparation. I wished that I could have spent the afternoon inspecting them; but I was only a second-lieutenant, and the bus carried me on to study explosions and smoke-clouds, and to hear a lecture about the tactical employment of the Mills' Bomb.

News of the Battalion came from the Quartermaster, to whom I had sent an account of my 'cushy' existence. Dottrell wrote that things had been quiet up in the Line, but advised me to make the most of my rest-cure, adding that he'd always noticed that the further you got from the front line the further you got from the War. In accordance with my instructions he was making good progress with the box of kippers (which Aunt Evelyn sent me twice a month); ditto the Devonshire cream, though some of it hadn't stood the journey well. His letter put me in the right frame of mind for returning to tours of trenches, though I should be sorry to say good-bye to young Allgood, with whom I was spending most of my spare time.

Allgood was quiet, thoughtful, and fond of watching birds. We had been to the same public school, though there were nearly ten years between us. He told me that he hoped to be a historian, and I listened respectfully while he talked about the Romans in Early Britain, which was his favourite subject. It was easy to imagine him as an undergraduate at Cambridge; travelling in Germany during the Long Vacation and taking a good Degree. But his Degree had been postponed indefinitely. He said he'd always wanted to go to Germany, and there seemed nothing incongruous in the remark; for the moment I forgot that every German we killed was a point scored to our side. Allgood never grumbled about the war, for he was a gentle soul, willing to take his share in it, though obviously unsuited to homicide. But there was an expression of veiled melancholy on his face, as if he were inwardly warned that he would never see his home in Wiltshire again. A couple of months afterwards I saw his name in one of the long lists of killed, and it seemed to me that I had expected it.

Our last day at the School was hot and cloudless. In the morning English and French Generals rolled up in their cars; there must have been about a hundred of them; it was not unlike an army of uniformed Uncles on Prizegiving Day. There were no prizes, naturally. But we did our best to show them how efficient we were, by running round the assault course in teams, stabbing the straw sacks. We also competed in putting up screw-pickets and barbed wire with rapidity and precision. Our exertions ended with a march past the Army Commander, and then we fell out to witness the explosion of two small mines. Earth and chalk heaved up at the blue sky, the ground vibrated, and there was a noise like a mad rainstorm, caused by the whizzing descent of clods and stones and the hiss of smaller particles. Finally, a fountain of dingy smoke arose and drifted away from the débris, and the Generals retired to have luncheon in the white château; and there, let us hope, they let their belts out a hole or two and allowed themselves a little relaxation from intellectual effort. Allgood said that he thought the French Generals looked much brainier than the British ones; but I told him that they must be cleverer than they looked, and anyhow, they'd all got plenty of medal-ribbons.

# PART TWO
# THE RAID

## I

I came back from the Army School at the end of a hot Saturday
afternoon. The bus turned off the bumpy main road from Corbie
and began to crawl down a steep winding lane. I looked, and
there was Morlancourt in the hollow. On the whole I considered
myself lucky to be returning to a place where I knew my way
about. It was no use regretting the little room at Flixécourt where
I had been able to sit alone every night, reading a good book and
calling my soul my own . . . Distant hills and hazy valleys were
dazzled with sun-rays and the glaring beams made a fiery mist in
the foreground. It was jolly fine country, I thought. I had become
quite fond of it, and the end-of-the-world along the horizon had
some obscure hold over my mind which drew my eyes to it almost
eagerly, for I could still think of trench warfare as an adventure.
The horizon was quiet just now, as if the dragons which lived
there were dozing.

The Battalion was out of the line, and I felt almost glad to be
back as I walked up to our old Company Mess with Flook
carrying my valise on his back. Flook and I were very good
friends, and his vigilance for my personal comfort was such that I
could more easily imagine him using his rifle in defence of my
valise than against the Germans.

Nobody was in when I got to our billets, but the place had
improved since I last saw it; the horse-chestnut in front of the
house was in flower and there were a few peonies and pink roses
in the neglected little garden at the back.

Dusk had fallen when I returned from a stroll in the fields; the candles were lit, there was a smell of cooking, and the servants were clattering tin plates in the sizzling kitchen. Durley, Birdie Mansfield, and young Ormand were sitting round the table, with a new officer who was meekly reading the newspaper which served as tablecloth. They all looked glum, but my advent caused some pumped-up cheeriness, and I was introduced to the newcomer whose name was Fewnings. (He wore spectacles and in private life had been a schoolmaster.) Not much was said until the end of the steak and onions; by then Mansfield had lowered the level of the whisky bottle by a couple of inches, while the rest of us drank lime-juice. Tinned peaches appeared, and I inquired where Barton was – with an uneasy feeling that something might have happened to him. Ormand replied that the old man was dining at Battalion Headquarters. 'And skiting to Kinjack about the Raid, I'll bet,' added Mansfield, tipping some more whisky into his mug. 'The Raid!' I exclaimed, suddenly excited, 'I haven't heard a word about it.' 'Well, you're the only human being in this Brigade who hasn't heard about it.' (Mansfield's remarks were emphasized by the usual epithets.) 'But what about it? Was it a success?' 'Holy Christ! Was it a success? The Kangaroo wants to know if it was a success!' He puffed out his plump cheeks and gazed at the others. 'This god-damned Raid's been a funny story for the last fortnight, and we've done everything except send word over to the Fritzes to say what time we're coming; and now it's fixed up for next Thursday, and Barton's hoping to get a D.S.O. out of it for his executive ability. I wish he'd arrange to go and fetch his (something) D.S.O. for himself!' From this I deduced that poor Birdie was to be in charge of the Raiding Party, and I soon knew all there was to be known. Ormand, who had obviously heard more than enough lately, took himself off, vocally announcing that he was 'Gilbert the filbert, the Nut with a K, the pride of Piccadilly, the blasé roué'.

Barton was still up at Headquarters when I went across the road to my billet. Flook had spread my 'flea-bag' on the tiled floor, and I had soon slipped into it and blown out my candle. Durley, on the other side of the room, was asleep in a few minutes, for he'd been out late on a working-party the night before. I was now full of information about the Raid, and I could think of nothing else. My month at Flixécourt was already obliterated. While I was away I had almost forgotten about the Raid; but it seemed now that I'd always regarded it as my private property, for when it had begun to be a probability in April, Barton had said that I should be sure to take charge of it. My feeling was much the same as it would have been if I had owned a horse and then been told that someone else was to ride it in a race.

Six years before I had ambitions of winning races because that had seemed a significant way of demonstrating my equality with my contemporaries. And now I wanted to make the World War serve a similar purpose, for if only I could get a Military Cross I should feel comparatively safe and confident. (At that time the Doctor was the only man in the Battalion who'd got one.) Trench warfare was mostly monotonous drudgery, and I preferred the exciting idea of crossing the mine-crates and getting into the German front line. In my simple-minded way I had identified myself with that strip of no-man's-land opposite Bois Français; and the mine-craters had always fascinated me, though I'd often feared that they'd be the death of me.

Mansfield had gloomily remarked that he'd something-well go on the razzle if he got through Thursday night with his procreative powers unimpaired. Wondering why he had been selected for the job, I wished I could take his place. I knew that he had more common-sense ability than I had, but he was podgily built and had never been an expert at crawling among shell-holes in the dark. He and Ormand and Corporal O'Brien had done two patrols last week but the bright moonlight had prevented them from properly inspecting the German wire. Birdie's language about moonlight and snipers was a masterpiece, but he hadn't a ghost of an idea whether we could get through the Boche wire. Nevertheless I felt that if I'd been there the patrolling would have been profitable, moon or no moon. I wouldn't mind going up there and doing it now, I thought, for I was wide awake and full of

energy after my easy life at the Army School . . . *Doing it now?*
The line was quiet to-night. Now and again the tapping of a
machine-gun. But the demented night-life was going on all the
time and the unsleeping strangeness of it struck my mind silent for
a moment, as I visualized a wiring-party standing stock still while
a flare quivered and sank, silvering the bleached sandbags of the
redoubt.

Warm and secure, I listened to the gentle whisper of the aspens
outside the window, and the fear of death and the horror of
mutilation took hold of my heart. Durley was muttering in his
sleep, something rapid and incoherent, and then telling someone
to get a move on; the war didn't allow people many pleasant
dreams. It was difficult to imagine old Julian killing a German,
even with an anonymous bullet. I didn't want to kill any Germans
myself, but one had to kill people in self-defence. Revolver
shooting wasn't so bad, and as for bombs, you just chucked them
and hoped for the best. Anyhow I meant to ask Kinjack to let me
go on the Raid. Supposing he *ordered* me to go on it? How should
I feel about it then? No good thinking any more about it now.
With some such ponderings as these I sighed and fell asleep.

## II

Next morning I went to the other end of the village to have a chat
with my friend the Quartermaster. Leaning against a bit of broken
wall outside his billet, we exchanged a few observations about the
larger aspects of the war and the possibilities of peace. Joe was
pessimistic as ever, airing his customary criticisms of profiteers,
politicians, and those whose military duties compelled them to
remain at the Base and in other back areas. He said that the
permanent staff at Fourth Army Headquarters now numbered
anything up to four thousand. With a ribald metaphor he
speculated on what they did with themselves all day. I said that
some of them were busy at the Army School. Joe supposed there
was no likelihood of their opening a rest-cure for Quartermasters.

When I asked his opinion about the Raid he looked serious, for he liked Mansfield and knew his value as an officer. 'From all I hear, Kangar,' he said, 'it's a baddish place for a show of that kind, but you know the ground better than I do. My own opinion is that the Boches would have come across themselves before now if they'd thought it worth trying. But Brigade have got the idea of a raid hot and strong, and they've nothing to lose by it one way or the other, except a few of our men.' I asked if these raids weren't a more or less new notion, and he told me that our Battalion had done several small ones up in Flanders during the first winter; Winchell, our late Colonel, had led one when he was still a company commander. The idea had been revived early this year, when some Canadian toughs had pulled off a fine effort, and since then such entertainments had become popular with the Staff. Our Second Battalion had done one, about a month ago, up at Cuinchy; their Quartermaster had sent Joe the details; five officers and sixty men went across, but casualties were numerous and no prisoners were brought back. He sighed and lit a cigarette. 'It's always the good lads who volunteer for these shows. One of the Transport men wanted to send his name in for this one; but I told him to think of his poor unfortunate wife, and we're pushing him off on a transport-course to learn cold-shoeing.'

Prodding the ground with my stick, I stared at the Transport lines below us – a few dirty white bell-tents and the limbers and wagons and picketed horses. I could see the horses' tails switching and the men stooping to groom their legs. Bees hummed in the neglected little garden; red and grey roofs clustered round the square church tower; everything looked Sunday-like and contented with the fine weather. When I divulged my idea of asking Kinjack to let me go on the Raid, Joe remarked that he'd guessed as much, and advised me to keep quiet about it as there was still a chance that it might be washed out. Kinjack wasn't keen about it and had talked pretty straight to the Brigade Major; he was never afraid of giving the brass-hats a bit of his mind. So I promised to say nothing till the last moment, and old Joe ended by reminding me that we'd all be over the top in a month or two. But I thought, as I walked away, how silly it would be if I got laid out by a stray bullet, or a rifle-grenade, or one of those clumsy 'canisters' that came over in the evening dusk with a little trail of sparks behind them.

We went into the line again on Tuesday. For the first three days Barton's Company was in reserve at 71. North, which was an assortment of dug-outs and earth-covered shelters about a thousand yards behind the front line. I never heard anyone ask the origin of its name, which for most of us had meant shivering boredom at regular intervals since January. Some map-making expert had christened it coldly, and it had unexpectedly failed to get itself called the Elephant and Castle or Hampton Court. Anyhow it was a safe and busy suburb of the front line, for the dug-outs were hidden by sloping ground and nicely tucked away under a steep bank. Shells dropped short or went well over; and as the days of aeroplane aggressiveness had not yet arrived, we could move about by daylight with moderate freedom. A little way down the road the Quartermaster-sergeant ruled the ration dump, and every evening Dottrell arrived with the ration-limbers. There, too, was the dressing station where Dick Tiltwood had died a couple of months ago; it seemed longer than that, I thought, as I passed it with my platoon and received a cheery greeting from our Medical Officer, who could always make one feel that Harley Street was still within reach.

The road which passed 71. North had once led to Fricourt; now it skulked along to the British Front Line, wandering evilly across no-man's-land, and then gave itself up to the Germans. In spite of this, the road had for me a queer daylight magic, especially in summer. Though grass-patched and derelict, something of its humanity remained. I imagined everyday rural life going along it in pre-war weather, until this businesslike open-air inferno made it an impossibility for a French farmer to jog into Fricourt in his hooded cart.

There was a single line railway on the other side of the road, but the only idea which it suggested to Barton was that if the war lasted a few more years we should be coming to the trenches every

day by train like city men going to the office. He was due for leave
next week and his mind was already half in England. The Raid
wasn't mentioned now, and there was little to be done about it
except wait for Thursday night. Mansfield had become loquacious about his past life, as though he were making a general audit
of his existence. I remember him talking about the hard times he'd
had in Canada, and how he used to get a meal for twelve cents. In
the meantime I made a few notes in my diary.

'*Tuesday evening, 8.30. At Bécordel crossroads*. On a working
party. A small bushy tree against a pale yellow sky; slate roofs
gleaming in the half-light. A noise of carts coming along with
rations. Occasional bang of our guns close to the village. The
church tower, gloomy, only the front remains; more than half of it
shot away and most of the church. In the foreground two broken
barns with skeleton roofs. A quiet cool evening after a shower.
Stars coming out. The R.E. stores are dumped around French
soldier-cemetery. Voices of men in the dusk. Dull rattle of
machine-guns on the left. Talking to a Northumberland Fusilier
officer who drops aitches. Too dark to write . . .

'*Wednesday, 6.15 p.m. On Crawley Ridge*. Ormand up here in
the Redoubt with a few men. I relieve him while he goes down to
get his dinner. Very still evening; sun rather hazy. Looking across
to Fricourt; trench mortars bursting in the cemetery; dull white
smoke slowly floats away over grey-green grass with buttercups
and saffron weeds. Fricourt; a huddle of reddish roofs; skeleton
village; church tower, almost demolished, a white patch against
green of Fricourt wood (full of German batteries). North, up the
hill, white seams and heapings of trenches dug in chalk. Sky full of
lark songs. Sometimes you can count thirty slowly and hear no
sound of a shot; then the muffled pop of a rifle or a slamming 5.9
or one of our 18-pounders. Then a burst of machine-gun fire.
Westward the yellow sky with a web of filmy cloud half across the
sun; the ridges with blurred outlines of trees. An aeroplane
droning overhead. A thistle sprouting through the chalk on the
parapet; a cockchafer sailing through the air. Down the hill, the
Bray-Fricourt road, white and hard. A partridge flies away,

calling. Lush grass and crops of nettles; a large black slug out for his evening walk (doing nearly a mile a month).'

## II

At ten o'clock on Thursday night I was alone with Durley in the sack-cloth smelling dug-out at 71. North. Rain was falling steadily. Everything felt fateful and final. A solitary candle stood on the table in its own grease, and by its golden glimmer I had just written a farewell letter to Aunt Evelyn. I did not read it through, and I am glad I cannot do so now, for it was in the 'happy warrior' style and my own fine feelings took precedence of hers. It was not humanly possible for me to wonder what Aunt Evelyn was doing while I wrote; to have done so would have cramped my style. But it is possible that she was calling her black Persian cat in from the dripping summer garden; when it scampered in from the darkness she would dry it carefully with a towel, whistling under her breath, while she did so, some indeterminate tune. Poor Aunt Evelyn was still comfortingly convinced that I was a transport officer, though I had given up that job nearly three months ago. Having licked and fastened the flimsy envelope I handed it to Durley, with a premonition that it would be posted. Durley received it with appropriate gravity.

In the meantime Mansfield was making a final reconnaissance of the ground with Sergeant Miles and Corporal O'Brien, while Barton (unaware of my intentions) was administering a drop of whisky to the raiding party in the large dug-out just along the road. It was time to be moving; so I took off my tunic, slipped my old raincoat on over my leather waistcoat, dumped my tin hat on my head, and picked up my nail-studded knobkerrie. Good old Durley wished me luck and economically blew out the candle. As we went along the road he remarked that it was lucky the night was dark and rainy.

Entering the other dug-out I was slightly startled, for I had forgotten that the raiders were to have blacked faces (to avoid the danger of their mistaking one another for Germans). Exchanging boisterous jokes, they were putting the finishing touches to their make-up with bits of burnt cork. Showing the whites of their eyes and pretending not to recognize one another, those twenty-five shiny-faced nigger minstrels might almost have been getting ready for a concert. Everyone seemed to expect the entertainment to be a roaring success. But there were no looking-glasses or banjos, and they were brandishing knobkerries, stuffing Mills' bombs into their pockets and hatches into their belts, and 'Who's for a Blighty one to-night?' was the stock joke (if such a well-worn wish could be called a joke).

At 10.30 there was a sudden silence, and Barton told me to take the party up to Battalion Headquarters. It surprises me when I remember that I set off without having had a drink, but I have always disliked the flavour of whisky, and in those days the helpfulness of alcohol in human affairs was a fact which had not yet been brought home to me. The raiders had been given only a small quantity, but it was enough to hearten them as they sploshed up the communication trench. None of us could know how insignificant we were in the so-called 'Great Adventure' which was sending up its uneasy flares along the Western Front. No doubt we thought ourselves something very special. But what we thought never mattered; nor does it matter what sort of an inflated fool I was when I blundered into Kinjack's Headquarters at Maple Redoubt to report the presence of the raiders and ask whether I might go across with them. 'Certainly not,' said the Colonel, 'your job is to stop in our trench and count the men as they come back.' He spoke with emphasis and he was not a man who expected to have to say a thing twice. We stared at one another for a moment; some freak of my brain made me remember that in peace time he had been an enthusiastic rose-grower – had won prizes with his roses, in fact; for he was a married man and had lived in a little house near the barracks.

My thought was nipped in the bud by his peremptory voice telling Major Robson, his second-in-command, to push off with the party. We were about 400 yards from the front line, and Robson now led us across the open to a point in the support trench, from which a red electric torch winked to guide us. Then up a trench to the starting point, the men's feet clumping and drumming on the duckboards. This noise, plus the clinking and drumming and creaking of weapons and equipment, suggested to my strained expectancy that the enemy would be well warned of our arrival. Mansfield and his two confederates now loomed squatly above us on the parapet; they had been laying a guiding line of lime across the craters. A gap had been cut in our wire, and it was believed that some sort of damage had been done to the German wire which had been 'strafed' by trench mortars during the day.

The raiders were divided into four parties of five men; operation orders had optimistically assumed that the hostile trenches would be entered without difficulty; 'A' party would go to the left, 'B' party to the right, and so on and so forth. The object of the raid was to enter the enemy loop on the edge of the crater; to enter Kiel Trench at two points; to examine the portions of trench thus isolated, capture prisoners, bomb dug-outs, and kill Germans. An 'evacuating party' (seven men carrying two ten-foot ladders and a red flash lamp) followed the others. The ladders were considered important, as the German front trench was believed to be deep and therefore difficult to get out of in a hurry. There were two mine-craters a few yards from our parapet; these craters were about fifty yards in diameter and about fifty feet deep; their sides were steep and composed of thin soft soil; there was water at the bottom of them. Our men crossed by a narrow bridge of earth between the craters; the distance to the German wire was about sixty yards.

It was now midnight. The five parties had vanished into the darkness on all fours. It was raining quietly and persistently. I sat on the parapet waiting for something to happen. Except for two men at a sentry post near by (they were now only spectators) there seemed to be no one about. 'They'll never keep that — — inside the trench,' muttered the sentry to his mate and even at that tense moment I valued the compliment. Major Robson and the stretcher-bearers had been called away by a message. There must be some trouble further along, I thought, wondering what it could be, for I hadn't heard a sound. Now and again I looked at my luminous watch. Five, ten, fifteen minutes passed in ominous silence. An occasional flare, never near our craters, revealed the streaming rain, blanched the tangles of wire that wound away into the gloom, and came to nothing, bringing down the night. Unable to remain inactive any longer, I crawled a little way out. As I went, a few shells began to drone across in their leisurely way. Our communication trench was being shelled. I joined the evacuating party; they were lying on the lip of the left-hand crater. A flare fizzed up, and I could see the rest of the men lying down, straight across the ridge, and was able to exchange a grimace with one of the black-faced ladder-carriers. Then some 'whizz-bangs' rushed over to our front trench; one or two fell on the craters; this made the obstinate silence of Kiel Trench more menacing. Soon afterwards one of the bayonet men came crawling rapidly back. I followed him to our trench where he whispered his message. 'They can't get through the second belt of wire; O'Brien says it's a washout; they're all going to throw a bomb and retire.'

I suppose I ought to have tried to get the ladder-carriers in before the trouble started; but the idea didn't strike me as I waited with bumping heart; and almost immediately the explosions began. A bomb burst in the water of the left-hand crater, sending up a phosphorescent spume. Then a concentration of angry flashes, thudding bangs, and cracking shots broke itself up in a hubbub and scurry, groans and curses, and stampeding confusion. Stumbling figures loomed up from below, scrambling clumsily over the parapet; black faces and whites of eyes showed grotesque in the antagonistic shining of alarm flares. Dodging to and fro, I counted fourteen men in; they all blundered away down the trench. I went out, found Mansfield badly hit, and left him with two others who soon got him in. Other wounded men were crawling back. Among them was a grey-haired lance-corporal, who had one of his feet almost blown off; I half carried him in, and when he was sitting on the firestep he said: 'Thank God

Almighty for this; I've been waiting eighteen months for it, and now I can go home.' I told him we'd get him away on a stretcher soon, and then he muttered: 'Mick O'Brien's somewhere down in the craters.'

All this had been quick work and not at all what I'd expected. Things were slowing down now. The excitement was finished, and O'Brien was somewhere down in the craters. The bombing and rifle fire had slackened when I started out to look for him. I went mechanically, as though I were drowning myself in the darkness. This is no fun at all, was my only thought as I groped my way down the soft clogging side of the left-hand crater; no fun at all, for they were still chucking an occasional bomb and firing circumspectly. I could hear the reloading click of rifle bolts on the lip of the crater above me as I crawled along with mud-clogged fingers, or crouched and held my breath painfully. Bullets hit the water and little showers of earth pattered down from the banks. I knew that nothing in my previous experience of patrolling had ever been so grim as this, and I lay quite still for a bit, miserably wondering whether my number was up; then I remembered that I was wearing my pre-war raincoat; I could feel the pipe and tobacco pouch in my pocket and somehow this made me less forlorn, though life seemed much further away than the low mumble of voices in our trench. A flare would have helped my searchings, but they had stopped sending them up; pawing the loose earth and dragging my legs after me, I worked my way round the crater. O'Brien wasn't there, so I got across into the other one, which was even more precipitous and squashy. Down there I discovered him. Another man was crouching beside him, wounded in one arm and patiently waiting for help. O'Brien moaned when I touched him; he seemed to have been hit in several places. His companion whispered huskily: 'Get a rope.' As I clambered heavily up the bank I noticed that it had stopped raining. Robson was peering out of the trench; he sent someone for a rope, urging him to be quick for already there was a faint beginning of daylight. With the rope, and a man to help, I got back to O'Brien, and we lifted him up the side of the crater.

It was heavy work, for he was tall and powerfully built, and the soft earth gave way under our feet as we lugged and hoisted the limp shattered body. The Germans must have seen us in the half light, but they had stopped firing; perhaps they felt sorry for us.

At last we lowered him over the parapet. A stretcher-bearer bent over him and then straightened himself, taking off his helmet with a gesture that vaguely surprised me by its reverent simplicity. O'Brien had been one of the best men in our Company. I looked down at him and then turned away; the face was grotesquely terrible, smeared with last night's burnt cork, the forehead matted with a tangle of dark hair.

I had now accounted for everyone. Two killed and ten wounded was the only result of the raid. In the other Company sector the Germans had blown in one of our mine-galleries, and about thirty of the tunnelling company had been gassed or buried. Robson had been called there with the stretcher-bearers just as the raid began.

Nothing now remained for me to do except to see Kinjack on my way back. Entering his dug-out I looked at him with less diffidence than I'd ever done before. He was sitting on his plank bed, wearing a brown woollen cap with a tuft on the top. His blond face was haggard; the last few hours had been no fun for him either. This was a Kinjack I'd never met before, and it was the first time I had ever shared any human equality with him. He spoke kindly to me in his rough way, and in doing so made me very thankful that I had done what I could to tidy up the mess in no-man's-land.

Larks were shrilling in the drizzling sky as I went down to 71. North. I felt a wild exultation. Behind me were the horror and the darkness. Kinjack had thanked me. It was splendid to be still alive, I thought, as I strode down the hill, skirting shell-holes and jumping over communication trenches, for I wasn't in a mood to bother about going along wet ditches. The landscape loomed around me, and the landscape was life, stretching away and away into freedom. Even the dreary little warren at 71. North seemed to await me with a welcome, and Flook was ready with some hot tea. Soon I was jabbering excitedly to Durley and old man Barton, who told me that the Doctor said Mansfield was a touch and go case, but already rejoicing at the prospect of getting across to Blighty, and cursing the bad wire-cutters which had been served out for the raid. I prided myself on having pulled off something rather heroic; but when all was said and done it was only the sort of thing which people often did during a fire or a railway accident.

Nothing important had happened on the British Front that night, so we were rewarded by a mention in the G.H.Q. *communiqué*. '*At Mametz we raised hostile trenches. Our party entered without difficulty and maintained a spirited bombing fight, and finally withdrew at the end of twenty-five minutes.*' This was their way of telling England. Aunt Evelyn probably read it automatically in her *Morning Post*, unaware that this minor event had almost caused her to receive a farewell letter from me. The next night our Company was in the front line and I recovered three hatchets and a knobkerrie from no-man's-land. Curiously enough, I hadn't yet seen a German. I had seen dim figures on my dark patrols; but no human faces.

# PART THREE
# BEFORE THE PUSH

## I

One evening about a fortnight later I was down in that too familiar front-line dug-out with Barton, who had just returned from leave and was unable to disguise his depression. I wasn't feeling over bright myself after tramping to and fro in the gluey trenches all day. A little rain made a big difference to life up there, and the weather had been wet enough to make the duckboards wobble when one stepped on them. I'd got sore feet and a trench mouth and food tasted filthy. And the Boche trench-mortars had been strafing us more than usual that evening. Probably I've been smoking too much lately, I thought, knocking my pipe out against one of the wooden props which held up the cramped little den, and staring irritably at my mud-encumbered boots, for I was always trying to keep squalor at bay, and the discomfort of feeling dirty and tickly all over was almost as bad as a bombardment. It certainly wasn't much of a place to be low-spirited in, so I tried reading the paper which the Company Sergeant-Major had just delivered when he came down for the rum ration. The rum jar lived under Barton's bed; having been poured into some tin receptacle, the rum was carried cautiously upstairs to be tipped into the men's tea-dixies.

'Fancy Kitchener being drowned in the North Sea!' I remarked, looking up from the *Daily Mail* which was making the most of that historic event. (It seemed a long time since I rode past his park wall in Kent when I was with the Yeomanry; it would be two years next September, though it wasn't much use looking as far ahead as that, with all these preparations going on for the 'Big

Push'.) Barton was scribbling away with his indelible pencil – filling in all that bosh which made Brigade think they were busy. 'If you want my opinion,' he grumbled, 'I believe those damned Irish had a hand in Kitchener being drowned. I'd like to see that fatuous island of theirs sunk under the sea.' Barton had an irrational dislike of the Irish, and he always blamed anything on them if he could. He couldn't even admit that Ireland was an agricultural country, and since the Easter Rebellion in Dublin it wasn't safe to show him a bottle of Irish whiskey. 'I've never met an Irishman with any more sense than that mouse!' he exclaimed. A mouse was standing on its head in the sugar basin, which was made of metal and contained soft sugar. He eyed the mouse morosely, as though accusing it of Irish ancestry. 'This time three nights ago my wife and I were having dinner at the Café Royal. Upstairs at the Café Royal – best food in London, and as good as ever even now. I tell you, Kangar, it's too much of a bloody contrast, coming back to all this.' There was a muffled 'Wump' and both candles went out. Something heavy had burst outside our door. Lighting the candles, I thought I'd just as soon be upstairs as down in this musty limbo. In about an hour I should be out with the wiring-party, dumping concertina wire in the shell-holes along the edge of the craters. I wondered if I should ever get a Blighty wound. One of our best officers had been hit last night while out with the wirers. This was Bill Eaves, who had been a Classical Scholar at Cambridge and had won medals there for writing Greek and Latin epigrams. Now he'd got a nice bullet wound in the shoulder, with the muscles damaged enough to keep him in England several months. And two nights ago Ormand and a Sandhurst boy named Harris had been hit while on a working party. Ormand's was a 'cushy' shell splinter; but Harris had got his knee smashed up, and the doctor said he would probably be out of the war for good. It was funny to think of young Harris being hit in the first twenty-four hours of his first tour of trenches.

Anyhow we were due for Divisional Rest, which would take us to the back area for three weeks, and the clogging monotony of life in the line would be cleaned out of our minds. And you never knew

– perhaps the war would end in those three weeks. The troops were beginning to need a rest badly, for most of them had been doing tours of trenches ever since the end of January, and even when we were at Morlancourt there was a working party every second night, which meant being out from seven o'clock till after midnight. And Miles, my platoon sergeant, hadn't been quite his usual self since the raid; but he'd been in France nearly a year, which was longer than most men could stick such a life. The chances are, I thought, that if Sergeant Miles is still here a few months hence, and I'm not, some fresh young officer from England will be accusing him of being windy. Sooner or later I should get windy myself. It was only a question of time. But could this sort of thing be measured by ordinary time, I wondered (as I lay on a bunk wishing to God Barton would stop blowing on his spectacles, which surely didn't need all that polishing). No; one couldn't reckon the effect of the war on people by weeks and months. I'd noticed that boys under twenty stood it worst, especially when the weather was bad. Mud and boredom and discomfort seemed to take all the guts out of them. If an officer crumpled up, Kinjack sent him home as useless, with a confidential report. Several such officers were usually drifting about at the Depot, and most of them ended up with safe jobs in England. But if a man became a dud in the ranks, he just remained where he was until he was killed or wounded. Delicate discrimination about private soldiers wasn't possible. A 'number nine pill' was all they could hope for if they went sick. Barton sometimes told me that I was too easy-going with the men when we were out of the Line, but it often seemed to me that I was asking them to do more than could be fairly expected of them. It's queer, I thought, how little one really knows about the men. In the Line one finds out which are the duds, and one builds up a sort of comradeship with the tough and willing ones. But back in billets the gap widens and one can't do much to cheer them up. I could never understand how they managed to keep as cheery as they did through such drudgery and discomfort, with nothing to look forward to but going over the top or being moved up to Flanders again.

26

Next evening, just before stand-to, I was watching a smouldering sunset and thinking that the sky was one of the redeeming features of the war. Behind the support line where I stood, the shell-pitted ground sloped sombrely into the dusk; the distances were blue and solemn, with a few trees grouped on a ridge, dark against the deep-glowing embers of another day endured. I was looking westward, away from the war, and the evening star twinkled serenely. Guns were grumbling miles away. Cartwheels could be heard on the roads behind Fricourt; it still made me feel strange when I remembered that they were German cartwheels.

Moments like those are unreproducible when I look back and try to recover their living texture. One's mind eliminates boredom and physical discomfort, retaining an incomplete impression of a strange, intense, and unique experience. If there be such a thing as ghostly revisitation of this earth, and if ghosts can traverse time and choose their ground, I would return to the Bois Français sector as it was then. But since I always assume that spectral presences have lost their sense of smell (and I am equally uncertain about their auditory equipment) such hauntings might be as inadequate as those which now absorb my mental energy. For trench life was an existence saturated by the external senses; and although our actions were domineered over by military discipline, our animal instincts were always uppermost. While I stood there then, I had no desire to diagnose my environment. Freedom from its oppressiveness was what I longed for. Listening to the German cartwheels rumbling remotely, I thought of an old German governess I had known, and how she used to talk about 'dear old Moltke and Bismarck' and her quiet home in Westphalia where her father had been a Protestant pastor. I wondered what sort of a place Westphalia was, and wished I'd seen more of the world before it became so busy with bloodshed. For until I came out to the war I had only the haziest notion of anything outside England.

Well, here I was, and my incomplete life might end any minute; for although the evening air was as quiet as a cathedral, a canister soon came over quite near enough to shatter my meditations with its unholy crash and cloud of black smoke. A rat scampered across the tin cans and burst sandbags, and trench atmosphere reasserted itself in a smell of chloride of lime. On my way to the dug-out, to fetch my revolver and attend the twilight ceremony of stand-to and rifle inspection, I heard the voice of Flook; just round a bend of the support trench he was asking one of the company bombers if he'd seen his officer bloke go along that way. Flook was in a hurry to tell me that I was to go on leave. I didn't wait to inspect my platoon's rifles and not many minutes later I was on my way down the Old Kent Road trench. Maple Redoubt was getting its usual evening bombardment, and as a man had been killed by a whizz-bang in the Old Kent Road a few minutes earlier, I was glad when I was riding back to Morlancourt with Dottrell; glad, too, to be driving to Méricourt station behind the sluggish pony next morning; to hear the mellow bells of Rouen on the evening air while the leave train stood still for half an hour before making up its mind to lumber on to Havre. And thus the gradations of thankfulness continued, until I found myself in a quiet house in Kensington where I was staying the night with an old friend of Aunt Evelyn's.

To be there, on a fine Sunday evening in June, with the drawing-room windows open and someone playing the piano next door, was an experience which now seemed as queer as the unnatural conditions I had returned from. Books, pictures, furniture, all seemed kind and permanent and unrelated to the present time and its troubles. I felt detached from my surroundings – rather as if I were in a doctor's waiting-room, expecting to be informed that I had some incurable disease. The sound of the piano suggested that the specialist had a happy home life of his own, but it had no connection with my coming and going. A sense of gentle security pervaded the room; but I could no longer call my life my own. The pensive music had caught me off my guard; I was only an intruder from the Western Front. But the room contained one object which unexpectedly reminded me of the trenches – a silent canary in a cage. I had seen canaries in cages being carried by the men of the tunnelling company when they emerged from their mine galleries.

## II

Correspondingly queer (though I didn't consciously observe it at the time) was the experience of returning to France after sleeping seven nights in a proper bed and wearing civilian clothes. The personal implications were obvious, since everybody at home seemed to know that the long-planned offensive was due to 'kick off' at the end of June. Officers going on leave had been cautioned to say nothing about it, but even Aunt Evelyn was aware of the impending onslaught. I was disinclined to talk about the trenches; nevertheless I permitted myself to drop a few heavy hints. No one had any notion what the Big Push would be like, except that it would be much bigger than anything which had happened before. And somehow those previous battles hadn't divulged themselves very distinctly to anyone except the actual participators, who had so far proved inarticulate reporters.

As regards my own adventures, I had decided to say nothing to my aunt about the raid. Nevertheless it all slipped out on the second evening, probably after she had been telling me how splendidly Mrs. Ampney's nephew had done out in Mesopotamia. Also I didn't omit to mention that I had been recommended for a Military Cross. 'But I thought you were only looking after the horses,' she expostulated, clutching my hand; her anxious face made me wish I'd held my tongue about it. Of course, Aunt Evelyn wanted me to do well in the war, but she couldn't enjoy being reminded that 'do be careful to wear your warm overcoat, dearie', was no precaution against German bombs and bullets. Afterwards I excused myself by thinking that she was bound to find out sooner or later, especially if I got killed.

Next day I walked across the fields to Butley and had tea with my old friend Captain Huxtable. I found him chubby-cheeked as ever, and keeping up what might be called a Justice of the Peace attitude toward the war. Any able-bodied man not serving in H.M. Forces should be required to show a thundering good reason for it, and the sooner conscription came in the better. That was his opinion; in the meantime he was working his farm with two elderly men and a boy; 'and that's about all an old crock like me can do for his country.' I gave him to understand that it was a jolly fine life out at the Front, and, for the moment, I probably believed what I was saying. I wasn't going to wreck my leave with facing facts, and I'd succeeded in convincing myself that I really wanted to go back. Captain Huxtable and I decided, between us, that the Push would finish the war by Christmas. While we talked, pacing to and fro in the garden, with his surly black retriever at our heels, the rooks cawed applaudingly in the clump of elms near by as though all were well with England on that June afternoon. I knew that the Captain would have asked nothing better than to go over the top with his old regiment, if only he'd been thirty years younger, and I wished I could have told him so, when we were standing at his gate. But English reticence prohibited all that sort of thing, and I merely remarked that Aunt Evelyn's lightning-conductor had been blown off the chimney in the spring and she said it wasn't worth while having it put up again. He laughed and said she must be getting war-weary; she had always been so particular about the lightning-conductor. 'We old 'uns can't expect to be feeling very cock-a-hoop in these days,' he added, wrinkling up his shrewd and kindly little eyes and giving my hand a farewell squeeze which meant more than he could say aloud.

When Aunt Evelyn wondered whether I'd like anyone to come to dinner on my last evening (she called it Friday night) I replied that I'd rather we were alone. There were very few to ask, and, as she said, people were difficult to get hold of nowadays. So, after a dinner which included two of my favourite puddings, we made the best of a bad job by playing cribbage (a game we had been addicted to when I was at home for my school holidays) while the black Persian cat washed his face with his paw and blinked contentedly at the fire which had been lit though there was no need for it, the night being warm and still. We also had the grey parrot brought up from the kitchen. Clinging sideways to the bars of his cage Popsy seemed less aware of the war than anyone I'd met. But perhaps he sensed the pang I felt when saying good-bye to him next morning; parrots understand more than they pretend to, and this one had always liked me. He wasn't much of a talker, though he could imitate Aunt Evelyn calling the cats.

Next morning she contrived to be stoically chatty until I had seen her turn back to the house door and the village taxi was rattling me down the hill. She had sensibly refrained from coming up to London to see me off. But at Waterloo Station I was visibly reminded that going back for the Push was rather rough on one's relations, however incapable they might be of sharing the experience. There were two leave trains and I watched the people coming away after the first one had gone out. Some sauntered away with assumed unconcern; they chatted and smiled. Others hurried past me with a crucified look; I noticed a well-dressed woman biting her gloved fingers; her eyes stared fixedly; she was returning alone to a silent house on a fine Sunday afternoon.

But I had nobody to see me off, so I could settle myself in the corner of a carriage, light my pipe and open a Sunday paper (though goodness knows what it contained, apart from *communiqués*, casualty lists, and reassuring news from Galicia, Bukovina, and other opaque arenas of war). It would have been nice to read the first-class cricket averages for a change, and their absence was an apt epitome of the life we were condemned to. While the train hurried out of London I watched the flitting gardens of suburban houses. In my fox-hunting days I had scorned the suburbs, but now there was something positively alluring in the spectacle of a City man taking it easy on his little lawn at Surbiton. Woking Cemetery was a less attractive scene, and my eyes recoiled from it to reassure themselves that my parcels were still safe on the rack, for those parcels were the important outcome of my previous day's shopping.

Armed with Aunt Evelyn's membership ticket (posted back to her afterwards) I had invaded the Army and Navy Stores and procured a superb salmon, two bottles of old brandy, an automatic pistol, and two pairs of wire-cutters with rubber-covered handles. The salmon was now my chief concern. I was concerned about its future freshness, for I had overstayed my leave by twenty-four hours. A rich restaurant dinner followed by a mechanical drawing-room comedy hadn't made the risk of Kinjack's displeasure seem worth while; but I felt that the salmon spelt safety at Battalion Headquarters. Probably the word *smelt* also entered my apprehensive mind. The brandy claimed that it had been born in 1838, so one day more or less couldn't affect its condition, as long as I kept an eye on it (for such bottles were liable to lose themselves on a leave boat). The wire-cutters were my private contribution to the Great Offensive. I had often cursed the savage bluntness of our Company's wire-cutters, and it occurred to me, in the Army and Navy Stores, that if we were going over the top we might want to cut our own wire first, to say nothing of the German wire (although our artillery would have made holes in that, I hoped). So I bought these very civilized ones, which looked almost too good for the Front Line. The man in the Weapon Department at the Stores had been persuasive about a periscope (probably prismatic) but I came to the conclusion that a periscope was a back number in my case. I shouldn't be in the trench long enough to need it. Apart from the wire-cutters and the pistol, all other 'trench requisites' appeared redundant. I couldn't see myself leading my platoon with *Mortleman's Patent Sound Absorbers* plugged in my ears, and a combined Compass-Barometer also failed to attract me. The automatic pistol wasn't 'warranted to stop a man', but it could be slipped into the pocket. It was only a plaything, but I was weary of my Colt revolver, with which I knew I couldn't hit anything, although I had blazed it off a few times in the dark when I was pretending to be important in no-man's-land. The only object I could be sure of hitting was myself, and I decided (in the Army and Navy Stores) that I might conceivably find it necessary to put myself out of my misery, if the worst came to the worst and I was lying out in a shell-hole with something more serious than a Blighty wound. To blow one's brains out with that clumsy Colt was unthinkable. The automatic pistol, on the other hand, was quite a charming little weapon. Not that I'd ever been fond of firearms. I had never shot at a bird or an animal in my life, though I'd often felt that my position as a sportsman would be stronger if I were 'a good man with a gun'.

The truth was that the only explosive weapon I owned before the war was a toy pistol which made a noise but discharged nothing. Sitting in the wrong-way leave train I remembered how, when about nine years old, I used to go up to the little sweet shop in the village and buy 'three penn'orth of percussion caps' for my pistol; and how the buxom old woman used to ask briskly, 'Anything else today, Master George?' Whereupon I would be compelled to decide between clove and peppermint bulls' eyes, with a bar of chocolate-cream to make it up to sixpence. Twenty years was a long time ago; but already the village green as I saw it last week was beginning to seem almost as remote . . . However, it was no use dreaming about all that now; Kinjack's salmon was my immediate problem, and as soon as I was on board the crowded boat, I consulted an obliging steward and my fishy insurance policy was providentially accommodated in the cold-storage cupboard. Consequently my mind was unperturbed when we steamed out of Southampton Water. I watched the woods on the Isle of Wight, hazily receding in the heat. And when the Isle of Wight was out of sight – well, there was nothing to be done about it.

At Havre I was instructed, by the all-knowing authority responsible for my return, to get out of the train at Corbie. Havre was a glitter of lights winking on dark slabbing water. Soon the glumly-laden train was groaning away from the wharves, and we nodded and snored through the night. Daylight came, and we crawled past green landscapes blurred with drizzling rain. Of my compartment companions I remember nothing except that one of them talked irrepressibly about his father's farm in Suffolk. His father, he said, owned a bull who had produced sixty black and white calves. This information was received with apathy. The Battalion was at Bussy, a three-mile walk in late afternoon sunshine. I kept to the shady side of the road, for the salmon in its hamper was still my constant care. Bussy came in sight as a pleasant little place on a tributary of the

Ancre. A few of our men were bathing, and I thought how young and light-hearted they looked, splashing one another and shouting as they rocked a crazy boat under some lofty poplars that shivered in a sunset breeze. How different to the trudging figures in full marching order; and how difficult to embody them in the crouching imprisonment of trench warfare!

With an unsoldierly sigh I picked up my packages and plodded on in search of C Company, who were billeted in some buildings round a friendly farmhouse. There I found Flook and despatched him to Kinjack's Headquarters with the hamper and a bottle of brandy. Barton, to whom I entrusted the second bottle, told me that I was a cunning old Kangaroo, and then regaled me with all the rumours about next week's operations. 'The bombardment begins on Saturday,' he said, 'so we're having Battalion Sports tomorrow, in case we get moved back to Morlancourt.' Then Durley came in with Jenkins, one of the new officers who had been posted to the Battalion while I was away. Fewnings, the gentle ex-schoolmaster, had been appointed Lewis gun officer, but he still messed with us; he now entered with the air of a man who had been teaching Euclid and Algebra all day. The Brigadier, he remarked, had ticked him off that afternoon, because he was wearing a light-coloured shirt; but no fault had been found with his Lewis gun team organization, and, as he remarked, it wouldn't make much odds what sort of shirt he was wearing in a week or two. Neither Durley nor I had ever been favoured with a word from our Brigadier, perhaps because our shirts were the orthodox colour. It was odd, how seldom those graduated autocrats found time to realize that a few kind words could make a platoon commander consider them jolly good Generals.

But there was harmony in our Company Mess, as if our certainty of a volcanic future had put an end to the occasional squabblings which occurred when we were on one another's nerves. A rank animal healthiness pervaded our existence during those days of busy living and inward foreboding. The behaviour of our servants expressed it; they were competing for the favours of a handsome young woman in the farmhouse, and a comedy of primitive courtship was being enacted in the kitchen. Death would be lying in wait for the troops next week, and now the flavour of life was doubly strong. As I went to my room across the road, the cool night smelt of mown grass and leafy gardens. Away toward Corbie there was the sound of a train, and bull-frogs croaked continuously in the marshes along the river. I wasn't sorry to be back; I was sure of that; we'd all got to go through it, and I was trying to convert the idea of death in battle into an emotional experience. Courage, I argued, is a beautiful thing, and next week's attack is what I have been waiting for since I first joined the army. I am happy to-night, and I don't suppose I'll be dead in a month's time. Going into my billet I almost fell over a goat which was tethered among some currant bushes in the garden.

Five days passed us by. We did easy field-training; the Battalion Sports were a great success, and we were defeated, in an officers' tug-of-war, by our 9th Battalion who were resting a few miles away. Saturday evening brought a feeling of finality, for we were moving up to Morlancourt on Monday and the intense bombardment had begun that morning. Barton and I (and our bottle of '38 brandy) dined at Battalion Headquarters. Kinjack was full of confidence; he told us that the French were holding on well at Verdun, which would make all the difference. But the doctor looked thoughtful, and even the brandy couldn't make Barton optimistic about his ability to command a company in open warfare.

# PART FOUR
## BATTLE

### I

On the morning of a Battalion move I made it my business to keep out of the way until the last moment. At the end of a march I had my definite duties, but before we started Barton was always in such a stew that my absence was a positive advantage to him. So on Monday, after bolting my breakfast while Flook waited to pack the mugs and plates in the mess-box, I left Barton shouting irritably for the Sergeant-Major and wandered away to sit by the river until the whistles began to blow. Durley and Jenkins had gone to make sure that the billets were being left clean and tidy. In the green orchard behind the farm buildings the men were putting their kits together, their voices sounding as jolly as though they were off for a summer holiday. For me it was a luxury to be alone for a few minutes, watching the yellow irises, and the ribbon weeds that swayed like fishes in the dimpling stream. I was sorry to be saying good-bye to the Marais and its grey-green pools and creeks and the congregation of poplar stems that upheld a cool whispering roof. Water-haunting birds whistled and piped, swinging on the bulrushes and tufted reeds, and a tribe of little green and gold frogs hopped about in the grass without caring whether they arrived anywhere. All this was obviously preferable to a battle, and it was a perfect morning to be reading a book beside the river.

But on the horizon the bombardment bumped and thudded in a continuous bubbling grumble. After a long stare at sun-flecked foliage and idly reflective alleys I bustled back to the farmyard to find my platoon all present and correct. Before I'd finished my formal inspection Barton emerged from the house with bulging pockets, his burly figure hung like a Christmas tree with haversack, water-bottle, revolver, field-glasses, gas-mask, map-case, and other oddments. The Battalion moved off at eight o'clock; by twelve-thirty it was at Morlancourt, which was now congested with infantry and supply columns, and 'lousy with guns' as the saying was. A colony of camouflage-daubed tents had sprung up close to the village; this was the New Main Dressing Station. We were in our usual billets – Durley and I in the room containing a representation of the Eiffel Tower and a ludicrous oleograph of our Saviour preaching from a boat, which we always referred to as jocular Jesus. After a sultry dinner, the day ended with torrents of rain. While I lay on the floor in my flea-bag the blackness of the night framed in the window was lit with the incessant glare and flash of guns. But I fell asleep to the sound of full gutters and rainwater gurgling and trickling into a well; and those were comfortable noises, for they signified that I had a roof over my head. As for my flea-bag, it was no hardship; I have never slept more soundly in any bed.

Operation Orders were circulated next morning. They notified us that Thursday was 'Z' (or zero) day. The Seventh Division Battle Plan didn't look aggressively unpleasant on paper as I transcribed it into my notebook. Rose Trench, Orchard Alley, Apple Alley, and Willow Avenue, were among the first objectives in our sector, and my mind very properly insisted on their gentler associations. Nevertheless this topographical Arcadia was to be seized, cleared, and occupied when the historic moment arrived and in conjunc-tion with the French the Fourth Army took the offensive, establishing as a primary objective a line Montauban-Pozières, passing to the south of Mametz Wood. There wasn't going to be any mistake about it this time. We decided, with quite a glow of excitement, that the Fourth Army was going to fairly wipe the floor with the Boches. In the meantime our Corps Intelligence Summary (known as *Comic Cuts*) reported on June 27th that three enemy balloons had been set on fire and destroyed on the previous afternoon; also that a large number of enemy batteries had been silenced by our artillery. The anonymous humorist who compiled *Comic Cuts* was also able to announce that the Russians had captured a redoubt and some heavy guns at Czartovijsk, which, he explained, was forty-four miles north-east of Luck. At Martinpuich a large yellowish explosion had been observed. On Tuesday afternoon I went up to the Line with Durley on some preliminary errand, for we were to relieve a battalion of the Border Regiment next day, in the sector in front of Fricourt Cemetery. Our Batteries were firing strenuously all along the countryside, with very little retaliation.

As we passed the gun-pits where some Heavies were hidden in a hollow called Gibraltar, I remarked on a sickly sweet smell which I attributed to the yellow weeds which were abundant there, but Durley explained that it was the lingering aroma of gas-shells. When we rode down the slope to 71. North, that familiar resort appeared much the same as usual, except for the impressive accumulations of war material which were dumped along the road. Durley remarked that he supposed the old spot would never be the same again after this week; and already it seemed to us as if the old days when Mansfield and Ormand were with our company had become an experience to be looked back on with regret. The Bois Français sector had been a sort of village, but we should soon be leaving it behind us in our vindictive explorations of Rose Trench, Apple Alley, and Willow Avenue.

On our way up to the Front Line we met a staff-officer who was wearing well-cut riding boots and evidently in a hurry to rejoin his horse. Larks were rejoicing aloft, and the usual symbolic scarlet poppies lolled over the sides of the communication trench; but he squeezed past us without so much as a nod, for the afternoon was too noisy to be idyllic, in spite of the larks and poppies which were so popular with war-correspondents. 'I suppose those brass-hats do know a hell of a lot about it all, don't they, Julian?' I queried. Durley replied that he hoped they'd learnt something since last autumn when they'd allowed the infantry to educate themselves at Loos, regardless of expense.

'They've got to learn their job as they go along, like the rest of us,' he added sagely. Five sausage balloons were visible beyond the sky-line, peacefully tethered to their mother earth. It was our duty to desire their destruction, and to believe that Corps Intelligence had the matter well in hand. What we did up in the Front Line I don't remember; but while we were remounting our horses at 71. North two privates were engaged in a good-humoured scuffle; one had the other's head under his arm. Why should I remember that and forget so much else?

Wednesday morning was miserably wet. Junior officers, being at a loss to know where to put themselves, were continually meeting one another along the muddy street, and gathering in groups to exchange cheerful remarks; there was little else to be done, and solitude produced the sinking sensation appropriate to the circumstances. The men were in their billets, and they too were keeping their spirits up as vocally as they could. At noon Barton came back from the Colonel's final conference of company commanders. A couple of hours later the anti-climax arrived. We were told that all arrangements for the show were in temporary abeyance. A popular song, *All dressed up and nowhere to go*, provided the obvious comment, and our confidence in Operation Orders oozed away. Was it the wet weather, we wondered, or had the artillery preparation been inadequate? Uncertainty ended with an inanimate message; we were to go up to the line that evening. The attack was postponed forty-eight hours. No one knew why.

At five o'clock C Company fell in, about eighty strong. The men were without packs; they carried extra ammunition, two Mills' bombs, two smoke helmets, and a waterproof sheet with a jersey rolled inside; their emergency rations consisted of two tins of bully beef, eight hard biscuits, and canteen packed with grocery ration. In spite of the anti-climax (which had made us feel that perhaps this was only going to be a second edition of the Battle of Loos) my personal impression was that we were setting out for the other end of nowhere. I had slipped a book into my haversack and it was a comfort to be carrying it, for Thomas Hardy's England

39

was between its covers. But if any familiar quotation was in my mind during the bustle of departure, it may well have been 'we brought nothing into this world, and it is certain we can carry nothing out of it'. We had trudged that way up to the Citadel and 71. North many times before; but never in such a blood-red light as now, when we halted with the sunset behind us and the whole sky mountainous with the magnificence of retreating rainclouds. Tours of trenches had been routine, with an ordinary chance of casualties. But this time we seemed to have left Morlancourt behind us for ever, and even a single company of Flintshire Fusiliers (with a ten minute interval between it and B and D Companies) was justified in feeling that the eyes of Europe were upon it. As for myself, I felt nothing worth recording – merely a sense of being irrevocably involved in something bigger than had ever happened before. And the symbolism of the sunset was wasted on the rank and file, who were concerned with the not infrequent badness of their boots, the discomfort caused by perspiration, and the toils and troubles of keeping pace with what was required of them till further notice. By nine o'clock we had relieved the Border Regiment. The mud was bad, but the sky was clear. The bombardment went on steadily, with periods of intensity; but that infernal shindy was taken for granted and was an aid to optimism. I felt rather lonely without Durley, who had been left behind with the dozen officers who were in reserve.

New Trench, which we took over, had been a good deal knocked about, but we passed an unharassed night. We were opposite Sunken Road Trench, which was 300 yards away up a slope. Gaps had been cut in our wire for the attacking battalion to pass through. Early on the next afternoon Kinjack came up to inspect the gaps. With the assistance of his big periscope he soon discovered that the wire wasn't properly cut. It must be done that night, he said. Barton brought me the news. I was huddled up in a little dog-kennel of a dug-out, reading *Tess of the D'Urbervilles* and trying to forget about the shells which were hurrying and hurrooshing overhead. I was meditating about England, visualizing a grey day down in Sussex; dark green woodlands with pigeons circling above the tree-tops; dogs barking, cocks crowing, and all the casual tappings and twinklings of the countryside. I thought of the huntsman walking out in his long white coat with the hounds; of Parson Colwood pulling up weeds in his garden till teatime; of Captain Huxtable helping his men get in the last load of hay while a shower of rain moved along the blurred Weald below his meadows. It was for all that, I supposed, that I was in the front-line with soaked feet, trench mouth, and feeling short of sleep, for the previous night had been vigilant though uneventful. Barton's head and shoulders butting past the gas-blanket in the dug-out doorway wrecked my reverie; he wanted me to come out and have a squint at the uncut wire, which was no day dream since it was going to affect the fortunes of a still undiminished New Army Battalion. Putting *Tess* in my pocket, I followed him to the fire-trench, which was cumbered with gas-cylinders and boxes of smoke-bombs. A smoke-cloud was to be let off later in the afternoon, for no special reason (except, perhaps, to make us cough and wipe our eyes, since what wind there was blew the smoke along our trench). Shells were banging away on the rising ground behind Fricourt and the low ridge of Contalmaison. A young yellow-hammer was fluttering about in the trench, and I wondered how it had got there: it seemed out of place, perching on a body which lay trussed in a waterproof sheet. As for the gaps in the wire, they looked too bad for words and only one night remained for widening them.

When I was back in the dug-out I found myself fingering with pardonable pride my two pairs of wire-cutters from the Army and Navy Stores. It is possible that I over-estimated their usefulness, but their presence did seem providential. Any fool could foresee what happened when troops got bunched up as they left their trench for a daylight attack; and I knew that, in spite of obstinate indentations to the source of supplies, we hadn't got a decent pair of wire-cutters in the Battalion.

The big-bugs back at Brigade and Divisional H.Q. were studying trench-maps with corrugated brows, for the 'greatest battle in history' was timed to explode on Saturday morning.

They were too busy to concern themselves with the ant-like activities of individual platoon commanders, and if they sent a sympathetic Staff Captain up to have a look round he couldn't produce wire-cutters like a conjuror. But the fact remained that insistence on small (and often irrelevant) details was a proverbial characteristic of Staff organization, and on the eve of battle poor old Barton would probably be filling in a 'return' stating how many men in his company had got varicose veins or married their deceased wife's sister. In the meantime my casual purchase at 'the Stores' had, perhaps, lessened the likelihood of the Manchesters getting bunched up and mown down by machine-guns when they went over the top to attack Sunken Road Trench. And what would the Manchesters say about the Flintshire Fusiliers if the wire wasn't properly cut? So it seemed to me that our prestige as a Regular Battalion had been entrusted to my care on a front of several hundred yards.

Anyhow, I was ready with my party as soon as it began to be dark. There were only eight of them (mostly from the other companies) and we were unable to do anything before midnight owing to rather lively shelling. I remember waiting there in the gloom and watching an unearthly little conflagration caused by some phosphorus bombs up the hill on our right. When we did get started I soon discovered that cutting tangles of barbed wire in the dark in a desperate hurry is a job that needs ingenuity, even when your wire-cutters have rubber-covered handles and are fresh from the Army and Navy Stores. More than once we were driven in by shells which landed in front of our trench (some of them were our own dropping short); two men were wounded and some of the others were reluctant to resume work. In the first greying of dawn only three of us were still at it. Kendle (a nineteen-year-old lance-corporal from my platoon) and Worgan (one of the tough characters of our company) were slicing away for all they were worth; but as the light increased I began to realize the unimpressive effect of the snippings and snatchings which had made such a mess of our leather gloves. We had been working three and a half hours but the hedge hadn't suffered much damage, it seemed. Kendle disappeared into the trench and sauntered back to me, puffing a surreptitious Woodbine. I was making a last onslaught on a clawing thicket which couldn't have been more hostile if it had been put there by the Germans. 'We can't do any more in this daylight,' said Kendle. I straightened my stiff and weary back and looked at him. His jaunty fag-smoking demeanour and freckled boyish face seemed to defy the darkness we had emerged from. That moment has impressed itself strongly on my memory; young Kendle was remarkable for his cheerfulness and courage, and his cheeky jokes. Many a company had its Kendle, until the war broke his spirit . . . The large solicitous countenance of old man Barton now appeared above the parapet; with almost aunt-like anxiety he urged us to come in before we got sniped. But there had been no sniping that night, and the machine-gun at Wing Corner had been silent. Wing Corner was at the edge of the skeleton village of Fricourt, whose ruinous church tower was now distinctly visible against the dark green wood. The Germans, coming up from their foundering dug-outs, would soon be staring grimly across at us while they waited for the relentless bombardment to begin again. As we got down into the trench young Kendle remarked that my new wire-cutters were a fair treat.

Next day, in warm and breezy weather, we moved to our battle-assembly position. For C Company 'battle-assembly position' meant being broken up into ammunition carrying parties, while Barton, Jenkins, and myself occupied an inglorious dug-out in the support line. The Manchesters were due to relieve us at 9 a.m., but there was still no sign of them at 10.30, so Barton, who was in a free and easy mood, (caused by our immunity from to-morrow's attack) led the company away and left New Trench to look after itself. I had made up my mind to have another cut at the wire, which I now regarded with personal enmity, enjoying at the same time a self-admiring belief that much depended on my efforts. Worgan stayed behind with me. Kendle was unwilling to be left out of the adventure, but two of us would be less conspicuous than three, and my feeling for Kendle was somewhat protective. It was queer to be in an empty front-line trench on a fine morning, with everything quite peaceful after a violent early bombardment. Queerer still to be creeping about in the long grass (which might well have been longer, I thought) and shearing savagely at the tangles which had bewildered us in the dark but were now at our mercy. As Worgan said, we were giving it a proper hair-cut this journey.

Lying on my stomach I glanced now and again at the hostile slope which overlooked us, wondering whether anyone would take a pot-shot at us, or speculating on a possible visitation of machine-gun bullets from Wing Corner. Barton's ignorance of what we were doing made it seem like an escapade, and the excitement was by no means disagreeable. It was rather like going out to weed a neglected garden after being warned that there might be a tiger among the gooseberry bushes. I should have been astonished if someone could have told me that I was an interesting example of human egotism. Yet such was the truth. I was cutting the wire by daylight because common sense warned me that the lives of several hundred soldiers might depend on it being done properly. I was excited and pleased with myself while I was doing it. And I had entirely forgotten that to-morrow six Army Corps would attack, and whatever else happened, a tragic slaughter was inevitable. But if I had been intelligent enough to realize all that, my talents would have been serving in some more exalted place, probably Corps Intelligence Headquarters. Anyhow, at the end of an hour and a half the gaps were real good ones, and Barton's red face and glittering pince-nez were bobbing up and down beyond the parapet with *sotto voce* incitements to prudence. Soon afterwards we dropped into the trench and the Manchesters began to arrive. It had been great fun, I said, flourishing my wire-cutters.

Early in the afternoon the Doctor bustled up from Battalion Headquarters to tell me that my M.C. had come through. This gratifying little event increased my blindness to the blood-stained future. Homeliness and humanity beamed in Barton's congratulations; and the little doctor, who would soon be dressing the wounds of moaning men, unpicked his own faded medal-ribbon, produced a needle and thread, and sewed the white and purple portent on to my tunic. For the rest of the day and, indeed, for the remainder of my military career, the left side of my chest was more often in my mind than the right – a habit which was common to a multitude of wearers of Military Cross ribbons. Books about war psychology ought to contain a chapter on 'medal-reflexes' and 'decoration complexes'. Much might be written, even here, about medals and their stimulating effect on those who really risked their lives for them. But the safest thing to be said is that nobody knew how much a decoration was worth except the man who received it. Outwardly the distribution of them became more and more fortuitous and debased as the War went on; and no one knew it better than the infantry, who rightly insisted that medal-ribbons earned at the Base ought to be a different colour.

But I must return to June 30th, which ended with a sullen bombardment from the British guns and a congestion of troops in the support-trench outside our dug-out. They had lost their way, and I remember how the exhausted men propped themselves against the sides of the trench while their exasperated Adjutant and a confused civilian Colonel grumbled to Barton about the ambiguity of their operation orders. They were to attack on our left, and they vanished in that direction, leaving me with my Military Cross and a foreboding that disaster awaited them. Since they came within the limited zone of my observations I can record the fact that they left their trench early next morning at a wrong zero hour and got badly cut up by the artillery support which ought to have made things easy for them.

II

On July the first the weather, after an early morning mist, was of the kind commonly called heavenly. Down in our frowsty cellar we breakfasted at six, unwashed and apprehensive. Our table, appropriately enough, was an empty ammunition box. At six-forty-five the final bombardment began, and there was nothing for us to do except sit round our candle until the tornado ended. For more than forty minutes the air vibrated and the earth rocked and shuddered. Through the sustained uproar the tap and rattle of machine-guns could be identified; but except for the whistle of bullets no retaliation came our way until a few 5.9 shells shook the roof of our dug-out. Barton and I sat speechless, deafened and stupefied by the seismic state of affairs, and when he lit a cigarette the match flame staggered crazily. Afterwards I asked him what he had been thinking about. His reply was 'Carpet slippers and kettle-holders'. My own mind had been working in much the same style, for during that cannonading cataclysm the following refrain was running in my head:

> They come as a boon and a blessing to men,
> The Something, the Owl, and the Waverley Pen.

For the life of me I couldn't remember what the first one was called. Was it the Shakespeare? Was it the Dickens? Anyhow it was an advertisement which I'd often seen in smoky railway stations. Then the bombardment lifted and lessened, our vertigo abated, and we looked at one another in dazed relief. Two Brigades of our Division were now going over the top on our right. Our Brigade was to attack 'when the main assault had reached its final objective'. In our fortunate role of privileged spectators Barton and I went up the stairs to see what we could from Kingston Road Trench. We left Jenkins crouching in a corner, where he remained most of the day. His haggard blinking face haunts my memory. He was an example of the paralysing effect which such an experience could produce on a nervous system sensitive to noise, for he was a good officer both before and afterwards. I felt no sympathy for him at the time, but I do now. From the support-trench, which Barton called 'our opera box', I observed as much of the battle as the formation of the country allowed, the rising ground on the right making it impossible to see anything of the attack towards Mametz. A small shiny black notebook contains my pencilled particulars, and nothing will be gained by embroidering them with afterthoughts. I cannot turn my field-glasses on to the past.

7.45. The barrage is now working to the right of Fricourt and beyond. I can see the 21st Division advancing about three-quarters of a mile away on the left and a few Germans coming to meet them, apparently surrendering. Our men in small parties (not extended in line) go steadily on to the German front-line. Brilliant sunshine and a haze of smoke drifting along the landscape. Some Yorkshires a little way below on the left, watching the show and cheering as if at a football match. The noise almost as bad as ever.

9.30. Came back to the dug-out and had a shave. 21st Division still going across the open, apparently without casualties. The sunlight flashes on bayonets as the tiny figures move quietly forward and disappear beyond mounds of trench débris. A few runners come back and ammunition parties go across. Trench-mortars are knocking hell out of Sunken Road Trench and the ground where the Manchesters will attack soon. Noise not so bad now and very little retaliation.

9.50. Fricourt half-hidden by clouds of drifting smoke, blue, pinkish and grey. Shrapnel bursting in small bluish-white puffs with tiny flashes. The birds seem bewildered; a lark begins to go up and then flies feebly along, thinking better of it. Others flutter above the trench with querulous cries, weak on the wing. I can see seven of our balloons, on the right. On the left our men still filing across in twenties and thirties. Another huge explosion in Fricourt and a cloud of brown-pink smoke. Some bursts are yellowish.

10.05. I can see the Manchesters down in New Trench, getting ready to go over. Figures filing down the trench. Two of them have gone out to look at our wire gaps! Have just eaten my last orange . . . I am staring at a sunlit picture of Hell, and still the breeze shakes the yellow weeds, and the poppies glow under Crawley Ridge where some shells fell a few minutes ago. Manchesters are sending forward some scouts. A bayonet glitters.

47

A runner comes back across the open to their Battalion Head-quarters close here on the right. 21st Division still trotting along the skyline toward La Boisselle. Barrage going strong to the right of Contalmaison Ridge. Heavy shelling toward Mametz.

12.15. Quieter the last two hours. Manchesters still waiting. Germans putting over a few shrapnel shells. Silly if I got hit! Weather cloudless and hot. A lark singing confidently overhead.

1.30. Manchesters attack at 2.30. Mametz and Montauban reported taken. Mametz consolidated.

2.30. Manchesters left New Trench and apparently took Sunken Road Trench, bearing rather to the right. Could see about 400. Many walked casually across with sloped arms. There were about forty casualties on the left (from machine-gun in Fricourt). Through my glasses I could see one man moving his left arm up and down as he lay on his side; his face was a crimson patch. Others lay still in the sunlight while the swarm of figures disappeared over the hill. Fricourt was a cloud of pinkish smoke. Lively machine-gun fire on the far side of the hill. At 2.50 no one to be seen in no-man's-land except the casualties (about half-way across). Our dug-out shelled again since 2.30.

5.0. I saw about thirty of our A Company crawl across to Sunken Road from New Trench. Germans put a few big shells on the Cemetery and traversed Kingston Road with machine-gun. Manchester wounded still out there. Remainder of A Company went across – about 100 altogether. Manchesters reported held up in Bois Français Support. Their Colonel went across and was killed.

8.0. Staff Captain of our Brigade has been along. Told Barton that Seventh Division has reached its objectives with some difficulty, except on this Brigade front. Manchesters are in trouble, and Fricourt attack has failed. Several hundred prisoners brought in on our sector.

9.30. Our A Company holds Rectangle and Sunken Road. Jenkins gone off in charge of a carrying-party. Seemed all right again. C Company now reduced to six runners, two stretcher-bearers, Company Sergeant-Major, signallers, and Barton's servant. Flook away on carrying-party. Sky cloudy westward. Red sunset. Heavy gun-fire on the left.

2.30. (Next afternoon.) Adjutant has just been up here, excited, optimistic, and unshaven. He went across last night to ginger up A Company who did very well, thanks to the bombers. About 40 casualties; only 4 killed. Fricourt and Rose Trench occupied this morning without resistance. I am now lying out in front of our trench in the long grass, basking in sunshine where yesterday there were bullets. Our new front-line on the hill is being shelled. Fricourt is full of troops wandering about in search of souvenirs. The village was a ruin and is now a dust heap. A gunner (Forward Observation Officer) has just been along here with a German helmet in his hand. Said Fricourt is full of dead; he saw one officer lying across a smashed machine-gun with his head bashed in – 'a fine looking chap,' he said, with some emotion, which rather surprised me.

8.15. Queer feeling, seeing people moving about freely between here and Fricourt. Dumps being made. Shacks and shelters being put up under skeleton trees and all sorts of transport arriving at Cemetery Cross Roads. We stay here till to-morrow morning. Feel a bit of a fraud.

### III

Early next morning we took leave of our subterranean sanctuary in Kingston Road, joined the Battalion at 71. North, and marched a couple of miles to a concentration point between Mametz and Carnoy. There, in a wide hollow, the four units of our Brigade piled arms, lay down on the grass, and took their boots off. Most of them had been without sleep for two nights and the immediate forecast was 'murky'. But every man had a waterproof sheet to sit on, helmets were exchanged for woollen caps, unshaven faces felt gratitude for generous sunshine, and bare feet stretched contented toes. Our Division having done well, there was a confident feeling in the air. But we had heard of partial and complete failures in other parts of the line, and the name of Gommecourt had already reached us with ugly implications. It was obvious that some of us would soon be lacing up our boots for the last time, and the current rumour, 'They say we've got to attack some Wood or other', could not fail to cause an uneasy visceral sensation. However, one felt that big things were happening, and my Military Cross was a comfort to me. It was a definite personal possession to be lived up to, I thought. I watched the men dozing in odd ungainly attitudes, half listened to their talk about the souvenirs they'd picked up in the German trenches, or stared at some captured guns being brought down the lane which led to Mametz.

A few of the men were wandering about, and my meditations were disturbed by Kinjack, who had given orders that everyone was to rest all day. 'Tell those men to lie down,' he shouted, adding – as he returned to his bivouac on the slope – 'The bastards'll be glad to before they're much older.' It was believed that his brusque manners had prevented him getting promotion, but everyone knew that it would be a bad day for the Battalion when Kinjack got his Brigade.

Evening fell calm and overcast, with a blurred orange sunset. Sitting among rank grass and thistles I stared pensively down at the four battalions grouped in the hollow. Thin smoke rose from the little bivouac fires which had been used for tea making; among the gruff murmuring which came up with the smoke, the nasal chant of a mouth organ did its best to 'keep the home fires burning'. In front of the hollow the open ground sloped treeless to Bazentin Ridge, dull green and striped with seams of trenches cut in the chalky soil. Field-guns were firing on the right and some aeroplanes hummed overhead. Beyond that hill our future awaited us. There would be no turning back from it . . . I would have liked Flook to bring me an orange, but he was away with Jenkins and the carrying-party, and oranges were almost as remote as the sunset. Poor Flook will be awfully worried about not being with his officer bloke, I thought, imagining his stolid red face puffing along under a box of ammunition . . . I went down the hill just in time to hear that we'd got orders to go up and dig a trench somewhere in front of Mametz.

For a few minutes the hollow was full of the subdued hubbub and commotion of troops getting into their equipment. Two battalions had been called out; the Royal Irish moved off ahead of us. As we went up the lane toward Mametz I felt that I was leaving all my previous war experience behind me. For the first time I was among the débris of an attack. After going a very short distance we made the first of many halts, and I saw, arranged by the roadside, about fifty of the British dead. Many of them were Gordon Highlanders. There were Devons and South Stafford-shires among them, but they were beyond regimental rivalry now – their fingers mingled in blood-stained bunches, as though acknowledging the companionship of death. There was much battle gear lying about, and some dead horses. There were rags and shreds of clothing, boots riddled and torn, and when we came to the old German front-line, a sour pervasive stench which differed from anything my nostrils had known before. Meanwhile we made our continually retarded progress up the hill, and I scrutinized these battle effects with partially complacent curiosity. I wanted to be able to say that I had seen 'the horrors of war'; and here they were, nearly three days old.

No one in the glumly halted column knew what was delaying us. After four hours we had only progressed 1,500 yards and were among some ruined buildings on the outskirts of the village. I have dim remembrance of the strangeness of the place and our uneasy dawdling in its midnight desolation. Kinjack was somewhere ahead of us with a guide. The guide, having presumably lost his way, was having a much hotter time than we were. So far we had done nothing except file past a tool-dump, where the men had collected picks, shovels, coils of wire, and corkscrew stakes. At 2 a.m. we really began to move, passing through Mametz and along a communication trench. There were some badly mangled bodies about. Although I'd been with the Battalion nearly eight months, these were the first newly dead Germans I had seen. It gave me a bit of a shock when I saw, in the glimmer of daybreak, a dumpy, baggy-trousered man lying half sideways with one elbow up as if defending his lolling head; the face was grey and waxen, with a stiff little moustache; he looked like a ghastly doll, grotesque and undignified. Beside him was a scorched and mutilated figure whose contorted attitude revealed bristly cheeks, a grinning blood-smeared mouth and clenched teeth. These dead were unlike our own; perhaps it was the strange uniform, perhaps their look of butchered hostility. Anyhow they were one with the little trench direction boards whose unfamiliar lettering seemed to epitomize that queer feeling I used to have when I stared across no-man's-land, ignorant of the humanity which was on the other side.

Leaving the trench we filed across the open hillside with Mametz Wood looming on the opposite slope. It was a dense wood of old trees and undergrowth. The Staff of our Division had assumed that the near side was now unoccupied. But as soon as we had halted in a sunken road an uproar broke out at the edge of the wood, which demonstrated with machine-guns and bombs that the Staff had guessed wrong.

Kinjack promptly ordered A Company forward to get in touch with the Royal Irish, whose covering parties were having a bombing fight in the Wood. Our men were fired on as they went along the road and forced to take cover in a quarry. I remember feeling nervous and incompetent while I wondered what on earth I should do if called on to lead a party out 'into the blue'. But the clouds were now reddening, and we were fed up with the whole performance. Messages went back and our guns chucked a lot of shrapnel which burst over the near side of the Wood and enabled the Irish to withdraw. We then, as Kinjack described it afterwards, 'did a guy'; but it was a slow one for we weren't back at our camping ground until 8.30 a.m. The expedition had lasted nearly eleven hours and we had walked less than three miles, which was about all we could congratulate ourselves on. The Royal Irish had had sixty casualties; we had one killed and four wounded. From a military point of view the operations had enabled the Staff to discover that Mametz Wood was still full of Germans, so that it was impossible to dig a trench on the bluff within fifty yards of it, as had been suggested. It was obvious now that a few strong patrols could have clarified the situation more economically than

1,000 men with picks and shovels. The necessary information had been obtained, however, and the Staff could hardly be expected to go up and investigate such enigmas for themselves. But this sort of warfare was a new experience for all of us, and the difficulties of extempore organization must have been considerable.

During the morning we were a silent battalion, except for snoring. Some eight-inch guns were firing about 200 yards from the hollow, but our slumbers were inured to noises which would have kept us wide awake in civilian life. We were lucky to be dry, for the sky was overcast. At one o'clock our old enemy the rain arrived in full force. Four hours' deluge left the troops drenched and disconsolate, and then Dottrell made one of his providential appearances with the rations. Dixies of hot tea, and the rum issue, made all the difference to our outlook. It seemed to me that the Quartermaster symbolized that region of temporary security which awaited us when our present adversities were ended. He had a cheery word for everyone, and his jocularity was judicious. What were the jokes he made, I wonder? Their helpfulness must be taken for granted. I can only remember his chaffing an officer named Woolman, whose dumpy figure had bulged abnormally since we came up to the battle area. Woolman's young lady in England had sent him a bullet-proof waistcoat; so far it had only caused its wearer to perspire profusely; and although reputed to be extremely vulnerable, it had inspired a humorist in his company to refer to him as 'Asbestos Bill'.

Time seems to have obliterated the laughter of the war. I cannot hear it in my head. How strange such laughter would sound, could I but recover it as it was on such an evening as I am describing, when we all knew that we'd got to do an attack that night; for short-sighted Barton and the other company commanders had just returned from a reconnaissance of the ground which had left them little wiser than when they started. In the meantime we'd got some rum inside us and could find something to laugh about. Our laughter leapt up, like the flames of camp fires in the dusk, soon to be stamped out, or extinguished by our impartial opponent, the rain. The consoling apparition of Dottrell departed and I don't suppose he did much laughing once he was alone with his homeward rattling limbers.

Zero hour was forty-five minutes after midnight. Two companies were to attack on a 600-yard front and the Royal Irish were to do the same on our right. Barton's company was to be in reserve; owing to the absence of the carrying-party it could only muster about thirty men.

At nine o'clock we started up the sunken road to Mametz. As a result of the rain, yesterday's dry going had been trodden to a quagmire. Progress was slow owing to the congestion of troops in front. We had only a couple of thousand yards to go, but at one time it seemed unlikely that the assaulting companies would be in position by zero hour. It was pitch dark as we struggled through the mud, and we got there with fifteen minutes to spare, having taken three and a half hours to go a mile and a quarter.

Barton arranged his men along a shallow support trench on the edge of Bottom Wood, which was a copse just to the left of the ground we'd visited the night before. Almost at once the short preliminary bombardment began and the darkness became diabolic with the din and flash of the old old story. Not for the first time – I wondered whether shells ever collided in the air. Silence and suspense came after. Barton and I talked in undertones; he thought I'd better borrow his electric torch and find out the nearest way to Battalion Headquarters.

Everyone was anonymous in the dark, but 'It's me, Kendle, sir,' from a looming figure beside me implied an intention to share my explorations. We groped our way into the wood, and very soon I muttered that unless we were careful we'd get lost, which was true enough, for my sense of direction had already become uncertain. While we hesitated, some shells exploded all round us in the undergrowth with an effect of crashing stupidity. But we laughed, encouraging each other with mutual bravado, until we found a path. Along this path came someone in a hurry. He bumped into me and I flashed the torch on his face. He was an officer who had joined us the week before. He had now lost all control of himself and I gathered from his incoherent utterances that he was on his way to Headquarters to tell Kinjack that his Company hadn't moved yet because they didn't know which way to go to find the Germans. This wasn't surprising; but I felt alarmed about his reception at Headquarters, for Kinjack had already got an idea that this poor devil was 'cold-footed'. So, with an assumption of ferocity, I pulled out my automatic pistol, gripped him by the shoulder, and told him that if he didn't go straight back to 'Asbestos Bill' I'd shoot him, adding that Kinjack would certainly shoot him if he rolled up at Headquarters with such a story and in such a state of 'wind-up'. This sobered him and he took my advice, though I doubt whether he did any damage to the Germans. (Ten days later he was killed in what I can only call a *bona fide* manner.) So far, I thought, my contribution to this attack is a queer one; I have saved one of our officers from being court-martialled for cowardice. I then remarked to Kendle that this seemed to be the shortest way to Battalion Headquarters and we found our own way back to Barton without further incident. I told Barton that 'Asbestos Bill' seemed to be marking time, in spite of his bullet-proof waistcoat.

The men were sitting on the rough-hewn fire-step, and soon we were all dozing. Barton's bulky figure nodded beside me, and Kendle fell fast asleep with his head against my shoulder. We remained like this until my luminous watch indicated twenty past two. Then a runner arrived with a verbal message. 'C Company bombers to go up at once.' With a dozen men behind me I followed him through Bottom Wood. Darkness was giving way to unrevealing twilight as we emerged from the trees and went up a shell-pitted slope. It was about 500 yards across the open to the newly captured Quadrangle Trench. Just before we got there a second runner overtook us to say that my bombers were to go back again. I sent them back. I cannot say why I went on myself; but I did, and Kendle stayed with me.

There wasn't much wire in front of Quadrangle Trench. I entered it at a strong point on the extreme left and found three officers sitting on the fire-step with hunched shoulders and glum unenterprising faces. Two others had gone away wounded. I was told that Edmunds, the Battalion Observation Officer, had gone down to explain the situation to Kinjack; we were in touch with the Northumberland Fusiliers on our left. Nevertheless I felt that there must be something to be done. Exploring to the right I found young Fernby, whose demeanour was a contrast to the apathetic trio in the sand-bagged strong-point. Fernby had only been out from England a few weeks but he appeared quite at home in his new surroundings. His face showed that he was exulting in the fact that he didn't feel afraid. He told me that no one knew what had happened on our right; the Royal Irish were believed to have failed. We went along the trench which was less than waist deep. The Germans had evidently been digging when we attacked, and had left their packs and other equipment ranged along the reverse edge of the trench. I stared about me; the smoke-drifted twilight was alive with intense movement, and there was a wild strangeness in the scene which somehow excited me. Our men seemed a bit out of hand and I couldn't see any of the responsible N.C.O.s; some of the troops were firing excitedly at the Wood; others were rummaging in the German packs. Fernby said that we were being sniped from the trees on both sides. Mametz Wood was a menacing wall of gloom, and now an outburst of rapid thudding explosions began from that direction. There was a sap from the Quadrangle to the Wood, and along this the Germans were bombing. In all this confusion I formed the obvious notion that we ought to be deepening the trench. Daylight would be on us at once, and we were along a slope exposed to enfilade fire from the Wood. I told Fernby to make the men dig for all they were worth, and went to the right with Kendle. The Germans had left a lot of shovels, but we were making no use of them. Two tough-looking privates were disputing the ownership of a pair of field-glasses, so I pulled out my pistol and urged them, with ferocious objurations, to chuck all that fooling and dig. I seemed to be getting pretty handy with my pistol, I thought, for the conditions in Quadrangle Trench were giving me a sort of angry impetus. In some places it was only a foot deep, and already men were lying wounded and killed by sniping. There were high-booted German bodies, too, and in the blear beginning of daylight they seemed as much the victims of a catastrophe as the men who had attacked them. As I stepped over one of the Germans an impulse made me lift him up from the miserable ditch. Propped against the bank, his blond face was undisfigured, except by the mud which I wiped from his eyes and mouth with my coat sleeve. He'd evidently been killed while digging, for his tunic was knotted loosely about his shoulders. He didn't look to be more than eighteen. Hoisting him a little higher, I thought what a gentle face he had, and remembered that this was the first time I'd ever touched one of our enemies with my hands. Perhaps I had some dim sense of the futility which had put an end to this good-looking youth. Anyhow I hadn't expected the Battle of the Somme to be quite like this . . . Kendle, who had been trying to do something for a badly wounded man, now rejoined me, and we continued, mostly on all fours, along the dwindling trench. We passed no one until we came to a bombing post – three serious-minded men who said that no one had been further than that yet. Being in an exploring frame of mind, I took a bag of bombs and crawled another sixty or seventy yards with Kendle close behind me. The trench became a shallow groove and ended where the ground overlooked a little valley along which there was a light railway line. We stared across at the Wood. From the other side of the valley came an occasional rifle-shot, and a helmet bobbed up for a moment. Kendle remarked that from that point anyone could see into the whole of our trench on the slope behind us. I said we must have our strong-post here and told him to go back for the bombers and a Lewis gun. I felt adventurous and it seemed as if Kendle and I were having great fun together. Kendle thought so too. The helmet bobbed up again. 'I'll just have a shot at him,' he said, wriggling away from the crumbling bank which gave us cover. At this moment Fernby appeared with two men and a Lewis gun. Kendle was half kneeling against some broken ground; I remember seeing him push his tin hat back from his forehead and then raise himself a few inches to take aim. After firing once he looked at us with a lively smile; a second later he fell sideways. A blotchy mark showed where the bullet had hit him just above the eyes.

The circumstances being what they were, I had no justification for feeling either shocked or astonished by the sudden extinction of Lance-Corporal Kendle. But after blank awareness that he was killed, all feelings tightened and contracted to a single intention – to 'settle that sniper' on the other side of the valley. If I had stopped to think, I shouldn't have gone at all. As it was, I discarded my tin hat and equipment, slung a bag of bombs across my shoulder, abruptly informed Fernby that I was going to find out who *was* there, and set off at a downhill double. While I was running I pulled the safety-pin out of a Mills' bomb; my right hand being loaded, I did the same for my left. I mention this because I was obliged to extract the second safety-pin with my teeth, and the grating sensation reminded me that I was half way across and not so reckless as I had been when I started. I was even a little out of breath as I trotted up the opposite slope. Just before I arrived at the top I slowed up and threw my two bombs. Then I rushed at the bank, vaguely expecting some sort of scuffle with my imagined enemy. I had lost my temper with the man who had shot Kendle; quite unexpectedly, I found myself looking down into a well-conducted trench with a great many Germans in it. Fortunately for me, they were already retreating. It had not occurred to them that they were being attacked by a single fool; and Fernby, with presence of mind which probably saved me, had covered my advance by traversing the top of the trench with his Lewis gun. I slung a few more bombs, but they fell short of the clumsy field-grey figures, some of whom half turned to fire their rifles over the left shoulder as they ran across the open toward the wood, while a crowd of jostling helmets vanished along the trench. Idiotically elated, I stood there with my finger in my right ear and emitted a series of 'view-holloas' (a gesture which ought to win the approval of people who still regard war as a form of outdoor sport). Having thus failed to commit suicide, I proceeded to occupy the trench – that is to say, I sat down on the fire-step, very much out of breath, and hoped to God the Germans wouldn't come back again.

The trench was deep and roomy, with a fine view of our men in the Quadrangle, but I had no idea what to do now I had got possession of it. The word 'consolidation' passed through my mind; but I couldn't consolidate by myself. Naturally, I didn't under-estimate the magnitude of my achievement in capturing the trench on which the Royal Irish had made a frontal attack in the dark. Nevertheless, although still unable to see that my success was only a lucky accident, I felt a bit queer in my solitude, so I reinforced my courage by counting the sets of equipment which had been left behind. There were between forty and fifty packs, tidily arranged in a row – a fact which I often mentioned (quite casually) when describing my exploit afterwards. There was the doorway of a dug-out, but I only peered in at it, feeling safer above ground. Then, with apprehensive caution, I explored about half way to the Wood without finding any dead bodies. Apparently no one was any the worse for my little bombing demonstration. Perhaps I was disappointed by this, though the discovery of a dead or wounded enemy might have caused a revival of humane emotion. Returning to the sniping post at the end of the trench I meditated for a few minutes, somewhat like a boy who has caught a fish too big to carry home (if such an improbable event has ever happened). Finally I took a deep breath and ran headlong back by the way I'd come.

Little Fernby's anxious face awaited me, and I flopped down beside him with an outburst of hysterical laughter. When he'd heard my story he asked whether we oughtn't to send a party across to occupy the trench, but I said that the Germans would be bound to come back quite soon. Moreover my rapid return had attracted the attention of a machine-gun which was now firing angrily along the valley from a position in front of the Wood. In my excitement I had forgotten about Kendle. The sight of his body gave me a bit of a shock. His face had gone a bluish colour; I told one of the bombers to cover it with something. Then I put on my web-equipment and its attachments, took a pull at my water-bottle, for my mouth had become suddenly intolerably dry, and set off on my return journey, leaving Fernby to look after the bombing post. It was now six o'clock in the morning, and a weary business it is, to be remembering and writing it down. There was nothing likeable about the Quadrangle, though it was comfortable, from what I have heard, compared with the hell which it became a few days afterwards. Alternately crouching and crawling, I worked my way back. I passed the young German whose body I had rescued from disfigurement a couple of hours before. He was down in the mud again and someone had trodden on his face. It disheartened me to see him, though his body had now lost all touch with life and was part of the wastage of the war. He and Kendle had cancelled one another out in the process called 'attrition of man-power'. Further along I found one of our men dying slowly with a hole in his forehead. His eyes were open and he breathed with a horrible snoring sound. Close by him knelt two of his former mates; one of them was hacking at the ground with an entrenching tool while the other scooped the earth out of the trench with his hands. They weren't worrying about souvenirs now.

Disregarding a written order from Barton, telling me to return, I remained up in Quadrangle Trench all the morning. The enemy made a few attempts to bomb their way up the sap from the Wood and in that restricted area I continued to expend energy which was a result of strained nerves. I mention this because, as the day went on, I definitely wanted to kill someone at close quarters. If this meant that I was really becoming a good 'fighting man', I can only suggest that, as a human being, I was both exhausted and exasperated. My courage was of the cock-fighting kind. Cock-fighting is illegal in England, but in July, 1916 the man who could boast that he'd killed a German in the Battle of the Somme would have been patted on the back by a bishop in a hospital ward.

German stick-bombs were easy to avoid; they took eight seconds to explode, and the throwers didn't hang on to them many seconds after pulling the string. Anyhow, my feverish performances were concluded by a peremptory message from Battalion H.Q. and I went down to Bottom Wood by a half-dug communication trench whose existence I have only this moment remembered (which shows how difficult it is to recover the details of war experience).

It was nearly two o'clock, and the daylight was devoid of mystery when I arrived at Kinjack's headquarters. The circumstances now made it permissible for me to feel tired and hungry, but for the moment I rather expected congratulations. My expectation was an error. Kinjack sat glowering in a surface dugout in a sand-pit at the edge of Bottom Wood. I went in from the sunlight. The overworked Adjutant eyed me sadly from a corner of an ammunition box table covered with a grey blanket, and the Colonel's face caused me to feel like a newly captured prisoner. Angrily he asked why I hadn't come back with my company bombers in the early morning. I said I'd stayed up there to see what was happening. Why hadn't I consolidated Wood Trench? Why the hell hadn't I sent back a message to let him know that it had been occupied? I made no attempt to answer these conundrums. Obviously I'd made a mess of the whole affair. The Corps Artillery bombardment had been held up for three hours because Kinjack couldn't report that 'my patrol' had returned to Quadrangle Trench, and altogether he couldn't be blamed for feeling annoyed with me, especially as he'd been ticked off over the telephone by the Brigadier (in Morse Code dots and dashes, I suppose). I looked at him with a sulky grin, and went along to Barton with a splitting headache and a notion that I ought to be thankful that I was back at all.

In the evening we were relieved. The incoming battalion numbered more than double our own strength (we were less than 400) and they were unseasoned New Army troops. Our little trench under the trees was inundated by a jostling company of exclamatory Welshmen. Kinjack would have called them a panicky rabble. They were mostly undersized men, and as I watched them arriving at the first stage of their battle experience I had a sense of their victimization. A little platoon officer was settling his men down with a valiant show of self-assurance. For the sake of appearances, orders of some kind had to be given, though in reality there was nothing to do except sit down and hope it wouldn't rain. He spoke sharply to some of them, and I felt that they were like a lot of children. It was going to be a bad look-out for two such bewildered companies, huddled up in the Quadrangle, which had been over-garrisoned by our own comparatively small contingent. Visualizing that forlorn crowd of khaki figures under the twilight of the trees, I can believe that I saw then, for the first time, how blindly war destroys its victims. The sun had gone down on my own reckless brandishings, and I understood the doomed condition of these half trained civilians who had been sent up to attack the Wood. As we moved out, Barton exclaimed, 'By God, Kangar, I'm sorry for those poor devils!' Dimly he pitied them, as well he might. Two days later the Welsh Division, of which they were a unit, was involved in massacre and confusion. Our own occupation of Quadrangle Trench was only a prelude to that pandemonium which converted the green thickets of Mametz Wood to a desolation of skeleton trees and blackening bodies.

In the meantime we willingly left them to their troubles and marched back twelve miles to peace and safety. Mametz was being heavily shelled when we stumbled wearily through its ruins, but we got off lightly, though the first four miles took us four hours, owing to congestion of transport and artillery on the roads round Fricourt. On the hill above Bécordel we dozed for an hour in long wet grass, with stars overhead and guns booming and flashing in the valleys below. Then, in the first glimmer of a cold misty dawn, we trudged on to Heilly. We were there by eight o'clock, in hot sunshine. Our camp was on a marsh by the river Ancre – not a good camp when it rained (as it did before long) but a much pleasanter place than the Somme battlefield . . . After three hours' sleep I was roused by Flook. All officers were required to attend the Brigadier's conference. At this function there was no need for me to open my mouth, except for an occasional yawn. Kinjack favoured me with a good-humoured grin. He only made one further comment on my non-consolidation of that fortuitously captured trench. He would probably leave me out of the 'next show' as a punishment, he said. Some people asserted that he had no sense of humour, but I venture to disagree with them.

## IV

Nobody had any illusions about the duration of our holiday at Heilly. Our Division had been congratulated by the Commander-in-Chief, and our Brigadier had made it clear that further efforts would be required of us in the near future. In the meantime the troops contrived to be cheerful; to be away from the battle and in a good village was all that mattered, for the moment. Our casualties had not been heavy (we had lost about 100 men but only a dozen of them had been killed). There was some grumbling on the second day, which was a wet one and reduced our camp to its natural condition – a swamp; but the Army Commander paid us a brief (and mercifully informal) visit, and this glimpse of his geniality made the men feel that they had done creditably. Nevertheless, as he squelched among the brown tents in his boots and spurs, more than one voice might have been heard muttering, 'Why couldn't the old – – have dumped us in a drier spot?' But the Fourth Army figure-head may well have been absent-minded that afternoon, since the Welsh Division had attacked Mametz Wood earlier in the day, and he must already have been digesting the first reports, which reached us in wild rumours next morning.

Basking in the sunshine after breakfast with Barton and Durley, I felt that to-day was all that concerned us. If there had been a disastrous muddle, with troops stampeding under machine-gun fire, it was twelve miles away and no business of ours until we were called upon to carry on the good work. There were no parades to-day, and we were going into Amiens for lunch – Dottrell and the Adjutant with us. Barton, with a brown field-service notebook on his knee, was writing a letter to his wife. 'Do you always light your pipe with your left hand, Kangar?' he asked, looking up as he tore another leaf out. I replied that I supposed so, though I'd never noticed it before. Then I rambled on for a bit about how unobservant one could be. I said (knowing that old man Barton liked hearing about such things) 'We've got a grandfather clock in the hall at home and for years and years I thought the maker's name was *Thos. Verney, London.* Then one day I decided to give the old brass face a polish up and I found that it was *Thos. Vernon, Ludlow!*' Barton thought this a pleasing coincidence because he lived in Shropshire and had been to Ludlow Races. A square mile of Shropshire, he asserted, was worth the whole of France. Durley (who was reading *Great Expectations* with a face that expressed release from reality) put in a mild plea for Stoke Newington, which was where he lived; it contained several quaint old corners if you knew where to look for them, and must, he said, have been quite a sleepy sort of place in Dickens's days. Reverting to my original topic, I remarked, 'We've got an old barometer, too, but it never works. Ever since I can remember, it's pointed to *Expect Wet from N.E.* Last time I was on leave I noticed that it's not *Expect* but *Except* – though goodness knows what that means!' My companions, who were disinclined to be talkative, assured me that with such a brain I ought to be on the Staff.

Strolling under the aspens that shivered and twinkled by the river, I allowed myself a little day dream, based on the leisurely ticking of the old Ludlow clock . . . Was it only three weeks ago that I had been standing there at the foot of the staircase, between the barometer and the clock, on just such a fine summer morning as this? Upstairs in the bathroom Aunt Evelyn was putting sweet-peas and roses in water, humming to herself while she arranged them to her liking. Visualizing the bathroom with its copper bath and basin, (which 'took such a lot of cleaning') its lead floor, and the blue and white Dutch tiles along the walls, and the elder tree outside the window, I found these familiar objects almost as dear to me as Aunt Evelyn herself, since they were one with her in my mind (though for years she'd been talking about doing away with the copper bath and basin).

Even now, perhaps, she was once again carrying a bowl of roses down to the drawing-room while the clock ticked slow, and the parrot whistled, and the cook chopped something on the kitchen table. There might also be the short-winded snorting of a traction-engine labouring up the hill outside the house ... Meeting a traction-engine had been quite an event in my childhood, when I was out for rides on my first pony. And the thought of the cook suggested the gardener clumping in with a trug of vegetables, and the gardener suggested birds in the strawberry nets, and altogether there was no definite end to that sort of day dream of an England where there was no war on and the village cricket ground was still being mown by a man who didn't know that he would some day join 'the Buffs', migrate to Mesopotamia, and march to Bagdad.

Amiens was eleven miles away and the horses none too sound; but Dottrell had arranged for us to motor the last seven of the miles – the former Quartermaster of our battalion (who had been Quartermaster at Fourth Army Headquarters ever since the Fourth Army had existed) having promised to lend us his car. So there was nothing wrong with the world as the five of us jogged along, and I allowed myself a momentary illusion that we were riding clean away from the War. Looking across a spacious and untroubled landscape chequered with ripening corn and blood-red clover, I wondered how that calm and beneficent light could be spreading as far as the battle zone. But a Staff car overtook us, and as it whirled importantly past in a cloud of dust I caught sight of a handcuffed German prisoner – soon to provide material for an optimistic paragraph in Corps Intelligence Summary, and to add his story to the omniscience of the powers who now issued operation orders with the assertion that we were 'pursuing a beaten enemy'. Soon we were at Querrieux, a big village cosily over-populated by the Fourth Army Staff. As we passed the General's white château Dottrell speculated ironically on the average income of his personal staff, adding that they must suffer terribly from insomnia with so many guns firing fifteen miles away. Leaving our horses to make the most of a Fourth Army feed, we went indoors to pay our respects to the opulent Quartermaster, who had retired from Battalion duties after the First Battle of Ypres. He assured us that he could easily spare his car for a few hours since he had the use of two; whereupon Dottrell said he'd been wondering how he managed to get on with only one car.

In Amiens, at the well-known Godbert Restaurant, we lunched like dukes in a green-shuttered private room. 'God only knows when we'll see a clean tablecloth again,' remarked Barton, as he ordered langoustes, roast duck, and two bottles of their best 'bubbly'. Heaven knows what else the meal contained; but I remember talking with a loosened tongue about sport, and old Joe telling us how he narrowly escaped being reduced to the ranks for 'making a book' when the Battalion was stationed in Ireland before the war. 'There were some fine riders in the regiment then; they talked and thought about nothing but hunting, racing, and polo,' he said; adding that it was lucky for some of us that horsemanship wasn't needed for winning the war, since most mounted officers now looked as if they were either rowing a boat or riding a bicycle uphill. Finally, when with flushed faces we sauntered out into the sunshine, he remarked that he'd half a mind to go and look for a young lady to make his wife jealous. I said that there was always the cathedral to look at, and discovered that I'd unintentionally made a very good joke.

## V

Two days later we vacated the camp at Heilly. The aspens by the river were shivering and showing the whites of their leaves, and it was good-bye to their cool showery sound when we marched away in our own dust at four o'clock on a glaring bright afternoon. The aspens waited, with their indifferent welcome, for some other dead beat and diminished battalion. Such was their habit, and so the war went on. It must be difficult, for those who did not experience it, to imagine the sensation of returning to a battle area, particularly when one started from a safe place like Heilly. Replenished by an unpromising draft from a home service battalion, our unit was well rested and, supposedly, as keen as mustard. Anyhow it suited everyone, including the troops themselves, to believe that victory was somewhere within sight. Retrospectively, however, I find it difficult to conceive them as an optimistic body of men, and it is certain that if the men of the new draft had any illusions about modern warfare, they would shortly lose them.

My exiguous diary has preserved a few details of that nine-mile march. Field-Marshal Haig passed us in his motor; and I saw a doctor in a long white coat standing in the church door at Morlancourt. Passing through the village, we went on by a track, known as 'the Red Road', arrived at the Citadel 'in rich yellow evening light', and bivouacked on the hill behind the Fricourt road. Two hours later we 'stood-to', and then started for Mametz, only to be brought back again after going half a mile. I fell asleep to the sound of heavy firing toward La Boisselle, rattling limbers on the Citadel road, and men shouting and looking for their kits in the dark. There are worse things than falling asleep under a summer sky. One awoke stiff and cold, but with a head miraculously clear.

Next day I moved to the Transport Lines, a couple of miles back, for I was one of eight officers kept in reserve. There I existed monotonously while the Battalion was engaged in the Battle of Bazentin Ridge. My boredom was combined with suspense, for after the first attack I might be sent for at any moment, so I could never wander far from the Transport Lines.

The battle didn't begin till Friday at dawn, so on Thursday Durley and I were free and we went up to look at the old Front Line. We agreed that it felt queer to be walking along no-man's-land and inspecting the old German trenches in a half-holiday mood. The ground was littered with unused ammunition, and a spirit of mischievous destruction possessed us. Pitching Stokes mortar shells down the dark and forbidding stairs of German dug-outs, we revelled in the boom of subterranean explosions. For a few minutes we felt as if we were getting a bit of our own back for what we'd endured opposite those trenches, and we chanced to be near the mine-craters where the raid had failed. But soon we were being shouted at by an indignant Salvage Corps Officer, and we decamped before he could identify us. Thus we 'put the lid on' our days and nights in the Bois Français sector, which was now nothing but a few hundred yards of waste ground – a jumble of derelict wire, meaningless ditches, and craters no longer formidable. There seemed no sense in the toil that had heaped those mounds of bleaching sandbags, and even the 1st of July had become an improbable memory, now that the dead bodies had been cleared away. Rank thistles were already thriving among the rusty rifles, torn clothing, and abandoned equipment of those who had fallen a couple of weeks ago.

That evening we heard that our Second Battalion had bivouacked about half a mile from the camp. Their Division had been brought down from Flanders and was on its way up to Bazentin. Returning from an after dinner stroll I found that several Second Battalion officers had come to visit us. It was almost dark; these officers were standing outside our tent with Durley and the others, and it sounded as if they were keeping up their courage with the volubility usual among soldiers who knew that they would soon be in an attack. Among them, big and impulsive, was David Cromlech, who had been with our Battalion for three months of the previous winter. As I approached the group I recognized his voice with a shock of delighted surprise. He and I had never been in the same Company, but we were close friends, although somehow or other I have hitherto left him out of my story. On this occasion his face was only dimly discernible, so I will not describe it, though it was a remarkable one. An instinct for aloofness which is part of my character caused me to remain in the background for a minute or two, and I now overheard his desperately cheerful ejaculations with that indefinite pang of affection often felt by a detached observer of such spontaneous behaviour. When I joined the group we had so much to tell one another that I very soon went back with him to his tentless hillside. On the way I gave him a breathless account of my adventures up at Mametz Wood, but neither of us really wanted to talk about the Somme Battle. We should probably get more than enough of it before we'd finished. He had only just joined the Second Battalion, and I was eager to hear about England. The men of his platoon were lying down a little way off; but soon their recumbent mutterings had ceased, and all around us in the gloom were sleeping soldiers and the pyramids of piled rifles. We knew that this might be our last meeting, and gradually an ultimate strangeness and simplicity overshadowed and contained our low-voiced colloquies. We talked of the wonderful things we'd do after the war; for to me David had often seemed to belong less to my war experience than to the freedom which would come after it. He had dropped his defensive exuberance now, and I felt that he was rather luckless and lonely – too young to be killed up on Bazentin Ridge. It was midnight when I left him. First thing in the morning I hurried up the hill in hope of seeing him again. Scarcely a trace remained of the battalion which had bivouacked there, and I couldn't so much as identify the spot where we'd sat on his ground sheet, until I discovered a scrap of silver paper which might possibly have belonged to the packet of chocolate we had munched while he was telling me about the month's holiday he'd had in Wales after he came out of hospital.

When I got back to our tent in the Transport Lines I found everyone in a state of excitement. Dottrell and the ration party had returned from their all-night pilgrimage with information about yesterday's attack. The Brigade had reached its first objectives. Two of our officers had been killed and several wounded. Old man Barton had got a nice comfortable one in the shoulder. Hawkes (a reliable and efficient chap who belonged to one of the other companies) had been sent for to take command of C Company, and was even now completing his rapid but methodical preparations for departure.

The reserve Echelon was an arid and irksome place to be loafing about in. Time hung heavy on our hands and we spent a lot of it lying in the tent on our outspread valises. During the sluggish mid-afternoon of the same Saturday I was thus occupied in economizing my energies. Durley had nicknamed our party 'the eight little nigger boys', and there were now only seven of us. Most of them were feeling more talkative than I was, and it happened that I emerged from a snooze to hear them discussing 'that queer bird Cromlech'. Their comments reminded me, not for the first time, of the diversified impressions which David made upon his fellow Fusiliers.

At his best I'd always found him an ideal companion, although his opinions were often disconcerting. But no one was worse than he was at hitting it off with officers who distrusted cleverness and disliked unreserved utterances. In fact he was a positive expert at putting people's backs up unintentionally. He was with our Second Battalion for a few months before they transferred him to 'the First', and during that period the Colonel was heard to remark that young Cromlech threw his tongue a hell of a lot too much, and that it was about time he gave up reading Shakespeare and took to using soap and water. He had, however, added, 'I'm agreeably surprised to find that he isn't windy in trenches.'

David certainly was deplorably untidy, and his absent-mindedness when off duty was another propensity which made him unpopular. Also, as I have already hinted, he wasn't good at being 'seen but not heard'. 'Far too fond of butting in with his opinion before he's been asked for it,' was often his only reward for an intelligent suggestion. Even Birdie Mansfield (who had knocked about the world too much to be intolerant) was once heard to exclaim, 'Unless you watch it, my son, you'll grow up into the most bumptious young prig God ever invented!' – this protest being a result of David's assertion that all sports except boxing, football and rock climbing were snobbish and silly.

From the floor of the tent, Holman (a spick and span boy who had been to Sandhurst and hadn't yet discovered that it was unwise to look down on temporary officers who 'wouldn't have been wanted in the Regiment in peace time') was now saying, 'Anyhow, I was at Clitherland with him last month, and he fairly got on people's nerves with his hot air about the Battle of Loos, and his brainwaves about who really wrote the Bible.' Durley then philosophically observed, 'Old Longneck certainly isn't the sort of man you meet every day. I can't always follow his theories myself, but I don't mind betting that he'll go a long way – provided he isn't pushing up daisies when Peace breaks out.' Holman (who had only been with us a few days and soon became more democratic) brushed Durley's defence aside with 'The blighter's never satisfied unless he's turning something upside down. I actually heard him say that Homer was a woman. Can you beat that? And if you'll believe me he had the darned sauce to give me a sort of pi-jaw about going out with girls in Liverpool. If you ask me, I think he's a rotten outsider, and the sooner he's pushing up daisies the better.' Whereupon Perrin (a quiet man of thirty-five who was sitting in a corner writing to his wife) stopped the discussion by saying, 'Oh, dry up, Holman! For all we know the poor devil may be dead by now.'

Late that night I was lying in the tent with *The Return of the Native* on my knee. The others were asleep, but my candle still guttered on the shell-box at my elbow. No one had mumbled 'For Christ's sake put that light out'; which was lucky, for I felt very wide awake. How were things going at Bazentin, I wondered? And should I be sent for to-morrow? A sort of numb funkiness invaded me. I didn't want to die – not before I'd finished reading *The Return of the Native* anyhow. 'The quick-silvery glaze on the rivers and pools vanished; from broad mirrors of light they changed to lustreless sheets of lead.' The words fitted my mood; but there was more in them than that. I wanted to explore the book slowly. It made me long for England, and it made the War seem a waste of time. Ever since my existence became precarious I had realized how little I'd used my brains in peace time, and now I was always trying to keep my mind from stagnation. But it wasn't easy to think one's own thoughts while on active service, and the outlook of my companions was mostly mechanical; they dulled everything with commonplace chatter and made even the vividness of the War ordinary. My encounter with David Cromlech – after three months' separation – had reawakened my relish for liveliness and originality. But I had no assurance of ever seeing him again, or of meeting anyone who could stir up my dormant apprehensions as he did. Was it a mistake, I wondered, to try and keep intelligence alive when I could no longer call my life my own? In the brown twilight of the tent I sat pondering with my one golden candle flame beside me. Last night's talk with David now assumed a somewhat ghostlike character. The sky had been starless and clouded and the air so still that a lighted match needed no hand to shield it. Ghosts don't strike matches, of course; and I knew that I'd smoked my pipe, and watched David's face – sallow, crooked, and whimsical – when he lit a cigarette. There must have been the usual noises going on, but they were as much a part of our surroundings as the weather, and it was easy to imagine that the silence had been unbroken by the banging of field batteries and the remote tack-tack of rifles and machine-guns. Had that sombre episode been some premonition of our both getting killed? For the country had loomed limitless and strange and sullenly imbued with the Stygian significance of the War. And the soldiers who slept around us in their hundreds – were they not like the dead, among whom in some dim region where time survived in ghostly remembrances, we two could still cheat ourselves with hopes and forecasts of a future exempt from antagonisms and perplexities? . . . On some such sonorous cadence as this my thoughts halted. Well, poor old David was up in the battle; perhaps my mind was somehow in touch with his (though he would have disparaged my 'fine style', I thought). More rationally reflective, I looked at my companions, rolled in their blankets, their faces turned to the earth or hidden by the folds. I thought of the doom that was always near them now, and how I might see them lying dead, with all their jollity silenced, and their talk, which had made me impatient, ended for ever. I looked at gallant young Fernby; and Durley, that kind and sensitive soul;

and my own despondency and discontent released me. I couldn't save them, but at least I could share the dangers and discomforts they endured. 'Outside in the gloom the guns are shaking the hills and making lurid flashes along the alleys. Inevitably, the War blunders on; but among the snoring sleepers I have had my little moment of magnanimity. What I feel is no more than the candle which makes tottering shadows in the tent. Yet it is something, perhaps, that one man can be awake there, though he can find no meaning in the immense destruction which he blindly accepts as part of some hidden purpose.' . . . Thus (rather portentously, perhaps) I recorded in my diary the outcome of my ruminations.

For another five days my war experience continued to mark time in that curious camp. I call the camp curious, for it seemed so, even then. There was a makeshift effect of men coming and going, loading and unloading limbers and wagons, carrying fodder, shouting at horses and mules, attending to fires, and causing a smell of cooking. A whiff from a certain sort of wood fire could make me see that camp clearly now, since it was strewn and piled with empty shell-boxes which were used for fuel, as well as for building bivouacs. Along the road from Fricourt to Méaulte, infantry columns continually came and went, processions of prisoners were brought down, and small parties of 'walking wounded' straggled thankfully toward the Casualty Clearing Station. The worn landscape looked parched and shabby; only the poppies made harsh spots of red, matching the head caps of the Indian cavalry who were camped near by.

Among all this activity time passed sluggishly for me. Inside our tent I used to stare at the camouflage paint smears which showed through the canvas, formulating patterns and pictures among which the whiteness of the sky showed in gaps and rents. The paint smears were like ungainly birds with wide spread wings, fishes floating, monkeys in scarecrow trees, or anything else my idle brain cared to contrive. In one corner a fight was going on (in a Futuristic style) and a figure brandished a club while his adversary took a side-leap, losing an arm and a leg from a bomb explosion. Then someone would darken the doorway with a rumour that the Battalion had been moved up to attack High Wood – a new name, and soon afterwards an ugly one. Night would fall, with the others playing 'Nap' and talking stale war stuff out of the *Daily Mail*, and the servants singing by a bright shell-box fire in the gusty twilight. And I would think about driving home from cricket matches before the War, wondering whether I'd ever go back to that sort of thing again.

I remember another evening (it was the last one I spent in that place) when the weather seemed awaiting some spectacular event in this world of blundering warfare. Or was it as though the desolation of numberless deaths had halted the clouded sky to an attitude of brooding inertia? I looked across at Albert; its tall trees were flat grey-blue outlines, and the broken tower of the basilica might have been a gigantic clump of foliage. Above this landscape of massed stillness and smoky silhouettes the observation balloons were swaying slowly, their noses pointing toward the line of battle. Only the distant thud of gun-fire disturbed the silence – like someone kicking footballs – a soft bumping, miles away. Walking along by the river I passed the horse-lines of the Indian cavalry; the barley field above couldn't raise a rustle, so still was the air. Low in the west, pale orange beams were streaming down on the country that receded with a sort of rich regretful beauty, like the background of a painted masterpiece. For me that evening expressed the indeterminate tragedy which was moving, with agony on agony, toward the autumn.

I leant on a wooden bridge, gazing down into the dark green glooms of the weedy little river, but my thoughts were powerless against unhappiness so huge. I couldn't alter European history, or order the artillery to stop firing. I could stare at the War as I stared at the sultry sky, longing for life and freedom and vaguely altruistic about my fellow-victims. But a second-lieutenant could attempt nothing – except to satisfy his superior officers; and altogether, I concluded, Armageddon was too immense for my solitary understanding. Then the sun came out for a last reddening look at the War, and I turned back to the camp with its clustering tents and crackling fires. I finished the day jawing to young Fernby about fox-hunting.

The Division had now been in action for a week. Next day they were to be relieved. Late in the afternoon Dottrell moved the Transport back about three miles, to a hill above Dernancourt. Thankful for something to do at last, I busied myself with the putting up of tents. When that was done I watched the sun going down in glory beyond the main road to Amiens. The horizon trees were dark blue against the glare, and the dust of the road floated in wreaths; motor-lorries crept continuously by, while the long shadows of trees made a sort of mirage on the golden haze of the dust. The country along the river swarmed with camps, but the low sun made it all seem pleasant and peaceful. After nightfall the landscape glowed and glinted with camp-fires, and a red half-moon appeared to bless the combatant armies with neutral beams. Then we were told to shift the tents higher up the hill and I became active again; for the Battalion was expected about midnight. After this little emergency scramble I went down to the crossroads with Dottrell, and there we waited hour after hour. The Quartermaster was in a state of subdued anxiety, for he'd been unable to get up to Battalion Headquarters for the last two days. We sat among some barley on the bank above the road, and as time passed we conversed companionably, keeping ourselves awake with an occasional drop of rum from his flask. I always enjoyed being with Dottrell, and that night the husky-voiced old campaigner was more eloquent than he realized. In the simplicity of his talk there was a universal tone which seemed to be summing up all the enduring experience of an Infantry Division. For him it was a big thing for the Battalion to be coming back from a battle, though, as he said, it was a new Battalion every few months now.

An hour before dawn the road was still an empty picture of moonlight. The distant gun-fire had crashed and rumbled all night, muffled and terrific with immense flashes, like waves of some tumult of water rolling along the horizon. Now there came an interval of silence in which I heard a horse neigh, shrill and scared and lonely. Then the procession of the returning troops began. The camp-fires were burning low when the grinding jolting column lumbered back. The field guns came first, with nodding men sitting stiffly on weary horses, followed by wagons and limbers and field-kitchens. After this rumble of wheels came the infantry, shambling, limping, straggling and out of step. If anyone spoke it was only a muttered word, and the mounted officers rode as if asleep. The men had carried their emergency water in petrol-cans, against which bayonets made a hollow clink; except for the shuffling of feet, this was the only sound. Thus, with an almost spectral appearance, the lurching brown figures flitted past with slung rifles and heads bent forward under basin-helmets. Moon-light and dawn began to mingle, and I could see the barley swaying indolently against the sky. A train groaned along the riverside, sending up a cloud of whitish fiery smoke against the gloom of the trees. The Flintshire Fusiliers were a long time arriving. On the hill behind us the kite balloon swayed slowly upward with straining ropes, its looming bulbous body reflecting the first pallor of daybreak. Then, as if answering our expectancy, a remote skirling of bagpipes began, and the Gordon Highlanders hobbled in. But we had been sitting at the crossroads nearly six hours, and faces were recognizable, when Dottrell hailed our leading Company.

Soon they had dispersed and settled down on the hillside, and were asleep in the daylight which made everything seem ordinary. None the less I had seen something that night which overawed me. It was all in the day's work – an exhausted Division returning from the Somme Offensive – but for me it was as though I had watched an army of ghosts. It was as though I had seen the War as it might be envisioned by the mind of some epic poet a hundred years hence.

# PART FIVE
# ESCAPE

## I

On Saturday afternoon we made a short train journey and then marched four easy miles to a village called La Chaussée. Twenty-four hours' rest and a shave had worked the usual miracle with the troops (psychological recovery was a problem which no one had time to recognize as existent) and now we were away from the Line for at least a fortnight. It was a dusty golden evening, and the road led us through quiet green country. Delusively harmonious, perhaps, is that retrospective picture of the Battalion marching at ease along an unfrequented road, at the end of a July afternoon, with Colonel Kinjack riding rather absent-mindedly in front, or pulling up to watch us go past him – his face thoughtful and indulgent and expressing something of the pride and satisfaction which he felt.

So it will go on, I thought; in and out, in and out, till something happens to me. We had come along the same road last January. Only five officers of that lot were with us now: not many of them had been killed, but they had 'faded away' somehow or other, and my awareness of this created a deceptive sense of 'the good old days'. Yesterday afternoon I'd heard that Cromlech had been killed up at High Wood. This piece of news had stupefied me, but the pain hadn't begun to make itself felt yet, and there was no spare time for personal grief when the Battalion was getting ready to move back to Divisional Rest. To have thought about Cromlech would have been calamitous. 'Rotten business about poor old "Longneck",' was the only comment that Durley, Dottrell and the others allowed themselves. And after all he wasn't the only one who'd gone west lately. It was queer how the men seemed to take their victimization for granted. In and out; in and out; singing and whistling, the column swayed in front of me, much the same length as usual, for we'd had less than a hundred casualties up at Bazentin. But it was a case of every man for himself, and the corporate effect was optimistic and untroubled. A London editor driving along the road in a Staff car would have remarked that the spirit of the troops was amazing. And so it was. But somehow the newspaper men always kept the horrifying realities of the War out of their articles, for it was unpatriotic to be bitter, and the dead were assumed to be gloriously happy. However, it was no use worrying about all that; I was part of the Battalion, and now I've got to see about getting the men settled into billets.

Some Australians had been in the billets at La Chaussée and (if they will pardon me for saying so) had left them in a very bad state. Sanitation had been neglected, and the inhabitants were complaining furiously that their furniture had been used for firewood. Did the Australians leave anything else behind them, I wonder? For some of them had been in Gallipoli, and it is possible that dysentery germs were part of the legacy they left us.

The fact remains that I awoke on Monday morning feeling far from well and, after a mechanical effort to go on parade in a glare of sunlight, took refuge in the cavernous bedroom which I occupied alone. Feeling worse and worse, in the evening I remembered that I possessed a thermometer, which had been handed over to me when I was Transport Officer. I had never taken the temperatures of any of the horses, but I now experimented shakily on myself. When I saw that it indicated 105° I decided that the thing was out of order; but next morning I was confusedly aware that Flook had fetched the doctor, and by the afternoon I was unbelievably at the New Zealand Hospital, which was in a substantial old building in the middle of Amiens.

The advantages of being ill were only too obvious. Lying awake in the large lofty ward on my fourth night, I was aware that I was feeling rather run down, but much better – almost too well, in fact. That evening my temperature had been normal, which reminded me that this change from active service to invalidism was an acute psychological experience. The door to safety was half open, and though an impartial New Zealand doctor decided one's destiny, there was a not unnatural impulse to fight for one's own life instead of against the Germans. Less than two weeks ago I'd been sitting in a tent thinking noble thoughts about sharing the adversities of my fellow Fusiliers. But that emotional defence wouldn't work now, and the unutterable words 'wangle my way home' forced their way obstinately to the foreground, supported by a crowd of smug-faced excuses.

Durley and the Adjutant had visited me that afternoon; they'd joked with me about how well I was looking. While they were with me I had talked about coming back in a few days, and I'd genuinely felt as if I wanted to. But they took my fortitude away with them, and now I was foreseeing that another night's rest would make me look indecently healthy for a man in a hospital. 'I suppose they'll all think I'm swinging the lead,' I thought. Turning the last few months over in my mind, I argued with myself that I had done all that was expected of me. 'Oh God,' I prayed, 'do get me sent down to the Base!' (How often was that petition whispered during the War?) To-day I had seen young Allgood's name in the Roll of Honour – a bit of news which had slammed the door on my four weeks at the Army School and provided me with a secondary sorrow, for I was already feeling sufficiently miserable about my friend Cromlech. I sympathized with myself about Allgood, for I had been fond of him. But he was only one among thousands of promising young men who had gone west since the 1st of July. Sooner or later I should probably get killed too. A breath of wind stirred the curtains, blowing them inward from the tall windows with a rustling sigh. The wind came from the direction of the Somme, and I could hear the remote thudding of the guns. Everyone in the ward seemed to be asleep except the boy whose bed had screens round it. The screens were red and a light glowed through them. Ever since he was brought in he'd been continually calling to the nurse on duty. Throughout the day this had gradually got on everyone's nerves, for the ward was already full of uncontrollable gasps and groans. Once I had caught a glimpse of his white face and miserable eyes. Whatever sort of wound he'd got he was making the most of it, had been the opinion of the man next to me (who had himself got more than he wanted, in both legs). But he must be jolly bad, I thought now, as the Sister came from behind the screen again. His voice went on, in the low rapid, even tone of delirium. Sometimes I could catch what he said, troubled and unhappy and complaining. Someone called Dicky was on his mind, and he kept on crying out to Dicky. 'Don't go out, Dicky; they snipe like hell!' And then, 'Curse the Wood . . . Dicky, you fool, don't go out!' . . . All the horror of the Somme attacks was in that raving; all the darkness and the dreadful daylight . . . I watched the Sister come back with a white-coated doctor; the screen glowed comfortingly; soon the disquieting voice became inaudible and I fell asleep. Next morning the screens had vanished, the bed was empty, and ready for someone else.

Not that day, but the next one, my supplication to the Almighty was put to the test. The doctor came along the ward on his cheerful morning inspection. Arriving at my bed he asked how I was feeling. I stared up at him, incapable of asserting that I felt ill and unwilling to admit that I felt well. Fortunately he didn't expect a reply. 'Well, we'll have to be moving you on,' he said with a smile; and before my heart had time to beat again he turned to the nurse with, 'Put him down for the afternoon train.' The nurse made a note of it, and my mind uttered a spontaneous Magnificat. Now, with any luck, I thought, I'll get a couple of weeks at one of those hospitals on the coast, at Étretat or Le Tréport, probably. The idea of reading a book by the seaside was blissful. No one could blame me for that, and I should be back with the Battalion by the end of August, if not earlier.

In my hurried exodus from my billet at La Chaussée, some of my belongings had been left behind, and good old Flook had brought them to the hospital next day. He had come treading in with clumsy embarrassment to deposit the packful of oddments by my bed, announcing in a hoarse undertone, 'Ah've brought the stoof,' and telling me that the lads in C Company were hoping to see me back soon. Somehow Flook, with his rough and ready devotion, had seemed my strongest link with the Battalion. When I shook his hand and said good-bye, he winked and advised me, confidentially, not to be in too much of a hurry about getting back. A good rest would do me no harm, he said; but as he tiptoed away I wondered when he himself would get a holiday, and whether he would ever return to his signal-box on the railway.

The details of my journey to the Base were as follows. First of all I was carried carefully down the stairs on a stretcher (though I could easily have walked to the ambulance, or even to the railway station, if such an effort had been demanded of me). Then the ambulance took me to Corbie, and from there the train (with 450 casualties on board) rumbled sedately to Rouen; we did the sixty miles in ten hours, and at two o'clock in the morning I was carried into No. 2 Red Cross Hospital. I remember that particular hospital with affection. During the morning a genial doctor came along and had a look at me. 'Well, me lad, what's wrong with you?' he asked. 'They call it enteritis,' I replied, with an indefinite grin. He had a newspaper in his hand as he glanced at the descriptive chart behind my bed. My name caused him to consult *The Times*. 'Is this you?' he asked. Sure enough, my name was there, in a list of Military Crosses which chanced to have appeared that day. The doctor patted me on the shoulder and informed me that I should be going across to England next day. Good luck had 'wangled me home'. Even now I cannot think of that moment without believing that I was involved in one of the lesser miracles of the Great War. For I am certain that I should have remained at Rouen if that observant and kind-hearted doctor hadn't noticed my name among the decorations. And in that case I should have been back with the Battalion in nice time for their operations at Delville Wood, which might quite conceivably have qualified my name for a place on the Butley village War Memorial.

The Hospital Ship left Rouen about midday. While we steamed down the Seine in fine weather I lay watching the landscape through a porthole with a sense of thankfulness which differed from any I had ever known before. A label was attached to me; I have kept that label, and it is in my left hand as I write these words. It is marked *Army Form W* 3083, though in shape and substance it is an ordinary civilian luggage label. It is stamped *Lying Train and Ship* in blue letters, with *Sick P.U.O.* on the other side. On the boat, my idle brain wondered what *P.U.O.* meant. There must, I thought, be a disease beginning with P. Perhaps it was 'Polypipsis unknown origin'. Between Rouen and Havre I devised several feebly funny solutions, such as 'Perfectly undamaged officer'. But my final choice was 'Poorly until October'.

At noon next day we reached Southampton. Nothing could be better than this, I thought, while being carried undeservedly from the ship to the train; and I could find no fault with Hampshire's quiet cornfields and unwarlike woods in the drowsy August afternoon. At first I guessed that we were on our way to London; but when the journey showed signs of cross-countrihood I preferred not to be told where we were going. Recumbent, I gazed gloatingly at England. Peaceable stay-at-homes waved to the Red Cross Train, standing still to watch it pass. It was nice to think that I'd been fighting for them, though exactly what I'd done to help them was difficult to define. An elderly man, cycling along a dusty road in a dark blue suit and a straw hat, removed one hand from the handle-bars to wave comprehensive gratitude. Everything seemed happy and homely. I was delivered from the idea of death, and that other thing which had haunted me, the dread of being blinded. I closed contented eyes, became sleepy, and awoke to find myself at Oxford. By five o'clock I was in a small white room on the ground floor of Somerville College. Listening to the tranquil tolling of Oxford bells and someone strumming melodiously on a piano across the lawn, with a glimpse of tall chestnut trees swaying against the blue sky, I whispered the word Paradise. Had I earned it? I was too grateful to care.

## II

In Oxford lived Mr. Farrell, an old friend of Aunt Evelyn's. Some years before the War he had lived near Butley, and he now came to pay me an afternoon visit at the Hospital, where I was reclining under a tree on the lawn, still keeping up appearances as an invalid officer. He sat beside me and we conversed rather laboriously about Aunt Evelyn and her neighbourhood. He was Irish and a voluble talker, but he seemed to have lost much of his former vivacity. I noticed that he was careful to keep the conversation safely on this side of the Channel, probably out of consideration for my feelings, although I wouldn't have minded telling him a thing or two about the Somme. Mr. Farrell was a retired Civil Servant and an authority on Military Records. He had written the lives of several famous Generals and an official History of the Indian Mutiny. But he showed no curiosity about the military operations of the moment. He was over seventy, and his face was unlit and fatigued as he talked about food restrictions in England. 'Sugar is getting scarce,' he remarked, 'but that doesn't affect me; my doctor knocked me off sugar several years ago.' I looked at his noticeably brown teeth, and then averted my eyes as if he could read my thoughts, for I was remembering how Aunt Evelyn used to scold me for calling him 'sugar-teeth'; his untidy teeth did look like lumps of sugar soaked in tea . . .

Dear old Mr. Farrell, with his red tie and the cameo ring round it, and his silver hair and ragged tobacco-stained moustache! As his large form lumbered away across the lawn, I thought that his clothes had got too big for him, though he'd always worn them rather baggy. Could it be possible that scrupulous people at home were getting thin while the soldiers got fat on their good rations at the Front? I began to suspect that England wasn't quite what it used to be. But my mind soon wandered indolently into the past which the veteran military historian had brought with him into the college garden. I remembered summer evenings when I was a little boy overhearing, from in bed upstairs, the mumble of voices down in the drawing-room, where Aunt Evelyn was having an after-dinner chat with Mr. Farrell and Captain Huxtable, who had walked across the fields from Butley in the twilight. Sometimes I tiptoed down the stairs and listened at the door (rather hoping to hear them saying something complimentary about myself) but they were nearly always gassing about politics, or India. Mr. Farrell had been in India for ages, and Captain Huxtable had been out there too; and Aunt Evelyn loved to hear about it. When we went to see Mr. Farrell he used to show us delightful old books with coloured plates of Indian scenes. What queer old codgers they were, sipping tea and puffing their cigars (which smelt quite nice) and talking all that rot about Lord Salisbury and his Government. 'Her-her-her,' laughed Mr. Farrell whenever he finished another of his funny stories which always ended with what someone had said to someone else or how he'd scored off someone at his club. They'd go on talking just the same, whatever happened; even if a Death's Head Hawk Moth flew into the room they wouldn't be a bit excited about it. It would be rather fun, I thought, if I were to fire my percussion-cap pistol outside the drawing-room door, just to give them a surprise. As I crept upstairs again in my nightgown, I wondered if I should ever be like that myself . . . Mr. Farrell was fond of playing tennis; he used to serve underhand, holding the ball a few inches above the ground as he struck it . . .

Emerging from my retrospective reverie, I felt that this war had made the past seem very peculiar. People weren't the same as they used to be, or else I had changed. Was it because I had experienced something that they couldn't share or imagine? Mr. Farrell had seemed diffident that afternoon, almost as if he were talking to a survivor from an incomprehensible disaster. Looking round me I began to feel that I wanted to be in some place where I needn't be reminded of the War all the time. For instance, there was that tall well-preserved man pushing his son very slowly across the lawn in a long wheeled bed. The son was sallow and sulky, as he well might be, having lost one of his legs. The father was all solicitude, but somehow I inferred that the pair of them hadn't hit it off too well before the War. More than once I had seen the son look at his father as though he disliked him. But the father was proud of his disabled son, and I heard him telling one of the nurses how splendidly the boy had done in the Gommecourt attack, showing her a letter, too, probably from the boy's colonel. I wondered whether he had ever allowed himself to find out that the Gommecourt show had been nothing but a massacre of good troops. Probably he kept a war map with little flags on it; when Mametz Wood was reported as captured he moved a little flag an inch forward after breakfast. For him the Wood was a small green patch on a piece of paper. For the Welsh Division it had been a bloody nightmare . . . 'Is the sun too strong for you here, Arthur?' Arthur shakes his head and frowns up at the sky. Then the father, with his neatly-trimmed beard and elegant buff linen waistcoat, begins to read him Haig's latest despatch. 'There is strong evidence that the enemy forces engaged on the battle-front have been severely shaken by the repeated successes gained by ourselves and our Allies . . .' The level cultivated voice palavers on until the nurse approaches brightly with a spouted feeding-cup. 'Time for some more beef-tea!' Nourishment is administered under approving parental eyes.

## III

During my last week I was allowed out of the hospital in the afternoons, and I used to go up the Cherwell in a canoe. I found this recreation rather heavy work, for the water was a jungle of weeds and on the higher reaches progress had become almost impossible. Certainly the Great War had made a difference to the charming River Cherwell. But I had been feeling much more cheerful lately, for my friend Cromlech had risen again from the dead. I had seen his name in the newspaper list of killed, but soon

85

afterwards someone telegraphed to tell me that he was in a London hospital and going on well. For fully a fortnight I had accustomed myself to the idea that his dead body was somewhere among the Somme shell-holes and it was a queer experience, to be disentangling myself from the mental obituary notices which I had evolved out of my luminous memories of our companionship in the First Battalion. 'Silly old devil,' I thought affectionately; 'he always manages to do things differently from other people.'

By the end of August I was back at Butley with a month's sick leave and the possibility of an extension. So for the first week or two I forgot the future and enjoyed being made a fuss of by Aunt Evelyn. My outlook on the War was limited to the Battalion I had served with. After being kept out of the Line for nearly five weeks, they were expecting to be moved up at any moment. This news came in a letter from Durley. Suppressing such disquietude as it caused me, I put the letter in my pocket and went out to potter round the garden. It was a fine early September morning – almost my favourite sort of weather, I thought. The garden was getting wild and overgrown, for there was only one old man working in it now. The day before I had begun an attempt to recivilize the tangled tennis-lawn, but it had been too much like canoeing on the Cherwell, and to-day I decided to cut dead wood out of the cedar. While I climbed about in the tree with a bill-hook in my hand I could hear old Huckett trundling the water-tank along the kitchen garden. Then Aunt Evelyn came along with her flower-basket full of dahlias; while she was gazing up at me another brittle bough cracked and fell scaring one of the cats who followed her about. She begged me to be careful, adding that it would be no joke to tumble out of such a big tree.

Later in the morning I visited the stables. Stagnation had settled there; nettles were thick under the apple-trees and the old mowing-machine pony grazed in shaggy solitude. In Dixon's little harness room, saddles were getting mouldy and there were rust-spots on the bits and stirrup-irons which he had kept so bright. A tin of *Harvey's Hoof Ointment* had obviously been there since 1914. It would take Dixon a long time to get the place straightened up, I thought, forgetting for a moment that he'd been dead six months ... It wasn't much fun, mooning about the stables. But a robin trilled his little autumn song from an apple-tree; beyond the fruit-laden branches I could see the sunlit untroubled Weald, and I looked lovingly at the cowls of hop-kilns which twinkled across those miles that were the country of my childhood. I could smell autumn in the air, too, and I thought I must try to get a few days' cubbing before I go back to the Depot. Down in Sussex there were a few people who would willingly lend me a horse, and I decided to write to old Colonel Hesmon about it. I went up to the schoolroom to do this; rummaging in a drawer for some note-paper, I discovered a little pocket mirror – a relic of my days in the ranks of the Yeomanry. Handling it absent-mindedly, I found myself using it to decipher the blotting paper, which had evidently been on the table some time, for the handwriting was Stephen Colwood's. '*P.S. The Old Guvnor is squaring up my annual indebtedness. Isn't he a brick?*' Stephen must have scribbled that when he was staying with us in the summer of 1914. Probably he had been writing to his soldier brother in Ireland. I imagined him adding the postscript and blotting it quickly. Queer how the past crops up, I thought, sadly, for my experience of such poignant associations was 'still in its infancy', as someone had said of Poison Gas when lecturing to cannon-fodder at the Army School.

Remembering myself at that particular moment, I realize the difficulty of recapturing war-time atmosphere as it was in England then. A war historian would inform us that 'the earlier excitement and suspense had now abated, and the nation had settled down to its organization of manpower and munition making'. I want to recover something more intimate than that, but I can't swear to anything unusual at Butley except a derelict cricket field, the absence of most of the younger inhabitants, and a certain amount of talk about food prospects for the winter. Two of our nearest neighbours had lost their only sons, and with them their main interest in life; but such tragedies as those remained intimate and unobtrusive. Ladies worked at the Local Hospital and elderly gentlemen superintended Recruiting Centres and Tribunals; but there was little outward change and no military training-camp within a radius of ten miles. So I think I am accurate when I say that Aunt Evelyn was jogging along much as usual (now that her mind was temporarily at rest about my own active service career). She was, of course, a bit intolerant about the Germans, having swallowed all the stories about atrocities in Belgium. It was her duty, as a patriotic Englishwoman, to agree with a certain prelate when he preached the axiom that 'every man who killed a German was performing a Christian act'. Nevertheless, if Aunt Evelyn had found a wounded Prussian when she was on her way to the post office, she would undoubtedly have behaved with her natural humanity (combined with enthusiasm for administering first aid). In the meantime we avoided controversial topics (such as that all Germans were fiends in human form) and while I was writing my letter to Colonel Hesmon she entered the schoolroom with her arms full of lavender which she strewed along the floor under the window. The sun would dry it nicely there, she said, adding that I must find her a very dull old party nowadays, since she had no conversation and seemed to spend all her time trying to catch a new housemaid. I assured her that it was a great relief after being incessantly ordered about in the Army, to be with someone who had no conversation.

But after dinner that evening I did find myself a bit dull, so I walked across the fields for a chat with Protheroe, a middle-aged bachelor who lived in a modest old house with his quiet sister. Before I started my aunt implored me to be careful about extinguishing the oil lamp in the drawing-room when I got back. Oil lamps were far from safe – downright dangerous, in fact!

The night was very still; as I went along the field path I was almost sure I could hear the guns. Not that I wanted to; but the newspapers reported that a new offensive had been started at Guillemont, and I couldn't help feeling that our Division was in it. (I still thought of it as 'our Division'.) Our village was quiet enough, anyhow, and so was Protheroe's white-faced house, with its creaking gate and red-blinded windows. I rapped with the

knocker and Miss Protheroe came to the door, quite surprised to
see me, though I'd seen her a few hours before when she called to
return last month's *Blackwood's Magazine*. Protheroe was in the
middle of a game of chess with the village doctor, a reticent little
man whose smallest actions were always extremely deliberate.
The doctor would make up his mind to move one of his men,
grasp it resolutely, become hesitative, release it, and then begin his
cogitative chin-rubbing and eye-puckering all over again, while
Protheroe drummed his fingers on the table and stared at a moth
which was bumping softly against the ceiling of the snug little
parlour, and his sister, with gentle careworn face, knitted something woollen for the brother who, though past forty, was serving
as a corporal in the infantry in France. My arrival put a stop to
the doctor's perplexities; and since I was welcomed rather as a
returned hero, I was inclined to be hearty. I slapped Protheroe on
the back, told him he'd got the best dug-out in Butley, and
allowed myself to be encouraged to discuss the War. I admitted
that it was pretty bad out there, with an inward feeling that such
horrors as I had been obliged to witness were now something to
be proud of. I even went so far as to assert that I wouldn't have
missed this War for anything. It brought things home to one
somehow, I remarked, frowning portentously as I lit my pipe, and
forgetting for the moment what a mercy it had been when it
brought me home myself. Oh yes, I knew all about the Battle of
the Somme, and could assure them that we should be in Bapaume
by October. Replying to their tributary questions, I felt that they
envied me my experience.

While I was on my way home, I felt elated at having outgrown
the parish boundaries of Butley. After all, it was a big thing, to
have been in the thick of a European War, and my peace-time
existence had been idle and purposeless. It was bad luck on
Protheroe and the doctor; they must hate being left out of it . . . I
suppose one must give this damned War its due, I thought, as I sat
in the schoolroom with one candle burning. I felt comfortable, for
Miss Protheroe had made me a cup of cocoa. I took Durley's letter
out of my pocket and had another look at it; but it wasn't easy to

speculate on its implications. The War's all right as long as one doesn't get killed or smashed up, I decided, blowing out the candle so that I could watch the moonlight which latticed the floor with shadows of the leaded windows. Where the moonbeams lay thickest they touched the litter of drying lavender. I opened the window and sniffed the autumn-smelling air. An owl hooted in the garden, and I could hear a train going along the Weald. Probably a hospital-train from Dover, I thought, as I closed the window and creaked upstairs on tiptoe so as not to disturb Aunt Evelyn.

About a week afterwards I received two letters from Dottrell, written on consecutive days, but delivered by the same post. The first one began: 'The old Batt. is having a rough time. We were up in the front a week ago, and lost 200 men in three days. The aid-post, a bit of a dug-out hastily made, was blown in. At the time it contained 5 wounded men, 5 stretcher-bearers, and the doctor. All were killed except the Doc. who was buried in the débris. He was so badly shaken when dug out that he had to be sent down, and will probably be in England by now. It is a hell of a place up there. The Batt. is attacking to-day. I hope they have better luck. The outlook is not rosy. Very glad to hear you are sitting up and taking nourishment. A lot of our best men have been knocked out recently. We shall soon want another Battn. All the boys send their love and best wishes in which your humble heartily joins.'

The second letter, which I chanced to open and read first, was the worst of the two.

'Dear Kangaroo . . . Just a line to let you know what rotten bad luck we had yesterday. We attacked Ginchy with a very weak Battn. (about 300) and captured the place but were forced out of half of it – due to the usual thing. Poor Edmunds was killed leading his Coy. Also Perrin. Durley was badly wounded, in neck and chest, I think. It is terrible to think of these two splendid chaps being cut off, but I hope Durley pulls through. Asbestos Bill died of wounds. Fernby, who was O.C. Bombers, very badly hit and not expected to live. Several others you don't know also killed. Only two officers got back without being hit. C.S.M. Miles and Danby both killed. The Battn. is *not now* over strength for rations! The rest of the Brigade suffered in proportion. Will write later. Very busy.' . . .

I walked about the room, whistling and putting the pictures straight. Then the gong rang for luncheon. Aunt Evelyn drew my attention to the figs, which were the best we'd had off the old tree that autumn.

## IV

October brought an extension of my sick leave and some mornings with the hounds. By the time I received another letter from Dottrell, Delville Wood had more or less buried its dead, in my mind if not altogether in reality. The old Quartermaster let off steam in a good grumble from which I quote a specimen.

'Well, we have been out at rest about 10 kilos from the place we were at last Xmas. We expected to be there three weeks but after 8 days have had sudden orders to move to the old spot with a *Why*. Kinjack left us to take command of a Brigade; a great loss to the Battn. They all come and go; stay in the Batt. long enough to get something out of it, and then disappear and will hardly give a thought to the men and officers who were the means of getting them higher rank. It's a selfish world, my friend. All successive C.O.s beg me to stay with the old Battalion they love so well. I do. So do they, till they get a better job. They neither know nor care what happens to me (who at their special request have stuck to "the dear old Corps") when I leave the Service on a pension of 30s. a week.'

I am afraid I wasn't worrying overmuch about 'the dear old Corps' myself, while out with the Ringwell Hounds on Colonel Hesmon's horses. In spite of the War, hunting was being carried on comfortably, though few people came out. 'The game was being kept alive for the sake of the boys at the Front', who certainly enjoyed the idea (if they happened to be keen fox-hunters and were still alive to appreciate the effort made on their behalf). As for me, I was armed with my uniform and the protective colouring of my Military Cross, and no one could do enough for me. I stayed as long as I liked with Moffat, the genial man who now combined the offices of Master and Secretary, and for a few weeks the pre-war past appeared to have been conjured up for my special benefit. It was difficult to believe that the misty autumn mornings, which made me free of those well-known woods and farms and downs, were simultaneously shedding an irrelevant brightness on the Ypres Salient and on Joe Dottrell riding wearily back with the ration-party somewhere near Plug Street Wood. I don't think I could see it quite like that at the time. What I am writing now is the result of a bird's-eye view of the past, and the cub-hunting subaltern. I see there is part of the 'selfish world' to which his attention had been drawn. He is listening to Colonel Hesmon while the hounds are being blown out of a big wood – hearing how well young Winchell has done with his Brigade (without wondering how many of them have been 'blown out' of their trenches) and being assured by the loquacious old Colonel that the German Count who used to live at Puxford Park was undoubtedly a spy and only hunted with the Ringwell for that reason; the Colonel now regretted that he didn't ride over to Puxford Park and break all the windows before war was declared. He also declared that any man under forty who wasn't wearing the King's uniform was nothing but a damned shirker. I remarked to Moffat afterwards that the Colonel seemed to be overdoing it a bit about the War. Moffat told me that the old boy was known to have practised revolver shooting in his garden, addressing insults to individual tree trunks and thus ventilating his opinion of Germany as a whole. He had been much the same about vulpicides and socialists in peace time. 'It's very odd; for Hesmon's an extraordinary kind-hearted man,' said Moffat, who himself regarded the War as an unmitigated nuisance, but didn't waste his energy abusing it or anybody else. He had enough to do already, for he found it far from easy to keep the Hunt on its legs, and what the hounds would get to eat next year he really didn't know. He added that 'the Missus's dachshunds only just escaped being interned as enemy aliens'.

Sport in Sussex was only a makeshift exhilaration, and early in November I went to London for a final Medical Board. At the Caxton Hall in Westminster I spent a few minutes gazing funereally round an empty waiting-room. Above the fireplace (there was no fire) hung a neatly-framed notice for the benefit of all whom it might concern. It stated the scale of prices for artificial limbs, with instructions as to how officers could obtain them free of cost. The room contained no other ornament. While I was adjusting my mind to what a journalist might have called 'the grim humour' of this footnote to Army life, a Girl Guide stepped in to say that Colonel Crossbones (or whatever his cognomen was) would see me now. A few formalities 'put paid to' my period of freedom, and I pretended to be feeling pleased as I walked away from Westminster, though wondering whether the politicians had any expectations that hostilities would be concluded by Christmas, and eyeing the Admiralty with a notion that it must be rather nice to be in the Navy.

Good-byes began all over again. A last day with the Ringwell ended at the crossroads by the old Harcombe point-to-point course. I went one way and the hounds went another. Jogging down the lane, they disappeared in the drizzling dusk. Moffat's 'Best of luck, old boy!' left me to ride on, alone with the creak of the saddle. I was due back at the Depot next day, but we'd had a good woodland hunt with one quite nice bit in the open, and I'd jumped a lot of timber and thoroughly enjoyed my day. Staring at the dim brown landscape I decided that the War was worth while if it was being carried on to safeguard this sort of thing. Was it? I wondered; and if a doubt arose it was dismissed before it had been formulated. Riding into Downfield where I was leaving the horse which had been lent me, I remembered how I'd slept on the floor of the Town Hall on the day war was declared. Two years and three months ago I had enlisted for 'three years or the duration'. It was beginning to look as if I had enlisted for a lifetime (though the word was one which had seen better days). Under the looming shadow of the hills the lights of the town twinkled cosily. But a distant bugle-call from some camp seemed to be summoning the last reluctant farm labourer. 'You'll all have to go in the end,' it seemed to say, and the comfortless call was being sounded far across Europe . . .

On my way home in the train I read about Roumania in the paper. Everyone, Aunt Evelyn included, had been delighted when Roumania came in on our side in August. But the results had not been reassuring. I couldn't help feeling annoyed with the Roumanian Army for allowing their country to be overrun by the Germans. They really might have put up a better show than that!

# PART SIX
## AT THE DEPOT

### I

Clitherland Camp had acquired a look of coercive stability; but this was only natural since for more than eighteen months it had been manufacturing Flintshire Fusiliers, many of whom it was now sending back to the Front for the second and third time. The Camp was as much an essential co-operator in the national effort as Brotherhood & Co.'s explosive factory, which flared and seethed and reeked with poisonous vapours a few hundred yards away. The third winter of the War had settled down on the lines of huts with calamitous drabness; fog-bleared sunsets were succeeded by cavernous and dispiriting nights when there was nothing to do and nowhere to do it.

Crouching as close as I could to the smoky stove in my hut I heard the wind moaning around the roof, feet clumping cheerlessly along the boards of the passage, and all the systematized noises and clatterings and bugle-blowings of the Camp. Factory-hooters and ship's fog-horns out on the Mersey sometimes combined in huge unhappy dissonances; their sound seemed one with the smoke-drifted munition works, the rubble of industrial suburbs, and the canal that crawled squalidly out into blighted and forbidding farmlands which were only waiting to be built over.

Except for the permanent staff, there weren't many officers I had known before this winter. But I shared my hut with David Cromlech, who was well enough to be able to play an energetic game of football, in spite of having had a bit of shell through his right lung. Bill Eaves, the Cambridge scholar, had also returned and was quietly making the most of his few remaining months. (He was killed in February while leading a little local attack.) And there was young Ormand, too, pulling wry faces about his next Medical Board, which would be sure to pass him for General Service. I could talk to these three about 'old times with the First Battalion', and those times had already acquired a delusive unobnoxiousness, compared with what was in store for us; for the 'Big Push' of last summer and autumn had now found a successor in 'the Spring Offensive' (which was, of course, going to 'get the Boches on the run').

Mess, at eight o'clock, was a function which could be used for filling up an hour and a half. While Ormand was making his periodic remark – that his only reason for wanting to go out again was that it would enable him to pay off his overdraft at Cox's Bank – my eyes would wander up to the top table where the Colonel sat among those good-natured easy-going Majors who might well have adopted as their motto the ditty sung by the troops: 'We're here because we're here because we're here because we're here.' At nine-thirty the Colonel went to the ante-room for his game of Bridge. But the second-in-command, Major Macartney, would sit on long afterwards, listening to one or two of his cronies and slowly imbibing port with a hand that trembled nervously. Probably his mind was often back in Ireland, snipe shooting and salmon fishing. There was nothing grim about the Major, though his features had a certain severity, slightly reminiscent of the late Lord Kitchener. He was a reserved and dignified man, much more so than the other Majors. These convivial characters were ostensibly directing the interior economy of the Camp, and as the troops were well fed and looked after they must be given credit for it. The training of recruits was left to sergeant-instructors, most of whom were Regular N.C.O.s of the best pattern, hard-worked men who were on their legs from morning to night, and strict because they had to be strict. The raw material to be trained was growing steadily worse. Most of those who came in now had joined the Army unwillingly, and there was no reason why they should find military service tolerable. The

War had become undisguisedly mechanical and inhuman. What in earlier days had been drafts of volunteers were now droves of victims. I was just beginning to be aware of this.

But Clitherland had accessible compensations. One of them was the Golf Course at Formby. The electric train took only twenty minutes to get there, and Formby was famous for its bracing air, comfortable Club House, and superlatively good war-time food. I went there at least one afternoon a week; usually I played alone, and often I had the links to myself, which was no disadvantage, since I have always been considerably addicted to my own company.

My main purpose, however, was a day with the hounds. For this I was readily given leave off Saturday morning duties, since an officer who wanted to go out hunting was rightly regarded as an upholder of pre-war regimental traditions. The Saturday Meets of the Cheshire Hounds were a long way off, but nothing short of impossibility deterred me, and the working out of my plans was an effective antidote to war-weariness. It was, in fact, very like achieving the impossible, when I sat in my hut of an evening, cogitating with luxurious deliberation, consulting a map and calculating how my hireling could meet me at such and such a station, measuring the distance from there to the meet, and so on in the manner known to enthusiastic young sportsmen. On such Saturdays I would get up in the dark with joyful alacrity. Leaving Liverpool by an early train, I would eagerly observe the disconsolate beginnings of a dull December day, encouraging as far as I could the illusion that I was escaping from everything associated with the uniform which I wore; and eyeing my brown Craxwell field-boots affectionately.

Under such conditions no day could be a bad one, and although more than one Saturday's hunting was stopped by frost, I derived singular consolation from the few hunts I had. My consolations included a heavy fall over some high timber which I ought to have had more sense than to tackle, since my hireling was a moderate though willing performer. Anyhow, the contrast between Clitherland Camp and the Cheshire Saturday country was like the difference between War and Peace – especially when – at the end of a good day – I jogged a few miles homeward with the hounds, conversing with the cheery huntsman in my best pre-war style.

Apart from these compensations I had the companionship of David who was now quite the 'old soldier' and as argumentative as ever. In fact, while I pored over my one-inch-to-the-mile map of Cheshire after dinner, he was usually sitting on in the Mess and taking an active part in the wordy warfare of other 'old soldiers', among whom he was now listened to as one having authority. It was something to have been in the Battle of the Somme; but to have been at the Battle of Loos as well made him feel quite a big gun. In our hut, however, we sought fresher subjects than bygone battles and obliterated trenches. I enjoyed talking about English literature, and listened to him as to an oracle which I could, now and then, venture to contradict. Although he was nine years younger than I was, I often found myself reversing our ages, since he knew so much more than I did about almost everything except fox-hunting. He made short work of most books which I had hitherto venerated, for David was a person who consumed his enthusiasms quickly, and he once fairly took my breath away by pooh-poohing *Paradise Lost* as 'that moribund academic concoction'. I hadn't realized that it was possible to speak disrespectfully about Milton. Anyhow, John Milton was consigned to perdition, and John Skelton was put forward as 'one of the few really good poets'. But somehow I could never quite accept his supremacy over Milton as an established fact. At that period Samuel Butler was the source of much of David's ingenuity at knocking highly-respected names and notions off their perches.

Anyhow, I was always ready to lose another literary illusion, for many of my friend's quiddities were as nicely rounded, and as evanescent, as the double smoke rings he was so adroit at blowing. He was full of such entertaining little tricks, and I never tired of hearing him imitate the talk of excitable Welshmen. He was fond of music, too; but it was a failure when we went to an orchestral concert in Liverpool. David said that it 'upset him psychologically'. It was no good as music either. No music was really any good except the Northern Folk-Ballad tunes which he was fond of singing at odd moments. 'The Bonny Earl of Murray' was one of his favourites, and he sang it in agreeably melancholy style. But much though I admired these plaintive ditties I could not believe that they abolished Beethoven's Fifth Symphony, which we'd heard at the Concert. I realize now that what I ought to have said was 'Oh rats, David!' Instead of which I clumsily tried to explain the merits of various composers other than the inventors of *The Minstrelsy of the Border*, which was exactly what he wanted me to do. Sometimes he made me quite angry. I remember one morning when he was shaving with one hand and reading *Robinson Crusoe* in the other. Crusoe was a real man, he remarked; fox-hunting was the sport of snobs and half-wits. Since it was too early in the day for having one's leg pulled, I answered huffily that I supposed Crusoe was all right, but a lot of people who hunted were jolly good sorts, and even great men in their own way. I tried to think of someone to support my argument, and after a moment exclaimed: 'Anthony Trollope, for instance! He used to hunt a lot, and you can't say he was a half-wit.' 'No, but he was probably a snob!' I nearly lost my temper while refuting the slur on Trollope's character, and David made things worse by saying that I had no idea how funny I was when I reverted to my peace-time self. 'I had an overdose of the hunting dope when I was with the Second Battalion in '15,' he added. 'If I'd been able to gas about Jorrocks and say I'd hunted with the Bedfordshire Hounds all my life, the Colonel and the Adjutant would have behaved quite decently to me.' 'You çan't be certain of that,' I replied, 'and anyway, there's no such thing as "the Bedfordshire Hounds". Bedfordshire's mostly the Oakley, and that isn't a first-class country either. You might as well get the names right when you're talking through your hat about things you don't understand.' What did it matter to David whether the Oakley was bordered by the Grafton, Fitzwilliam, and Whaddon Chase – none of which I'd ever hunted with, but I knew they were good countries and I didn't pretend that I wasn't interested in

99

them, and I strongly objected to them being sneered at by a crank – yes, a fad-ridden crank – like David. 'You're a fad-ridden crank,' I remarked aloud. But as he always took my admonitions for what they were worth, the matter ended amicably, and a minute later I was able to remind him that he was going on parade without a tie.

I have already said that, as a rule, we avoided war-talk. Outwardly our opinions did not noticeably differ, though his sense of 'the regimental tradition' was stronger than mine, and he 'had no use for anti-war idealism'. But each of us had his own attitude toward the War. My attitude (which had not always been easy to sustain) was that I wanted to have fine feelings about it. I wanted the War to be an impressive experience – terrible, but not horrible enough to interfere with my heroic emotions. David, on the other hand, distrusted sublimation and seemed to want the War to be even uglier than it really was. His mind loathed and yet attached itself to rank smells and squalid details. Like his face (which had a twist to it, as though seen in a slightly distorting mirror) his mental war-pictures were a little uncouth and out of focus. Though in some ways more easily shocked than I was, he had, as I once informed him, 'a first-rate nose for anything nasty'. It is only fair to add that this was when he'd been discoursing about the ubiquity of certain establishments in France. His information was all second-hand; but to hear him talk – round-eyed but quite the man of experience – one might have imagined that Amiens, Abbeville, Béthune, and Armentières were mainly illuminated by 'Blue Lamps' and 'Red Lamps', and that for a good young man to go through Havre or Rouen was a sort of Puritan's Progress from this world to the next.

## II

Going into Liverpool was, for most of us, the only antidote to the daily tedium of the Depot. Liverpool usually meant the Olympic Hotel. This palatial contrast to the Camp was the chief cause of the overdrafts of Ormand and other young officers. Never having crossed the Atlantic, I did not realize that the Hotel was an American importation, but I know now that the whole thing might have been brought over from New York in the mind of a first-class passenger. Once inside the Olympic, one trod on black and white squares of synthetic rubber, and the warm interior smelt of this pseudo-luxurious flooring. Everything was white and gilt and smooth; it was, so to speak, an air-tight Paradise made of imitation marble. Its loftiness made resonance languid; one of its attractions was a swimming-bath, and the whole place seemed to have the acoustics of a swimming bath; noise was muffled and diluted to an aqueous undertone, and even the languishing intermezzos of the string band throbbed and dilated as though a degree removed from ordinary audibility. Or so it seemed to the Clitherland subaltern who lounged in an ultra-padded chair eating rich cakes with his tea, after drifting from swimming-bath to hairdresser, buying a few fiction-magazines on his way. Later on the cocktail bar would claim him; and after that he would compensate himself for Clitherland with a dinner that defied digestion.

'Fivers' melted rapidly at the Olympic, and many of them were being melted by people whose share in the national effort was difficult to diagnose. In the dining-room I began to observe that some non-combatants were doing themselves pretty well out of the War. They were people whose faces lacked nobility, as they ordered lobsters and selected colossal cigars. I remember drawing Durley's attention to some such group when he dined with me among the mirrors and mock magnificence. They had concluded their spectacular feed with an ice-cream concoction, and now they were indulging in an afterthought – stout and oysters. I said that I supposed they must be profiteers. For a moment Durley regarded them with unspeculative eyes, but he made no comment; if he found them incredible, it wasn't surprising; both his brothers had been killed in action and his sense of humour had suffered in proportion. I remarked that we weren't doing so badly ourselves and replenished his champagne glass. Durley was on sick leave and had come to Liverpool for a night so as to see me and one or two others at the Depot. The War was very much on his mind, but we avoided discussing it during dinner. Afterwards, when we were sitting in a quiet corner, he gave me an account of the show at Delville Wood on September 3rd. Owing to his having been wounded in the throat, he spoke in a strained whisper. His narrative was something like this:

'After our first time up there – digging a trench in front of Delville Wood – we came back to Bonté Redoubt and got there soon after daylight on the 30th. That day and the next we were being shelled by long-range guns. About ten o'clock on the night of the 31st, Kinjack decided to shift camp. That took us two hours, though it was only 1,500 yards away, but it was pitch dark and pouring with rain. I'd got into "slacks" and was just settling down in a bell-tent when we got the order to move up to Montauban in double quick time. Kinjack went on ahead. You can imagine the sort of mix-up it was – the men going as fast as they could, getting strung out and losing touch in the dark, and the Adjutant galloping up and down cursing everyone; I never saw him in such a state before – you know what a quiet chap he usually is. We'd started in such a hurry that I'd got my puttees on over my "slacks"! It must have been nearly five miles, but we did it in just over the hour. When we got there no one could say what all the "wind-up" was about; we were in reserve all next day and didn't move up to the Wood till the evening after that. We were to attack from the right-hand corner of the Wood, with the East Surreys covering our left and the Manchesters attacking Ginchy on our right. Our objective was Pint Trench, taking Bitter and Beer and clearing Ale and Vat, and also Pilsen Lane in which the Brigade thought there were some big dug-outs. When I showed the battle-plan to the Sergeant-Major, all he said was "We'll have a rough house from Ale Alley". But no one had any idea it was going to be such a schimozzle as it was! . . . Anyhow by 8.30 on the night of September 2nd I got C Company inside the Wood, with Perrin and his Company just in front of us. A lot of the trees were knocked to splinters and most of the undergrowth had gone, so it wasn't difficult to get about. But while we were getting into position in shell-holes and a trench through the Wood there were shells coming from every direction and Very lights going up all round the Wood, and more than once I had to get down and use my luminous compass before I could say which side was which. Young Fernby and the Battalion bombers were on my right, and I saw more of him than of Perrin during the night; he was quite cheerful; we'd been told it was going to be a decent show. The only trouble we struck that night was when a shell landed among some men in a shell-hole; two of the stretcher-bearers were crying and saying it was bloody murder.

'Next day began grey and cheerless; shells screeching overhead, the earth going up in front of the Wood, and twigs falling on my tin hat. When it got near zero, the earth was going up continuously. Boughs were coming down. You couldn't hear the shells coming – simply felt the earth quake when they arrived. There was some sort of smoke-screen but it only let the Boches know we were coming. No one seems to be able to explain exactly what happened, but the Companies on the left never had a hope. They got enfiladed from Ale Alley, so the Sergeant-Major was right about the "rough house". Edmunds was killed almost at once and his Company and B were knocked to bits as soon as they came out of the Wood. I took C along just behind Perrin and his crowd. We advanced in three rushes. It was nothing but scrambling in and out of shell-holes, with the ground all soft like potting-mould. The broken ground and the slope of the hill saved us a bit from their fire. Bitter Trench was simply like a filled-in ditch where we crossed it. The contact-aeroplane was just over our heads all the time, firing down at the Boches. After the second rush I looked round and saw that a few of the men were hanging back a bit, and no wonder, for a lot of them were only just out from England! I wondered if I ought to go back to them, but the only thing I'd got in my head was a tag from what some instructor had told me when I was a private in the Artists' Rifles before the War. *In an attack always keep going forward!* Except for that, I couldn't think much; the noise was appalling and I've never had such a dry tongue in my life. I knew one thing, that we must keep up with the barrage. We had over 500 yards to go before the first lift and had been specially told we must follow the barrage close up. It was a sort of cinema effect; all noise and no noise. One of my runners was shot through the face from Ale Alley; I remember something like a half-brick flying over my head, and the bullets from the enfilade fire sort of smashing the air in front of my face. I saw a man just ahead topple over slowly, almost gracefully, and thought 'poor little chap, that's his last Cup Tie'. Anyhow, the two companies were all mixed up by the time we made the third rush, and we suddenly found ourselves looking down into Beer Trench with the Boches kneeling below us. Just on my left, Perrin, on top, and a big Boche, standing in the trench, fired at one another; down went the Boche. Then they cleared off along Vat Alley, and we blundered after them. I saw one of our chaps crumpled up, with a lot of blood on the back of his neck, and I took his rifle and bandolier and went on with Johnson, my runner. The trench had fallen in in a lot of places. They kept turning round and firing back at us. Once, when Johnson was just behind me, he fired (a cool careful shot – both elbows rested) and hit one of them slick in the face; the red jumped out of his face and up went his arms. After that they disappeared. Soon afterwards we were held up by a machine-gun firing dead on the trench where it was badly damaged, and took refuge in a big shell-hole that had broken into it. Johnson went to fetch Lewis guns and bombers. I could see four or five heads bobbing up and down a little way off so I fired at them and never hit one. The rifle I'd got was one of those "wirer's rifles" which hadn't been properly looked after, and very soon nothing happened when I pressed the trigger which had come loose somehow and wouldn't fire the charge. I reloaded and tried again, then threw the thing away and got back into the trench. There was a man kneeling with his rifle sticking up, so I thought I'd use that; but as I was turning to take it another peace-time tag came into my head – *Never deprive a man of his weapon in a post of danger!*

'The next thing I knew was when I came to and found myself

remembering a tremendous blow in the throat and right shoulder, and feeling speechless and paralysed. Men were moving to and fro about me. Then there was a wild yell – "They're coming back!" and I was alone. I thought "I shall be bombed to bits lying here" and just managed to get along to where a Lewis gun was firing. I fell down and Johnson came along and cut my equipment off and tied up my throat. Someone put my pistol in my side pocket, but when Johnson got me on to my legs it was too heavy and pulled me over so he threw it away. I remember him saying, "Make way; let him come," and men saying "Good luck, sir" – pretty decent of them under such conditions! Got along the trench and out at the back somehow – everything very hazy – drifting smoke and shell-holes – down the hill – thinking "I must get back to Mother" – kept falling down and getting up – Johnson always helping. Got to Battalion Headquarters; R.S.M. outside; he took me very gently by the left hand and led me along, looking terribly concerned. Out in the open again at the back of the hill I knew I was safe. Fell down and couldn't get up any more. Johnson disappeared. I felt it was all over with me till I heard his voice saying, "Here he is," and the stretcher-bearers picked me up . . . When I was at the dressing-station they took a scrap of paper out of my pocket and read it to me. "I saved your life under heavy fire"; signed and dated. The stretcher-bearers do that sometimes, I'm told!'

He laughed huskily, his face lighting up with a gleam of his old humour . . .

I asked whether the attack had been considered successful. He thought not. The Manchesters had failed, and Ginchy wasn't properly taken till about a week later. 'When I was in hospital in London,' he went on, 'I talked to a son of a gun from the Brigade Staff; he'd been slightly gassed. He told me we'd done all that was expected of us; it was only a holding attack in our sector, so as to stop the Boches from firing down the hill into the backs of our men who were attacking Guillemont. They knew we hadn't a hope of getting Ale Alley.'

He had told it in a simple unemphatic way, illustrating the story with unconscious gestures – taking aim with a rifle, and so on. But the nightmare of smoke and sunlight had been in his eyes, with a sense of confusion and calamity of which I could only guess at the reality. He was the shattered survivor of a broken battalion which had 'done all that was expected of it'.

I asked about young Fernby. Durley had been in the same hospital with him at Rouen and had seen him once. 'They were trying to rouse him up a bit, as he didn't seem to recognize anybody. They knew we'd been in the same Battalion, so I was taken into his ward one night. His head was all over shrapnel wounds. I spoke to him and tried to get him to recognize me, but he didn't know who I was; he died a few hours later.'

Silence was the only comment possible; but I saw the red screens round the bed and Durley whispering to Fernby's bandaged head and irrevocable eyes, while the nurse stood by with folded hands.

### III

At the beginning of January David got himself passed for General Service abroad. I was completely taken by surprise when he came back and told me. Apparently the doctor asked him whether he wanted some more home service, but a sudden angry pride made him ask to be given G.S. A couple of weeks later he'd had his final leave and I was seeing him off at Liverpool Station.

A glum twenty-one-year-old veteran (unofficially in charge of a batch of young officers going out for the first time) he butted his way along the crowded platform with shoulders hunched, collar turned up to his ears, and hands plunged in pockets. A certain philosophic finality was combined with the fidgety out-of-luck look which was not unusual with him. 'I've reduced my kit to a minimum this time. No revolver. I've worked it out that the chances are about five to one against my ever using it,' he remarked, as he stood shuffling his feet to try and keep them warm. He hadn't explained how he'd worked the chances out, but he was always fond of a formula. Then the train began to move and he climbed awkwardly into his compartment. 'Give my love to old Joe when you get to the First Battalion,' was my final effort at heartiness. He nodded with a crooked smile. Going out for the third time was a rotten business and his face showed it.

'I ought to be going with him,' I thought, knowing that I could have got G.S. at my last Board if I'd had the guts to ask for it. But how could one ask for it when there was a hope of getting a few more days with the Cheshire and the weather was so perishing cold out in France? 'What a queer mixture he is,' I thought, as I wandered absent-mindedly away from the station. Nothing could have been more cheerless than the rumbling cobbled street by the Docks, with dingy warehouses shutting out the dregs of daylight and an ash-coloured sky which foretold some more snow.

I remember going back to the hut that night after Mess. There was snow on the ground, and the shuttered glare and muffled din of the explosive works seemed more than usually grim. Sitting by the stove I began to read a magazine which David had left behind. It was a propagandist weekly containing translations from the Foreign Press. A Copenhagen paper said: 'The sons of Europe are being crucified on the barbed wire because the misguided masses are shouting for it. They do not know what they do, and the statesmen wash their hands. They dare not deliver them from their martyr's death . . .' Was this really the truth, I wondered; wild talk like that was new to me. I thought of Dick Tiltwood, and how he used to come into this hut with such shining evidences of youth in his face; and of dark-haired little Fernby who was just such another; and of Lance-Corporal Kendle, and all those others whose violent deaths had saddened my experience. David was now returning to be a candidate for this military martyrdom, and so (I remembered it with a sick assurance) was I.

Lying awake while the stove-light died redly in the corner of the room, I remembered the wine-faced Army Commander with his rows of medal-ribbons, and how young Allgood and I had marched past him at the Army School last May, with the sun shining and the band playing. He had taken the salute from four hundred officers and N.C.O.s of his Army. How many of them had been killed since then, and how deeply was he responsible for their deaths? Did he know what he was doing, or was he merely a successful old cavalryman whose peace-time popularity had pushed him up on to his present perch?

It was natural that I should remember Flixécourt. Those four weeks had kept their hold on my mind, and they now seemed like the First Act of a play – a light-hearted First Act which was unwilling to look ahead from its background of sunlight and the glorying beauty of beech forests. Life at the Army School, with its superb physical health, had been like a prelude to some really conclusive sacrifice of high-spirited youth. Act II had carried me along to the fateful First of July. Act III had sent me home to think things over. The autumn attacks had been a sprawling muddle of attrition and inconclusiveness. In the early summer the Fourth Army had been ready to advance with a new impetus. Now it was stuck in the frozen mud in front of Bapaume, like a derelict tank. And the story was the same all the way up to Ypres. Bellicose politicians and journalists were fond of using the word 'crusade'. But the 'chivalry' (which I'd seen in epitome at the Army School) had been mown down and blown up in July, August, and September, and its remnant had finished the year's 'crusade' in a morass of torment and frustration. Yet I was haunted by the memory of those Flixécourt weeks – almost as though I were remembering a time when I'd been in love. Was it with life that I'd been in love then? – for the days had seemed saturated with the fecundity of physical health and fine weather, and it had been almost as if my own germinant aliveness were interfused with some sacrificial rite which was to celebrate the harvest. 'Germinating and German-hating,' I thought, recovering my sense of reality with a feeble joke. After that I fell asleep.

I had an uncomfortable habit of remembering, when I woke up in the morning, that the War was still going on and waiting for me to go back to it; but apart from that and the times when my inmost thoughts got the upper hand of me, life at the Camp was comparatively cheerful, and I allowed myself to be carried along by its noisy current of good-humoured life. At the end of each day I found consolation in the fact that I had shortened the winter, for the new year had begun with a spell of perishing cold weather. Our First Battalion, which had been up to its neck in mud in front of Beaumont-Hamel, was now experiencing fifteen degrees of frost while carrying on minor operations connected with straightening the line. Dottrell wrote that they 'weren't thinking beyond the mail and the rum ration', and advised me to stay away until the weather improved. It wasn't difficult to feel like following his advice; but soon afterwards I went into Liverpool for what I knew to be my final Medical Board. It was a dark freezing day, and all the officers in the waiting-room looked as if they wanted to feel their worst for the occasion. A sallow youth confided in me that he'd been out on the razzle the night before and was hoping to get away with another four weeks' home service.

There were two silver-haired Army doctors sitting at a table, poring over blue and white documents. One, with a waxed moustache, eyed me wearily when I came into the office. With a jerk of the head he indicated a chair by the table. 'Feel fit to go out again?' 'Yes; quite well, thank you.' His pen began to move across the blue paper. 'Has been passed fit for General Ser . . .' He looked up irritably. 'Don't shake the table!' (I was tapping it with my fingers.) The other Colonel gazed mildly at me over his pince-nez. Waxed moustache grunted and went on writing. Shaking the table wouldn't stop that pen of his!

# PART SEVEN
# ROUEN IN FEBRUARY

## I

Sometime in the second week of February I crossed to Havre on a detestable boat named *Archangel*. As soon as the boat began to move I was aware of a sense of relief. It was no use worrying about the War now; I was in the Machine again, and all responsibility for my future was in the haphazard control of whatever powers manipulated the British Expeditionary Force. Most of us felt like that, I imagine, and the experience was known as 'being for it again'. Apart from that, my only recollection of the crossing is that someone relieved me of my new trench-coat while I was asleep.

At nine o'clock in the evening of the next day I reported myself at the 5th Infantry Base Depot at Rouen. The journey from London had lasted thirty-three hours (a detail which I record for the benefit of those who like slow-motion war-time details). The Base Camp was a couple of miles from the town, on the edge of a pine forest. In the office where I reported I was informed that I'd been posted to our Second Battalion; this gave me something definite to grumble about, for I wanted to go where I was already known, and the prospect of joining a strange battalion made me feel more homeless than ever. The 5th I.B.D. Adjutant advised me to draw some blankets; the store-room was just round the corner, he said. After groping about in the dark and tripping over tent ropes I was beginning to lose my temper when I opened a door and found myself in a Guard Room. A man, naked to the waist, was kneeling in the middle of the floor, clutching at his chest and weeping uncontrollably. The Guard were standing around with embarrassed looks, and the Sergeant was beside him, patient and unpitying. While he was leading me to the blanket store I asked him what was wrong. 'Why, sir, the man's been under detention for assaulting the military police, and now 'e's just 'ad news of his brother being killed. Seems to take it to 'eart more than most would. 'Arf crazy, 'e's been, tearing 'is clothes off and cursing the War and the Fritzes. Almost like a shell-shock case, 'e seems. It's his third time out. A Blighty one don't last a man long nowadays, sir.' As I went off into the gloom I could still hear the uncouth howlings.

'Well, well; this is a damned depressing spot to arrive at!' I thought, while I lay awake trying to keep warm and munching a bit of chocolate, in a narrow segment of a canvas shed about four feet high. Beyond the army-blanket which served as a partition, two officers were chattering interminably in rapid Welsh voices. They were comparing their experiences at some squalid pleasure house in Rouen, and their disclosures didn't make the War seem any jollier. It was, in fact, the most disgusting little conversation I'd ever listened to. But what right had I to blame the poor devils for trying to have a good time before they went up to the Line? . . . Nevertheless, the War seemed to be doing its best to make me feel unheroic.

Next day I found the 5th I.B.D. Mess dispiriting. I knew nobody, and it wasn't a place where people felt inclined to be interested in one another, since none of them were there for more than a few days. They agreed in grumbling about the alcoholic R.C. padre who managed the mess; the food was bad, and four and threepence a day was considered an exorbitant charge. When they weren't on the training ground (known as 'the Bull Ring') officers sat about in the Mess Room playing cards, cursing the cold weather, and talking tediously about the War with an admixture of ineffective cynicism which hadn't existed twelve months before. I watched them crowding round the notice board after a paper had been pinned to it. They were looking to see if their names were on the list of those going up to the Line next day. Those who were on the list laughed harshly and sat down, with simulated unconcern, to read a stale picture paper. On the same notice board were the names of three private soldiers who had been shot for cowardice since the end of January. 'The sentence was duly carried out . . .' In the meantime we could just hear the grumbling of the guns and there was the Spring Offensive to look forward to.

I was feeling as if I'd got a touch of fever, and next morning the doctor told me I'd got German measles. So I transferred myself ingloriously to No. 25 Stationary Hospital, which was a compound of tents with a barbed wire fence round it, about 300 yards from the Camp. There were six in the tent already and my arrival wasn't popular. An extra bed had to be brought in, and the four card players huddled against a smoky stove were interrupted by a gust of Arctic wind. There was snow on the ground and the tent was none too warm at the best of times. 'Now, Mr. Parkins, I'm afraid you must shift round a bit to make room for the new patient,' said the nurse. While my bed was being lugged into position by an orderly, Mr. Parkins made it plain that six had been company in that tent and seven was an inconvenience. One of his opponents told him to stop chewing the rag and deal again. The cards had been blown off the table and Parkins had lost what, he said, was the first decent hand he'd held that morning. But the additional overcrowding soon ceased to be a grievance, and I didn't spoil their well established circle by offering to butt in at bridge, for I was content to read a book and observe my fellow-invalids.

The quietest of them was Strangford, a specimen of adolescent simplicity, lanky and overgrown and credulous. He wore a kilt, but came of good North Irish stock. Though barely nineteen, he had done several months in the trenches. His father kept a pack of harriers in County Down, and his face would light up when I encouraged him to tell me about them. But unless he was talking or had some little job to keep him busy, his brain appeared to cease working altogether. He would sit on the edge of his bed, slowly rubbing his knee which had a bad sore on it; a mop of untidy brown hair hung over his forehead, and his huge clumsy hands and red wrists had outgrown his tunic. After rubbing his knee, he takes a letter from his breast pocket, bending his gawky, unformed face over it; once he smiles secretly, but when he has read it through he is solemn – wondering, perhaps, when he will see his home and the harriers again.

Parkins was an obvious contrast to this modest youth. Pent up in the accidental intimacy of army life, men were usually anxious to exhibit themselves to the best advantage, particularly as regards their civilian antecedents. 'I'll bet he was jolly well-dressed before the war,' was a type of remark frequently made by young platoon commanders. Parkins was about thirty, and often reminded us that he had been to Cambridge; in private life he had been a schoolmaster. Plausible at first, he soon revealed his defects, for the slovenly tedium of that tent brought greed and selfishness to the surface. With his muddy eyes and small dark moustache, he wasn't a man one took to. But he was self-satisfied, and did his best to amuse us with indecent rhymes and anecdotes. He was also fond of using certain stilted expressions, such as 'for the nonce' and 'anent'. 'I've no complaints to make anent this hand,' he would say when playing cards. He posed as a gay dog, chaffing the nurses when they brought in the food, and quoting Omar Khayyám at them – 'a jug of wine, a loaf of bread and thou beside me, singing in the Wilderness' – and referring to the tent as 'this battered Caravanserai whose portals are alternate Night and Day'. Parkins did not conceal his dislike of the Front Line, and was now in hopes of getting a job as Railway Transport Officer. But he was the sort of man who would get killed in some unutterably wretched attack after doing his best to dodge it.

Young Holt was another second-rate character, plump, smooth-faced and spuriously smart. He had escaped from the Infantry into the Balloon Section, and now fancied himself in a leather overcoat with a fur collar – playing at 'being in the Royal Flying Corps'. He felt that R.F.C. officers had a social superiority to the Infantry. Being up in a balloon elevated a man in more ways than one, and he often aired his discrimination in such matters. Speaking of the Artillery, he would say: 'Yes, there's more *tone* in the R.F.A. – much more tone than you find in the Garrison Gunners!' Holt was a harmless easy-going creature, but we got very tired of his incessant repetition of a stale joke which consisted in saying in a loud voice, *I will rise and will go unto my father and will say unto him: Father, stand-at-ease!*

Then there was White, a sensible Territorial Captain who had been in charge of Heavy Trench Mortars. Short and thick-set, with a deep, humorous voice, he talked in a muddled way about the War – sardonic about English methods, but easily impressed by notable 'public names' of politicians and generals. He liked discussing Trench Mortar technicalities, and from the way he spoke about his men I knew that he had earned their gratitude.

There was another youngish man who had been a clerk in the Colonial Office and had gone to Egypt as a Yeomanry Sergeant before getting his Infantry commission. He talked to me, in a cockney accent, about his young wife, and was evidently kindly and reliable, though incapable of understanding an original idea. Two days after I'd seen the last of him, I couldn't remember either his face or his name.

The last of my six companions was Patterson, aged nineteen and fresh from Edinburgh University with a commission in the Field Artillery. His home was in Perth and he admitted that he loved porridge, when asking the nurse to try and wangle him a second helping of it. He talked broad Scots and made simple-minded war jokes, and then surprised me by quoting Milton and Keats. Self-reliant with a sort of pleasant truculence, he was thorough and careful in everything he did. With his crisp fair hair, grey eyes, and fresh complexion, he was a pattern of charming youthfulness. If he lived, he would be a shrewd, kindly man. Did he live, I wonder? . . .

After the first few days I used to slip through the wire fence and walk in the clean-smelling pine-woods. The surf-like sighing of the lofty colonnades could tranquillize my thoughts after the boredom of the tent and the chatter of the card players crouching by the stove. The pine-trees are patiently waiting for the guns to stop, I thought, and I felt less resentment against the War than I had done since I left England . . . One afternoon I followed an alley which led downhill to a big shuttered house. Blackbirds were scolding among the bushes as I trespassed in the untidy garden, and someone was chopping timber in a brown copse below the house. A dog barked from the stable-yard; hens clucked, and a cow lowed. Such homely sounds were comforting when one was in the exile of army life. I thought of the lengthening spring twilights and the lovely wakening of the year, forgetful of the 'Spring Offensive'. But it was only for a short while, and the bitter reality returned to me as I squeezed myself through the hospital's barbed wire fence. I was losing my belief in the War, and I longed for mental acquiescence – to be like young Patterson, who had come out to fight for his country undoubting, who could still kneel by his bed and say his simple prayers, steadfastly believing that he was in the Field Artillery to make the world a better place. I had believed like that, once upon a time, but now the only prayer which seemed worth uttering was Omar Khayyám's:

> For all the Sin wherewith the face of Man
> Is blackened – Man's forgiveness give – and take.

## II

Back at the Infantry Base Depot after my ten days of German measles, I stared at the notice board on nine successive mornings before my own name (typewritten and slightly misspelt Sharston) caused me to saunter away with the correct air of unconcern. At that moment the Medical Officer came in, shaking some snow off his coat. Sturdy, pink-faced and chubby, he looked a typical optimist. He had been two years with a fighting battalion and was now down at the Base for good, with a well earned D.S.O. He and I got on well together, but his appearance was deceptive, for he was a profound pessimist. He now exclaimed, rather crustily, that he supposed there'd only be one more winter out here, if we were lucky. I'd heard this remark from him before, and the first time had made me feel gloomy, for I had been hoping that the War would be over by next autumn. When the Mess waiter had brought him a whisky I ventured to ask his opinion about the German withdrawal on the Ancre; for at that time they were retiring to the Hindenburg Line, and sanguine subalterns were rejoicing over this proof that we'd 'got them on the run'. The Doctor assured me that the Germans were 'pulling our legs properly'. The idea seemed to please him; he always looked his brightest when he was announcing that we were certain to lose the War. We were now joined by a Rifle Brigade Major with an Irish brogue, who had been a cavalryman in the South African War. He had got his skull fractured by a bit of shell at the first battle of Ypres, but in spite of this he was a resolute optimist and was delighted to be back in France as second-in-command of a New Army Battalion. England, he said, was no place for an honest man; the sight of all those dirty dogs swindling the Government made him sick. When the Doctor grumbled about the rotten outlook, the Major would say: 'Yes, things couldn't be much worse, but another two or three years ought to see the job finished.' I found him surly and contradictory at first, but he softened when he got to know me, though he wasn't an easy man to discuss anything with, for he simply stated his opinions in a loud voice and only listened to one's replies in a detached one-eared way (which was literally true, since he was stone deaf on one side of his head, and had only got himself passed for active service after a tussle with the War Office). His rough and ready philosophy was refreshing, and he was a wholesome example of human inconsistency. He was a good-hearted man, I felt; but his attitude toward Conscientious Objectors was frankly brutal. He described, with evident relish, his methods of dealing with two of them who had turned up at the Rifle Brigade Depot. One had been a tough nut to crack, for he was a well-educated man, and the authorities were afraid of him. But the Major had got him run in for two years' hard labour. He'd have knocked him about a bit if he'd been allowed to, he said. The other one was some humble inarticulate wretch who refused to march. So the Major had him tied to the back of a wagon and dragged along a road until he was badly cut about. 'After a few hundred yards he cried enough, and afterwards turned out to be quite a decent soldier. Made good, and was killed in the trenches.' He smiled grimly. Discipline had to be enforced by brutality, said the Major; and, as I have already remarked, he wasn't amenable to argument.

I hadn't formed any opinion about Conscientious Objectors, but I couldn't help thinking that they must be braver men than some I'd seen wearing uniforms in safe places and taking salutes from genuine soldiers.

Resolved to make the most of my last day at the Base, I went down to Rouen early in the afternoon without having wasted any time in applying for leave from the Adjutant. A tram took me most of the way; the city looked fine as we crossed the river. There wasn't so very much to be done when I got there, but the first thing was to have a hair-cut. I'd had one a week ago, but this one might have to last me a longish while, for I wasn't keen on Battalion barbers. So I told the man to cut off as much as he could, and while he clipped and snipped I gazed gloomily at myself in the glass, speculating prosaically on the probabilities of my head of hair ever needing another trim up. A captain in the next chair had been through the whole repertoire – hair-cut, shave, shampoo, face-massage, and friction. 'Now I feel a quid better,' he remarked when he got up to go. He was wearing trench boots and was evidently on his way to the Line. I had heard him treating the barber, who spoke English, to a panegyric on the prospects of an Allied success in the Spring. 'We're going to give them the knock all right this journey!' The barber asked him about a long scar which seamed his head. He smiled: 'A souvenir of Devil's Wood.' I wondered how much longer he would retain his enthusiasm for the Western Front. Personally I preferred rambling around Rouen and pretending that I was an ordinary peace-time tourist. In the old quarters of the town one could stroll about without meeting many English soldiers.

Later on I was going to the Hôtel de la Poste for a valedictory bath and dinner. In the meantime I was content to stare at shop-

windows and explore side streets. It was a Saturday afternoon
and the people were busy marketing. At the end of my wanderings
I went into the Cathedral, leaving behind me the bustling Square
and the sallow gusty sunset which flared above the roofs. In the
Cathedral, perhaps, I could escape from the War for a while,
although the Christian Religion had apparently no claim to be
regarded as a Benevolent Neutral Power.

It was some Saint's Day, and the nave was crowded with
drifting figures, their footfalls echoing in the dusk. Sometimes a
chair scrooped when a worshipper moved away. Candles burned
in clear clusters, like flickering gold flowers, in the shrines where
kneeling women gazed and whispered and moved their hands
devoutly. In the pulpit a priest was urging the Lenten significance
of 'Jésu', tilting his pallid square face from side to side and
gesticulating mechanically. A congregation sat or stood to hear
him; among them, at my elbow, a small child stared up at the
priest with stupid innocent eyes. That child couldn't understand
the sermon any more than it understood the War. It saw a man,
high up and alone, clenching his hands and speaking vehemently;
it also saw the figures of people called soldiers who belonged to
something that made a much bigger noise than the preacher, who
now stopped suddenly, and the monotonous chanting began
again in front of the altar (sounding, I thought, rather harsh and
hopeless).

The preacher, I inferred, had been reminding us that we ought
to love one another and be like little children. 'Jésu' had said so,
and He had died to save us (but not to save the Germans or the
Austrians or any of that lot). It was no good trying to feel uplifted,
when such thoughts grimaced at me; but there was a certain
consolation in the solemnity of the Cathedral, and I remained
there after the service had ended. Gradually, the glory faded from
the rose-window above the organ. I looked at all the windows,
until their lights were only blurs and patches, and the prophets
and martyrs robed in blue and crimson and green were merged in
outer darkness.

The Hôtel de la Poste hadn't altogether modernized its interior, but it contained much solid comfort and supplied the richest meals in Rouen. Consequently it was frequented by every British officer employed in the district, and had become a sort of club for those indispensable residents – so much so that strong suggestions had been advanced by senior officers to the effect that the *Poste* should be put out of bounds for all Infantry subalterns on their way to the Line. The place, they felt, was becoming too crowded, and the deportment of a 'temporary gentleman' enjoying his last decent dinner was apt to be more suitable to a dug-out than a military club.

Leaning back in a wicker chair, I enjoyed the after-effects of a hot bath and wondered what I'd have for dinner. The lift came sliding down from nowhere to stop with a dull bump. A bulky grey-haired Colonel, with green tabs and a Coronation Medal, stepped heavily out, leaning on a stick and glaring around him from under a green and gold cap and aggressive eyebrows. His disapproval focused itself on a group of infantry subalterns whose ungainly legs were cumbered with high trench boots; trench-coats and haversacks were slung untidily across their chairs; to-night, or to-morrow, or 'some old time or other' they'd be crawling up to the War in an over-ventilated reinforcement train, gazing enviously at the Red Cross trains which passed them – going the other way – and disparaging the French landscape, 'so different to good old Blighty'. Compared with 'the troops', who travelled in vans designed for horses and cattle, they were in clover. The Colonel, on the other hand, probably supervised an office full of clerks who made lists of killed, wounded, and reinforcements. I had visited such a place myself in an attempt to get my name transferred to the First Battalion, and had been received with no civility at all. They were all much too busy to rearrange the private affairs of a dissatisfied second-lieutenant, as might have been expected. But the contrast between the Front Line and the Base was an old story, and at any rate the Base Details were at a disadvantage as regards the honour and glory which made the War such an uplifting experience for those in close contact with it.

I smiled sardonically at the green and gold Colonel's back view. The lift ascended again, leaving a confused murmur of male voices and a clatter of feet on the polished wood floor. Officers pushed through the swing-doors in twos and threes, paused to buy an English paper from the concierge, vanished to hang up their overcoats, and straddled in again, pulling down their tunics and smoothing their hair, conscious of gaiters, neatly-fitting or otherwise. Young cavalrymen were numerous, their superior social connections demonstrated by well-cut riding boots and predominantly small heads. Nice-looking young chaps with nice manners, they sipped cocktails and stood up respectfully when a Cavalry Brigadier strode past them. The Cavalry were still waiting for their chance on the Western Front . . . Would they ever get it, I wondered. Personally, I thought it would be a pity if they did, for I disliked the idea of a lot of good horses being killed and wounded, and I had always been soft-hearted about horses. By the time I'd finished my dinner and a bottle of Burgundy, I felt soft-hearted about almost everything. The large dining-room was full of London Clubmen dressed as Colonels, Majors, and Captains with a conscientious objection to physical discomfort. But, after all, somebody had to be at the Base; modern warfare offered a niche for everyone, and many of them looked better qualified for a card-table than a military campaign. They were as much the victims of circumstances as the unfortunate troops in the trenches. Puffing a cigar, I decided that there was a tolerant view to be taken about almost everybody, especially after a good dinner at the Hôtel de la Poste.

# PART EIGHT
# THE SECOND BATTALION

## I

Although the War has been described as the greatest event in history, it could be tedious and repetitional for an ordinary Infantry Officer like myself.

From Corbie Station the War had started me on my home journey in a Hospital Train. Rather more than seven months later, at midnight, it again deposited me at Corbie Station after eight hours in an unlit and overcrowded carriage which had no glass in its windows. My valise was on a truck and though I made a scrambling attempt to get it unloaded the train clanked away into the gloom with all my belongings on board. We slept on the floor of the Field Ambulance Hut outside the station; my companions grumbled a good deal, for several of them were out again after being wounded last year, and one of them claimed to have been hit in both lungs. Two cadet-officers were going with me to the Second Battalion, but I had little in common with them except our lost valises, which were returned to us a week later (with one sample of everything abstracted by someone at the Army Service Corps Dump). Next morning, after glumly congratulating myself that I'd packed my safety razor in my haversack, I walked to my new unit, which was seven miles away. I was wearing my best friends, a pair of greased marching boots whose supple strength had never failed to keep the water out; how much those boots meant to me can only be understood by persons who have shared my type of experience; I can only say that they never gave me sore feet; and if this sounds irrelevant, I must remind the reader that a platoon commander's feet were his fortune.

The Second Battalion of the Flintshire Fusiliers had recently returned from two months in the Cléry sector of the Somme Front, where they had endured some of the severest weather of the War. Battalion records relate that there were no braziers in the trenches, fuel was so scarce that wooden crosses were taken from casual graves, and except for the tepid tea that came up in tins wrapped in straw, food was mostly cold. Major-General Whincop, who commanded the Division, had made himself obnoxiously conspicuous by forbidding the Rum Ration. He was, of course, over anxious to demonstrate his elasticity of mind, but the 'No Rum Division' failed to appreciate their uniqueness in the Expeditionary Force. He also thought that smoking impaired the efficiency of the troops and would have liked to restrict their consumption of cigarettes. General Whincop had likewise demonstrated his independence of mind earlier in the War by forbidding the issue of steel helmets to his Division. His conservative objection (which was based on a belief that this new War Office luxury would weaken the men's fighting spirit – 'make them soft', in fact) was, of course, only a flash in the pan (or brain-pan) and Whincop's reputation as an innovator was mainly kept alive by his veto on the Rum Ration. G.O.C.s, like platoon commanders, were obliged to devise 'stunts' to show their keenness, and opportunities for originality were infrequent. But since 1918 Generals have received their full share of ridicule and abuse, and it would not surprise me if someone were to start a Society for the Prevention of Cruelty to Great War Generals. If such a Society were formed, I, for one, would gladly contribute my modest half-guinea per annum; for it must be remembered that many an unsuccessful General had previously been the competent Colonel of an Infantry Battalion, thereby earning the gratitude and admiration of his men.

Anyhow, the frost had been intense, and owing to the rationing of coal in England the issue to the Army had been limited and coke-issues had caused many cases of coke-fume poisoning where the men slept in unventilated dug-outs. After this miserable experience (which had ended with a thaw and a hundred cases of trench-feet) the Second Battalion was now resting at Camp 13, about two miles from Morlancourt. The huts of Camp 13 had been erected since last summer; they disfigured what I had formerly known as an inoffensive hollow about half a mile from the reedy windings of the Somme. No one had a good word for the place. The Battalion was in low spirits because the Colonel had been wounded a few weeks before, and he had been so popular that everyone regarded him as irreplaceable. His successor was indulgent and conciliatory, but it seemed that greater aggressiveness would have been preferable. Contrasting him with the rough-tongued efficiency of Kinjack, I began to realize that, in a Commanding Officer, amiability is not enough.

Meanwhile we were in what was called 'Corps Reserve', and Colonel Easby had issued the order 'carry on with platoon training' (a pronouncement which left us free to kill time as best we could). No. 8 Platoon, which was my own compact little command, was not impressive on parade. Of its thirty-four N.C.O.s and men, eight were Lewis gunners and paraded elsewhere. Eight was likewise the number of Private Joneses in my platoon, and my first difficulty was to differentiate between them. The depleted Battalion had been strengthened by a draft from England, and these men were mostly undersized, dull-witted, and barely capable of carrying the heavy weight of their equipment. As an example of their proficiency, I can say that in one case platoon training began with the man being taught how to load his rifle. Afterwards I felt that he would have been less dangerous in his pre-existing ignorance.

It was difficult to know what to do with my bored and apathetic platoon. I wasn't a competent instructor, and my sergeant was conscientious but unenterprising. *Infantry Training*, which was the only manual available, had been written years before trench-warfare 'came into its own' as a factor in world affairs, and the condensed and practical *Handbook for the Training of Platoons* was not issued until nearly twelve months afterwards. One grey afternoon, when we had gone through all our monotonous exercises and the men's eyes were more than usually mindless, I had a bright unmilitary idea and ordered them to play hide-and-seek among some trees. After a self-conscious beginning they livened up and actually enjoyed themselves. When I watched them falling in again with flushed and jolly faces I was aware that a sense of humanity had been restored to them, and realized how intolerable the ordinary exercises were unless the instructor was an expert. Even football matches were impossible, since there was no suitable ground.

The main characteristics of Camp 13 were mud and smoke. Mud was everywhere. All the Company officers lived in one long gloomy draughty hut with an earth floor. Smoke was always drifting in from the braziers of the adjoining kitchen. After dark we sat and shivered in our 'British Warm' coats, reading, playing cards, and writing letters with watering eyes by the feeble glimmer of guttering candles. Orderlies brought in a clutter of tin mugs and plates, and Maconochie stew was consumed in morose discomfort. It was an existence which suffocated all pleasant thoughts; nothing survived except animal cravings for warmth, food, and something to break the monotony of Corps Rest routine.

The only compensation for me was that my body became healthy, in spite of lesser discomforts such as a continuous cold in the head. The landscape was a compensation too, for I liked its heaving grey and brown billows, dotted with corn-stacks, patched and striped by plough and stubble and green crops, and crossed by bridle tracks and lonely wandering roads. Hares and partridges hurried away as I watched them. Along the horizon the guns still boomed and thudded, and bursting shells made tiny puffs of smoke above ridges topped by processions of trees, with here and there the dark line of woods. But from some windy upland I looked down on villages, scattered in the folds of hill and valley like handfuls of pebbles, grey and dull red, and from such things I got what consolation I could.

One Sunday afternoon I walked across to Heilly. I'd been there for a few days with the First Battalion last July, before we marched back to the Line in dust and glare. The water still sang its undertones by the bridge and went twinkling to the bend, passing the garden by the house where the Field Cashier used to hand us our money. I remembered going there with Dick Tiltwood, just a year ago. Ormand was with me this time, for he had joined the Second Battalion soon after I did. He had still got his little gramophone, and we reminded ourselves how Mansfield and Barton used to be forever 'chipping' him about it. 'I must say I used to get jolly fed-up with them sometimes; they overdid it, especially about that record *Lots of Loving*.' He laughed, rolling his good-humoured eyes round at me under the strongly marked black eyebrows which indicated that he had a strong temper when roused. The joke about *Lots of Loving* had consisted in the others pretending that it contained an unprintable epithet. On one occasion they conspired with the Adjutant, who asked Ormand to play *Lots of Loving* and then simulated astonishment at a certain adjective which was indistinct owing to the worn condition of the disc. Whereupon Ormand explained angrily, 'I ask you, is it bloody likely that "His Master's Voice" would send out a record with the word — — in it?'

As we trudged back from Heilly the sun was sinking red beyond the hazy valleys, a shrewd wind blowing, and plough teams turning a last furrow along the ridges. We'd had quite a good afternoon, but Ormand's cheerfulness diminished as we neared the Camp. He didn't fancy his chance in the Spring Offensive and he wanted to be back with the 'good old First Battalion', though he wouldn't find many of the good old faces when he got there. He spoke gloomily about his longing for an ordinary civilian career and his hatred of 'this silly stunt which the blasted Bishops call the Great Adventure'. He had been on a Court Martial the day before, and though nothing had been required of him except to make up the quorum of officers trying the case, he had been upset by it. Some poor wretch had been condemned to be shot for cowardice. The court had recommended the prisoner to mercy, but the proceedings had been bad for young Ormand. However, he relieved the situation by explaining, 'And to-morrow I've got to have my . . . anti-typhoid injection!' and I reminded him that he was reducing his overdraft at Cox's by being at the Front. So our walk ended; we passed the looming aerodrome, and the lines of lorries under the trees along the main road, and the sentry who stood by a glowing brazier at the crossroads. Down in the hollow crouched the Camp; a disgusting dinner in the smoky hut and then early to bed, was all it could offer us. 'Summer time' began at midnight, which meant one hour less sleep and absolutely nothing else.

## II

Palm Sunday was on April 1st that year. On April 2nd we left Camp 13. No one wanted to see it again, and as we went up hill to the Corbie road the smoke from the incinerators made the place look as if we had set fire to it.

I had a feeling that we were marching away to a better land. Camp 13 had clogged our minds, but the troops were in better spirits to-day and the Battalion seemed to have recovered its consciousness as a unit. The wind was blowing cold enough for snow, but the sun shone and wintry weather couldn't last much longer. Where were we walking to, I wondered; for this was known to be the first stage of a longish migration northwards. Arras, perhaps; rumours of an impending battle there had been active lately. As second-in-command of the Company I went along behind it, rather at my ease. Watching the men as they plodded patiently on under their packs, I felt as if my own identity was becoming merged in the Battalion. We were on the move and the same future awaited all of us (though most of the men had bad boots and mine were quite comfortable).

More light-hearted than I'd been for some time, I contemplated my Company Commander, who was in undisputed occupation of a horse which looked scarcely up to his weight. Captain Leake had begun by being rude to me. I never discovered the reason. But he had been a Special Reserve officer before the War, and he couldn't get certain regimental traditions out of his head. In the good old days, all second-lieutenants had been called 'warts', and for their first six months a senior officer never spoke to them, except on parade. Leake evidently liked the idea, for he was a man who enjoyed standing on his dignity; but such behaviour was inappropriate to active service, and six months at the Front usually sufficed to finish the career of a second-lieutenant. On my second morning at Camp 13 Leake had remarked (for my special benefit) that 'these newly joined warts were getting too big for their boots'. This was incorrect, for I was bemoaning the loss of my valise, and the M.O. had just given me my anti-typhoid injection. Leake also resented the fact that I had served with the First Battalion, which he appeared to regard as a hated rival. He thawed gradually after my first week, and was now verging on cordiality, which I did my best to encourage. The other Company Commanders had been friendly from the first, for I had known them at Clitherland in 1915.

Then there was the Doctor, who was now away on leave but would certainly be back before things became lively. Captain Munro had been with the Second Battalion about eighteen months. The first time I saw him was when he gave me my anti-typhoid injection. I looked at him with interest, for he was already known to me by reputation. 'Hullo, here's Sherston, the man who did stunts with the First Battalion,' he remarked, as I unbuttoned my shirt for the perforation process. He was giving double injections, so as to save us the trouble of feeling unwell twice. 'That'll keep you quiet for forty-eight hours,' he observed; and I retired, with a sickly grin. The M.O. was a famous character in the Battalion, and I was hoping to get to know him better. (At the time of writing I can indeed claim to have achieved my hope. But the Doctor is a man adverse to the idea of being applauded in print, and he would regard any reference to his local renown as irrelevant to this narrative.)

Equally popular was Bates, the Quartermaster, who was a burlier prototype of Joe Dottrell, with fewer political prejudices. When, at Camp 13, there had been rumours of a Divisional Race Meeting, Bates had asked me to ride his mare. The Races had been cancelled, but the notion had delighted me for a day or two.

This mare could gallop quite well and was the apple of the Quartermaster's eye. It was said that on one occasion, when the Transport was having a rough time, Bates had rigged up a tarpaulin shelter for his mare and slept out in the open himself. I was mentally comparing Bates and Dottrell, to their mutual credit, when we came to the end of our first fifty minutes and the men fell out at the side of the road and slipped their packs off. A gang of red and blue capped German prisoners was at work on the road close by, and their sullen under-nourished faces made our own troops look as if they were lucky in some sort of liberty. But whistles blew, pack straps were adjusted, and on we went. By half-past one the Battalion was in its billet in Corbie.

Before dinner Ralph Wilmot came round to our Company Mess to suggest that Leake and myself should join 'a bit of a jolly' which he'd arranged for that evening. Wilmot was a dark, monocled young man, mature for his years. His war experience had begun with despatch riding on a motor-bicycle in 1914. Afterwards he had gone to Gallipoli, where he had survived until the historic Evacuation. He had now done a long spell of service in France, and was a popular character in the Second Battalion. He had the whimsical smile which illuminated a half-melancholy temperament, and could give an amusing twist to the sorriest situation, since he liked to see life as a tragi-comedy and himself as a debonair philosopher, a man with a gay past who had learned to look at the world more in sorrow than in anger. His unobtrusive jests were enunciated with a stammer which somehow increased their effect. With some difficulty he now told us that he had discovered a place where we could 'buy some bubbly and tickle the ivories'. The ivory-tickling would be his own contribution, for he had a passion for playing the piano. So we spent the evening in a sparsely furnished little parlour on the ground-floor of a wine-merchant's house. The wine-merchant's wife, a sallow silent woman, brought in bottle after bottle of 'bubbly' which, whatever its quality, produced conviviality. We drank farewell to civilization with an air of finality, while Wilmot performed on an upright piano, the tone of which was meretriciously agreeable, like the flavour of the champagne. He played, mostly by ear, familiar passages from *Tosca* and *Bohème*, musical comedy extracts, and sentimental ballads. We all became confidential and almost emotional. I felt that at last I was really getting on good terms with Leake; every glass of wine made us dislike one another a little less. Thus the proceedings continued until after midnight, while Wilmot became more and more attached to a certain popular song. We sang the chorus over and over again:

> *Moon, moon, see-reen-ly shy-ning,*
> *Don't go home too soo-oon;*
> *You've such a charm about you*
> *That we – can't get – on with-out you.*
> *Da-da-da, de-dum . . .* etc.

The atmosphere of the room had become tropical, for we had all been smoking like chimneys. But Wilmot couldn't tear himself away from that piano, and while he caressed the keys with lingering affection, the wine-merchant's wife received I don't know how many francs and we all wrote our names in her album. From the number of shaky signatures in it I judged that she must have made a handsome profit out of the War.

Out in the white moonlight, Leake and I meandered along the empty street, accompanied by our tipsy shadows. At the door of my billet we shook hands 'sholemnly', and I assured him that he could always rely on me to 'blurry well do my damnedest for him'. He vanished heavily, and I spent several minutes prodding at the key-hole of the greengrocer's shop. Once inside the door, my difficulties were almost ended. I remember balancing myself in the dark little shop, which was full of strong-smelling vegetables, and remarking aloud, 'Well, old boy, here you are, and now you gotter get up the stairs.' My room was an unventilated cupboard which reeked of onions; the stairs were steep, but my flea-bag was on the floor and I fell asleep fully dressed. What with the smell of onions and the bad champagne, I awoke feeling like nothing on earth, and to say that Leake was grumpy at breakfast would be to put it mildly. But we were on the march by nine, in cold bright weather, and by the first halt I was feeling surprisingly clear-headed and alert.

We had halted on some high ground above Pont Noyelles: I can remember the invigorating freshness of the air and the delicate outlines of the landscape towards Amiens, and how I gazed at a line of tall trees by the river beyond which not two miles away, was the village of Bussy where I'd been last June before the Somme battle began. At such a moment as that the War felt quite a friendly affair and I could assure myself that being in the infantry was much better than loafing about at home. And at the second half I was able to observe what a pleasant picture the men made, for some of them were resting in warm sunlight under a crucifix and an old apple-tree. But by midday the march had become tedious; the road was dusty, the sun glared down on us, and I was occupied in preventing exhausted men from falling out. It was difficult to keep some of them in the ranks, and by the time we reached Villers-Bocage (nearly fourteen miles from Corbie) I was pushing two undersized men along in front of me, another one staggered behind hanging on to my belt, and the Company Sergeant-Major was carrying three rifles as well as his own. By two o'clock they were all sitting on dirty straw in a sun-chinked barn, with their boots and socks off. Their feet were the most important part of them, I thought, as I made my sympathetic inspection of sores and blisters. The old soldiers grinned at me philosophically, puffing their Woodbines. It was all in the day's work, and the War was the War. The newly-joined men were different; white and jaded, they stared up at me with stupid trusting eyes. I wished I could make things easier for them, but I could do nothing beyond sending a big batch of excruciating boots to the Battalion boot-menders, knowing that they'd come back roughly botched, if anything were done to them at all. But one Company's blisters were a small event in the procession of sore feet that was passing through Villers-Bocage. The woman in my billet told me in broken English that troops had been going through for fifteen days, never stopping more than one night and always marching towards Doullens and Arras. My only other recollection of Villers-Bocage is the room in which our Company's officers dined and slept. It contained an assortment of stuffed and mouldy birds with outspread wings. There was a stork, a jay, and a sparrow-hawk; also a pair of squirrels. Lying awake on the tiled floor I could watch a seagull suspended by a string from the ceiling; very slowly it revolved in the draughty air; and while it revolved I fell asleep, for the day had been a long one.

Next day's march took us to Beauval, along a monotonous eight-mile stretch of the main road from Amiens to St. Pol. Wet snow was falling all the way. We passed into another 'Army area'; the realm of Rawlinson was left behind us and our self-sacrificing exertions were now to be directed to Allenby. Soon after entering the Allenby Area we sighted a group of mounted officers who had stationed themselves under the trees by the roadside. Word was passed back that it was the Corps Commander. Since there were only three Corps Commanders in each Army they were seldom seen, so it was with quite a lively interest that we put ourselves on the alert to eyes-left this one. While we were trudging stolidly nearer to the great man, Colonel Easby detached himself from the head of the column, rode up to the General, and saluted hopefully. The Corps Commander (who was nothing much to look at, for his interesting accumulation of medal-ribbons was concealed by a waterproof coat) ignored our eyes-lefting of him; he was too busy bellowing at poor Colonel Easby, whom he welcomed thus. C.C. 'Are you stuck to that bloody horse?' *Col. E.* 'No, sir.' (Dismounts hastily and salutes again.) As Leake's Company went by, the General was yelling something about why the hell hadn't the men got the muzzles of their rifles covered (this being one of his 'special ideas'). 'Pity he don't keep his own muzzle covered,' remarked someone in the ranks, thereby voicing a prevalent feeling. The Corps Commander was equally abusive because the 'Cookers' were carrying brooms and other utilitarian objects. Also the Companies were marching with fifty-yard intervals between them (by a special order of the late Rawlinson). In Allenby's Army the intervals between Companies had to be considerably less, as our Colonel was now finding out. However, the episode was soon behind us and the 'Cookers' rumbled peacefully on their way, brooms and all, emitting smoke and stewing away at the men's dinners. Very few of us ever saw the Corps Commander again. It was a comfort to know that Allenby, at any rate, could be rude to him if he wanted to.

We started from Beauval at four o'clock on a sunny afternoon and went another eight miles to a place called Lucheux . . . There is nothing in all this, the reader will expostulate. But there was a lot in it, for us. We were moving steadily nearer to the Spring Offensive; for those who thought about it the days had an ever intensifying significance. For me, the idea of death made everything seem vivid and valuable. The War could be like that to a man, until it drove him to drink and suffocated his finer apprehensions.

Among the troops I observed a growing and almost eager expectancy; their cheerfulness increased; something was going to happen to them; perhaps they believed that the Arras Battle would end the War. It was the same spirit which had animated the Army before the Battle of the Somme. And now, once again, we could hear along the horizon that blundering doom which bludgeoned armies into material for military histories. 'That way to the Sausage Machine!' some old soldier exclaimed as we passed a signpost marked *Arras, 32 k*. We were entering Doullens with the brightness of the setting sun on our faces. As we came down the hill our second-in-command (a gentle middle-aged country solicitor) was walking beside me, consoling himself with reminiscences of cricket and hunting.

Thus the Battalion slogged on into an ominous Easter, and every man carried his own hazardous hope of survival. Overshadowed by the knowledge of what was ahead of us, I became increasingly convinced that a humble soldier holding up a blistered foot could have greater dignity than a blustering Corps Commander.

That night we were in huts among some wooded hills. I can remember how we had supper out in the moonlight sitting round a brazier with plates of ration stew on our knees. The wind was from the east and we could hear the huge bombardment up at Arras. Brown and leafless, the sombre woods hemmed us in. Soon the beeches would be swaying and quivering with the lovely miracle of spring. How many of us will return to that, I wondered, forgetting my hatred of the War in a memory of all that April had ever meant for me . . .

On Good Friday morning I woke with sunshine streaming in at the door and broad Scots being shouted by some Cameronians in the next hut. Someone was practising the bagpipes at the edge of the wood, and a mule contributed a short solo from the Transport Lines.

On Saturday afternoon we came to Saulty, which was only ten miles from Arras and contained copious indications of the Offensive, in the form of ammunition and food dumps and the tents of a Casualty Clearing Station. A large Y.M.C.A. canteen gladdened the rank and file, and I sent my servant there to buy a pack full of Woodbines for an emergency which was a certainty. Canteens and *estaminets* would be remote fantasies when we were in the devastated area. Twelve dozen packets of Woodbines in a pale green cardboard box were all that I could store up for the future consolation of B Company; but they were better than nothing and the box was no weight for my servant to carry.

Having seen the men settled into their chilly barns and sheds, I stuffed myself with coffee and eggs and betook myself to a tree stump in the peaceful park of a white château close to the village. Next day we were moving to our concentration area, so I was in a meditative mood and disposed to ask myself a few introspective questions. The sun was just above the tree-tops; a few small deer were grazing; a rook flapped overhead; and some thrushes and blackbirds were singing in the brown undergrowth. Nothing was near to remind me of the War; only the enormous thudding on the horizon and an aeroplane humming across the clear sky. For some obscure reason I felt confident and serene. My thoughts assured me that I wouldn't go back to England to-morrow if I were offered an improbable choice between that and the battle. Why should I feel elated at the prospect of the battle, I wondered. It couldn't be only the coffee and eggs which had caused me to feel so acquiescent. Last year, before the Somme, I hadn't known what I was in for. I knew now; and the idea was giving me emotional satisfaction! I had often read those farewell letters from second-lieutenants to their relatives which the newspapers were so fond of printing. 'Never has life brought me such an abundance of noble feelings,' and so on. I had always found it difficult to believe that these young men had really felt happy with death staring them in the face, and I resented any sentimentalizing of infantry attacks. But here I was, working myself up into a similar mental condition, as though going over the top were a species of religious experience. Was it some suicidal self-deceiving escape from the limitless malevolence of the Front Line? . . . Well, whatever it was, it was some compensation for the loss of last year's day dreams about England (which I could no longer indulge in, owing to an indefinite hostility to 'people at home who couldn't understand'). I was beginning to feel rather arrogant toward 'people at home'. But my mind was in a muddle; the War was too big an event for one man to stand alone in. All I knew was that I'd lost my faith in it and there was nothing left to believe in except 'the Battalion spirit'. The Battalion spirit meant living oneself into comfortable companionship with the officers and N.C.O.s around one; it meant winning the respect, or even the affection, of platoon and company. But while exploring my way into the War I had discovered the impermanence of its humanities. One evening we could be all together in a cosy room in Corbie, with Wilmot playing the piano and Dunning telling me about the eccentric old ladies who lived in his mother's boarding house in Bloomsbury. A single machine-gun or a few shells might wipe out the whole picture within a week. Last summer the First Battalion had been part of my life; by the middle of September it had been almost obliterated. I knew that a soldier signed away his independence;

we were at the front to fight, not to think. But it became a bit awkward when one couldn't look even a week ahead. And now there was a steel curtain down between April and May. On the other side of the curtain, if I was lucky, I should meet the survivors, and we should begin to build up our little humanities all over again.

That was the bleak truth, and there was only one method of evading it; to make a little drama out of my own experience – that was the way out. I must play at being a hero in shining armour, as I'd done last year; if I didn't, I might crumple up altogether. (Self-inflicted wounds weren't uncommon on the Western Front, and brave men had put bullets through their own heads before now, especially when winter made trench warfare unendurable.) Having thus decided on death or glory, I knocked my pipe out and got up from the tree stump with a sense of having solved my problems. The deer were still grazing peacefully in the park; but the sun was a glint of scarlet beyond the strip of woodland and the air was turning chilly. Along the edge of the world that infernal banging was going on for all it was worth. Three Army Corps were to attack on Easter Monday.

On a sunny Easter morning we moved another seven miles, to Basseux, a village which had been quite close to the trenches before the Germans withdrew to the Hindenburg Line. The Sausage Machine was now only eight miles away from us, and the preliminary bombardment was, as someone in the ranks remarked, 'a fair bloody treat to listen to'. We insisted on being optimistic. The Tanks were going to put the fear of God into the Boches, and the Cavalry would get their opportunity at last. We passed a squadron of Lancers on the road. Oh yes, they were massing for a break-through. Allenby knew what he was up to all right. And our Divisional General had told someone that it would be a walk-over for the infantry this time.

That afternoon I strolled out to inspect our old front-line trenches. As usual they gave me a queer feeling; it would be almost accurate to say that they fascinated me. Derelict ditches as they now were, battalion after battalion had endured intensities of experience in that intensified strip of territory. Night after night the tea-dixies had been carried up that twisting communication trench. Night after night sentries had stared over sodden parapets until the sky reddened and the hostile territory emerged, familiar and yet foreign. Not a very good sector to hold, I thought, observing how our cramped trench system had been overlooked by the Germans. That mile-and-a-bit back to Basseux hadn't been so easy a couple of months ago.

In peace time the village must have been quite a pretty little place, and even now it wasn't very badly damaged. All our officers were billeted in a dilapidated white château, which I now explored until I was sitting with my feet out of the window of an attic. Down in the courtyard Ormand and Dunning and one or two others were playing cricket with a stump and a wooden ball, using an old brazier as a wicket. Wilmot had found a ramshackle piano from which he was extracting his favourite melodies. Pigeons fluttered around the red tiled roofs and cooed in the warm evening sunshine. Three yellow balloons were visible. Then the little Adjutant bustled across the courtyard with a bunch of papers in his hand. There was no time for relaxation in the orderly room, for after to-day we were under orders to move at the shortest notice . . . Young Ormand shouted up at me, 'Come down and have a knock at the nets.'

The Battle of Arras began at 5.30 next morning. For two days we hung about the château, listening to the noise (of Military History being manufactured regardless of expense) and waiting for the latest rumours. With forced uneasy gaiety we talked loudly about the successes reported from the Line. 'Our objectives gained at Neuville-Vitasse', 'five thousand prisoners taken', and so on. But every one of us had something in his mind which he couldn't utter, even to his best friend.

Meanwhile the weather was misbehaving itself badly. Snow showers passed by on a bitterly cold wind, and I began an intimate battle in which a chill on the intestines got the better of me. It wasn't so easy to feel like a happy warrior turning his necessities to glorious gain, when doomed to go in company with gastritis, a sore throat, and several festering scratches on each hand. No more clean socks or handkerchiefs either. A big mail came in on Tuesday – the first we'd had for a week – and this kept us quiet for an interval of flimsy consolation. My only letter was from Aunt Evelyn, who apologized as usual for having so little to say. She had been reading *The Life of Disraeli* – 'such a relief to get away from all these present-day horrors. What a wonderful man he was. Are you still in the Rest Camp? I do hope so.' She added that spring-cleaning had been going on vigorously, with the usual floods of conversation from the maids . . . This didn't help my gastritis, which was getting beyond a joke. The M.O. wasn't back from leave yet, but one of his orderlies handed me an opium pill of such constipating omnipotence that my intestines were soon stabilized to a condition suitable for open warfare.

In the middle of Wednesday afternoon we were having an eleven-a-side single-brazier cricket match on a flat piece of ground in the château garden. The sun was shining between snow showers, and most of the men were watching from the grassy bank above. One of the Company Sergeant-Majors was playing a lively innings, though the ball was beginning to split badly. Then a whistle blew and the match ended abruptly. Less than an hour later the Battalion marched away from Basseux.

III

A heavy snowstorm set in soon after we started. A snowstorm on April 11th was the sort of thing that one expected in the War and it couldn't be classed as a major misfortune. Nevertheless we could have done without it, since we were marching away from all comfort and safety; greatcoats had been left behind and we had nothing but what we stood up in. As we slogged along narrow winding lanes the snow melted on the shiny waterproof sheets which kept the men uncomfortably warm. We were now in the devastated area; villages had been levelled to heaps of bricks;

fruit trees, and even pollard-willows, had been hacked down, and there was still a chance that we might be the victims of a booby trap in the shape of a dynamite charge under a causeway. A signpost pointed to Blairville; but a couple of inches of snow was enough to blot out Blairville. The next village was Ficheux (the men called it 'Fish Hooks' – any joke being better than none in that snowstorm); but Ficheux wasn't there at all; it had vanished from the landscape.

The snow had stopped when, after marching eight miles, we bivouacked in the dregs of daylight by a sunken road near Mercatel, a place which offered no shelter except the humanity of its name. After dark I found my way into a small dug-out occupied by a Trench Mortar Sergeant-Major and two signallers who were working a field telephone. With Shirley (one of our Company officers) I considered myself lucky to be there, crouching by a brazier, while the Sergeant-Major regaled us, in omniscient tones, with rumours about the desperate fighting at Wancourt and Heninel, names which meant nothing to me. I dozed through the night without ever being unaware of the coke fumes from the brazier and the tick-tack of the telephone.

Daylight discovered us blear-eyed and (to abbreviate a contemporary phrase) 'fed up and far from home'. We got through the morning somehow and I issued some of my 'emergency Woodbines'. Rifle-cleaning and inspection was the only occupation possible. Early in the afternoon the Battalion moved on four miles to St. Martin-Cojeul. The snow had melted, leaving much mud which rain made worse. St. Martin was a demolished village about a mile behind the battle-line. As we entered it I noticed an English soldier lying by the road with a horribly smashed head; soon such sights would be too frequent to attract attention, but this first one was perceptibly unpleasant. At the risk of being thought squeamish or even unsoldierly, I still maintain that an ordinary human being has a right to be momentarily horrified by a mangled body seen on an afternoon walk, although people with sound common sense can always refute me by saying that life is full of gruesome sights and violent catastrophes. But I am no believer in wild denunciations of the War; I am merely describing my own experiences of it; and in 1917 I was only beginning to learn that life, for the majority of the population, is an unlovely struggle against unfair odds, culminating in a cheap funeral. Anyhow, the man with his head bashed in had achieved theoretical glory by dying for his country in the Battle of Arras, and we who marched past him had an excellent chance of following his example.

We took over an old German reserve trench (captured on Easter Monday). Company Headquarters was a sort of rabbit-hole, just wide enough to accommodate Leake, a tiny stove, and myself. Leake occupied himself in enlarging it with a rusty entrenching tool. When dusk was falling I went out to the underground dressing-station to get my festering fingers attended to. I felt an interloper, for the place was crowded with groaning wounded. As I made my way back to the trench a few shells exploded among the ruinous remains of brickwork. All this, I thought, is disgustingly unpleasant, but it doesn't really count as war experience. I knew that if I could get the better of my physical discomforts I should find the War intensely interesting. B Company hadn't arrived at the groaning stage yet; in fact, they were grimly cheerful, though they'd only had one meal that day and the next was to-morrow morning. Leake and I had one small slice of ration bacon between us; I was frizzling my fragment when it fell off the fork and disappeared into the stove. Regardless of my unfortunate fingers I retrieved and ate it with great relish.

The night was cold and sleep impossible, since there was no space to lie down in. Leake, however, had a talent for falling asleep in any position. Chiselling away at the walls by candlelight, I kept myself warm, and in a couple of hours I had scooped out sufficient space for the other two officers. They were a well contrasted couple. Rees was a garrulous and excitable little Welshman; it would be flattery to call him anything except uncouth, and he made no pretensions to being 'a gentleman'. But he was good-natured and moderately efficient. Shirley, on the other hand, had been educated at Winchester and the War had interrupted his first year at Oxford. He was a delicate-featured and fastidious young man, an only child, and heir to a comfortable estate in Flintshire. Rees rather got on our nerves with his table manners, and Shirley deprecated the way he licked his thumb when dealing the cards for their games of nap. But social incompatibilities were now merged in communal discomfort. Both of them were new to the line, so I felt that I ought to look after them, if possible. I noticed that Rees kept his courage up by talking incessantly and making jokes about the battle; while Shirley, true to the traditions of his class, simulated nonchalance, discussing with Leake (also an Oxford man) the comparative merits of Magdalen and Christ Church, or Balliol and New College. But he couldn't get the nonchalance into his eyes . . . Both Shirley and Rees were killed before the autumn.

From our obsolete trench we looked toward the naked ground which rose to the ridge. Along that ridge ran the Hindenburg Line (a mile and a half away) from which new attacks were now being attempted. There was another attack next morning. Rees was detailed for an ammunition-carrying party, and he returned noisier than ever. It had been his first experience of shell-fire. Narrating his numerous escapes from hostile explosives, he continually invoked the name of the founder of his religion; now that it was all over he enjoyed the retrospective excitement roaring with laughter while he told us how he and his men had flung themselves on their faces in the mud. Rees never minded making himself look ridiculous, and I began to feel that he was capable of taking care of himself. Shirley raised his eyebrows during the recital, evidently disapproving of such volubility and not at all sure that officers ought to throw themselves flat on their faces when shells burst. Later in the day I took him for a walk up the hill; I wanted to educate him in unpleasant sights. The wind had dropped and the sunset sky was mountainous with calm clouds. We inspected a tank which had got stuck in the mud while crossing a wide trench. We succeeded in finding this ungainly monster interesting. Higher up the hill the open ground was dotted with British dead. It was an unexpectedly tidy scene, since most of them had been killed by machine-gun fire. Stretcher-bearers had been identifying the bodies and had arranged them in happy warrior attitudes, hands crossed and heads pillowed on haversacks. Often the contents of a man's haversack were scattered around him. There were letters lying about; the pathos of those last letters from home was obvious enough. It was a queer thing, I thought, that I should be taking a young Oxford man for this conducted tour of a battlefield on a fine April evening. Here we were, walking about in a sort of visible fraction of the Roll of Honour, and my pupil was doing his best to behave as if it were all quite ordinary and part of the public-school tradition. He was being politely introduced to the horrors of war, and he made no comment on them. Earlier in the day an attack on Fontaine-les-Croiselles had fizzled out in failure. Except for the intermittent chatter of machine-guns, the country ahead of us was quiet. Then, somewhere beyond the ridge, a huge explosion sent up a shapeless tower of yellow vapour. I remarked sagely that a German dump had probably been blown up. Shirley watched it intently as though the experience would be of use to him during future operations.

At five-thirty next morning our Brigade renewed the attack on Fontaine-les-Croiselles, but we remained in reserve. Enveloped by the din of the bombardment I leaned my elbows on the parapet and looked at the ridge. A glowering red sun was rising; the low undulant hills were grey-blue and deeply shadowed; the landscape was full of gun flashes and drifting smoke. It was a genuine battle picture, and I was aware of its angry beauty. Not much more than a mile away, on the further side of that menacing slope, lines of muttering men were waiting, strained to an intolerable expectancy, until the whistles blew and the barrage crept forward, and they stumbled across the open with the good wishes of General Allenby and the bad wishes of the machine-guns in the German strong-posts. Perhaps I tried to visualize their grim adventure. In my pocket I had a copy of a recent *communiqué* (circulated for instructive purposes) and I may as well quote it now. 'That night three unsuccessful bombing attacks were made on the Tower at Wancourt. During the Battalion relief next night the enemy opened a heavy bombardment on the Tower and its immediate vicinity, following it up with an attack which succeeded, mainly owing to the relief being in progress. A local counter-attack delivered by the incoming battalion failed owing to the darkness, pouring rain, and lack of knowledge of the ground. It was then decided that nothing could be done till daylight.' The lesson to be drawn from this episode was, I think, that lack of Artillery preparation is a mistake . . . The Wancourt Tower was only a couple of miles away on our left, so I felt vaguely impressed by being so close to events which were, undoubtedly, of historic importance in the annals of the War. And anyone who has been in the front line can amplify that *communiqué* for himself.


IV

On Saturday afternoon the order to move up took us by surprise. Two days of stagnation in the cramped little trench had relaxed expectancy, which now renewed itself in our compact preparations for departure. As usual on such occasions, the Company Sergeant-Major was busier than anybody else. I have probably said so before, but it cannot be too often repeated that C.S.M.s were the hardest worked men in the infantry; everything depended on them, and if anyone deserved a K.C.B. it was a good C.S.M.

At 9 p.m. the Company fell in at the top of the ruined street of St. Martin. Two guides from the outgoing battalion awaited us. We were to relieve some Northumberland Fusiliers in the Hindenburg Trench – the companies going up independently.

It was a grey evening, dry and windless. The village of St. Martin was a shattered relic; but even in the devastated area one could be conscious of the arrival of spring, and as I took up my position in the rear of the moving column there was something in the sober twilight which could remind me of April evenings in

England and the Butley cricket field where a few of us had been having our first knock at the nets. The cricket season had begun . . . But the Company had left the shell-pitted road and was going uphill across open ground. Already the guides were making the pace too hot for the rear platoon; like most guides they were inconveniently nimble owing to their freedom from accoutrement, and insecurely confident that they knew the way. The muttered message 'pass it along – steady the pace in front' was accompanied by the usual muffled clinkings and rattlings of arms and equipment. Unwillingly retarded, the guides led us into the deepening dusk. We hadn't more than two miles to go, but gradually the guides grew less authoritative. Several times they stopped to get their bearings. Leake fussed and fumed and they became more and more flurried. I began to suspect that our progress was circular.

At a midnight halt the hill still loomed in front of us; the guides confessed that they had lost their way, and Leake decided to sit down and wait for daylight. (There were few things more uncomfortable in the life of an officer than to be walking in front of a party of men all of whom knew that he was leading them in the wrong direction.) With Leake's permission I blundered experimentally into the gloom, fully expecting to lose both myself and the Company. By a lucky accident, I soon fell headlong into a sunken road and found myself among a small party of Sappers who could tell me where I was. It was a case of 'Please, can you tell me the way to the Hindenburg Trench?' Congratulating myself on my cleverness I took one of the Sappers back to poor benighted B Company, and we were led to our Battalion rendezvous.

The rendezvous took some finding, since wrong map references had been issued by the Brigade Staff; but at last, after many delays, the Companies filed along to their ordained (and otherwise anathematized) positions.

We were at the end of a journey which had begun twelve days before, when we started from Camp 13. Stage by stage, we had marched to the life-denying region which from far away had threatened us with the blink and growl of its bombardments. Now we were groping and stumbling along a deep ditch to the place appointed for us in the zone of inhuman havoc. There must have been some hazy moonlight, for I remember the figures of men huddled against the sides of communication trenches; seeing them in some sort of ghastly glimmer (was it, perhaps, the diffused whiteness of a sinking flare beyond the ridge?) I was doubtful whether they were asleep or dead, for the attitudes of many were like death, grotesque and distorted. But this is nothing new to write about, you will say; just a weary company, squeezing past dead or drowsing men while it sloshes and stumbles to a front-line trench. Nevertheless that night relief had its significance for me, though in human experience it had been multiplied a millionfold. I, a single human being with my little stock of earthly experience in my head, was entering once again the veritable gloom and disaster of the thing called Armageddon. And I saw it then, as I see it now – a dreadful place, a place of horror and desolation which no imagination could have invented. Also it was a place where a man of strong spirit might know himself utterly powerless against death and destruction and yet stand up and defy gross darkness and stupefying shell-fire, discovering in himself the invincible resistance of an animal or an insect, and an endurance which he might, in days afterwards, forget or disbelieve.

Anyhow, there I was, leading that little procession of Flintshire Fusiliers many of whom had never seen a front-line trench before. At that juncture they asked no compensation for their efforts except a mug of hot tea. The tea would have been a miracle, and we didn't get it till next morning, but there was some comfort in the fact that it wasn't raining.

It was nearly four o'clock when we found ourselves in the Hindenburg Main Trench. After telling me to post the sentries, Leake disappeared down some stairs to the Tunnel (which will be described later on). The Company we were relieving had already departed, so there was no one to give me any information. At first I didn't even know for certain that we were in the Front Line. The trench was a sort of gully, deep, wide, and unfinished looking. The sentries had to clamber up a bank of loose earth before they could see over the top. Our Company was only about eighty strong and its sector was fully 600 yards. The distance between the sentry-posts made me aware of our inadequacy in that wilderness. I had no right to feel homeless, but I did; and if I had needed to be reminded of my forlorn situation as a living creature I could have done it merely by thinking of a Field Cashier. Fifty franc notes were comfortable things, but they were no earthly use up here, and the words 'Field Cashier' would have epitomized my remoteness from snugness and security, and from all assurance that I should be alive and kicking the week after next. But it would soon be Sunday morning; such ideas weren't wholesome, and there was a certain haggard curiosity attached to the proceedings; combined with the self-dramatizing desperation which enabled a good many of us to worry our way through much worse emergencies than mine.

When I had posted the exhausted sentries, with as much cheeriness as I could muster, I went along to look for the Company on our left. Rather expecting to find one of our own companies, I came round a corner to a place where the trench was unusually wide. There I found myself among a sort of panic party which I was able to identify as a platoon (thirty or forty strong). They were jostling one another in their haste to get through a cavernous doorway, and as I stood astonished one of them breathlessly told me that 'the Germans were coming over'. Two officers were shepherding them downstairs and before I'd had time to think the whole lot had vanished. The Battalion they belonged to was one of those amateur ones which were at such a disadvantage owing to lack of discipline and the absence of trained N.C.O.s. Anyhow, their behaviour seemed to indicate that the Tunnel in the Hindenburg Trench was having a lowering effect on their *morale*.

Out in no-man's-land there was no sign of any German activity. The only remarkable thing was the unbroken silence. I was in a sort of twilight, for there was a moony glimmer in the low-clouded sky; but the unknown territory in front was dark, and I stared out at it like a man looking from the side of a ship. Returning to my own sector I met a runner with a verbal message from Battalion H.Q. B Company's front was to be thoroughly patrolled at once. Realizing the futility of sending any of my few spare men out on patrol (they'd been walking about for seven hours and were dead beat) I lost my temper, quietly and inwardly. Shirley and Rees were nowhere to be seen and it wouldn't have been fair to send them out, inexperienced as they were. So I stumped along to our right flank post, told them to pass it along that a patrol was going out from right to left, and then started sulkily out for a solitary stroll in no-man's-land. I felt more annoyed with Battalion Headquarters than with the enemy. There was no wire in front of the trench, which was, of course, constructed for people facing the other way. I counted my steps; 200 steps straight ahead; then I began to walk the presumptive 600 steps to the left. But it isn't easy to count your steps in the dark among shell-holes, and after a problematic 400 I lost confidence in my automatic pistol, which I was grasping in my right-hand breeches pocket. Here I am, I thought, alone out in this God-forsaken bit of ground, with quite a good chance of bumping into a Boche strong-post. Apparently there was only one reassuring action which I could perform; so I expressed my opinion of the War by relieving myself (for it must be remembered that there are other reliefs beside Battalion reliefs). I insured my sense of direction by placing my pistol on the ground with its muzzle pointing the way I was going. Feeling less lonely and afraid, I finished my patrol without having met so much as a dead body, and regained the trench exactly opposite our left-hand post, after being huskily challenged by an irresolute sentry, who, as I realized at the time was the greatest danger I had encountered. It was now just beginning to be more daylight than darkness, and when I stumbled down a shaft to the underground trench I left the sentries shivering under a red and rainy-looking sky.

There were fifty steps down the shaft; the earthy smell of that triumph of Teutonic military engineering was strongly suggestive of appearing in the Roll of Honour and being buried until the Day of Judgement. Dry-mouthed and chilled to the bone, I lay in a wire-netting bunk and listened to the dismal snorings of my companions. Along the Tunnel the air blew deathly cold and seasoned with mephitic odours. In vain I envied the snorers; but I was getting accustomed to lack of sleep, and three hours later I was gulping some peculiar tea with morose enjoyment. Owing to the scarcity of water (which had to be brought up by the Transport who were eight miles back, at Blairville) washing wasn't possible; but I contrived a refreshing shave, utilizing the dregs of my tea.

By ten o'clock I was above ground again, in charge of a fatigue party. We went half-way back to St. Martin, to an ammunition dump, whence we carried up boxes of trench mortar bombs. I carried a box myself, as the conditions were vile and it seemed the only method of convincing the men that it had to be done. We were out nearly seven hours; it rained all day and the trenches were a morass of glue-like mud. The unmitigated misery of that carrying party was a typical infantry experience of discomfort without actual danger. Even if the ground had been dry the boxes would have been too heavy for most of the men; but we were lucky in one way; the wet weather was causing the artillery to spend an inactive Sunday. It was a yellow corpse-like day, more like November than April, and the landscape was desolate and treeless. What we were doing was quite unexceptional; millions of soldiers endured the same sort of thing and got badly shelled into the bargain. Nevertheless I can believe that my party, staggering and floundering under its loads, would have made an impressive picture of 'Despair'. The background, too, was appropriate. We were among the débris of the intense bombardment of ten days before, for we were passing along and across the Hindenburg Outpost Trench, with its belt of wire (fifty yards deep in places); here and there these rusty jungles had been flattened by tanks. The Outpost Trench was about 200 yards from the Main Trench, which was now our front line. It had been solidly made, ten feet deep, with timbered fire-steps, splayed sides, and timbered steps at intervals to front and rear and to machine-gun emplacements. Now it was wrecked as though by earthquake and eruption. Concrete strong-posts were smashed and tilted sideways; everywhere the chalky soil was pocked and pitted with huge shellholes; and wherever we looked the mangled effigies of the dead were our *memento mori*. Shell-twisted and dismembered, the Germans maintained the violent attitudes in which they had died. The British had mostly been killed by bullets or bombs, so they looked more resigned. But I can remember a pair of hands (nationality unknown) which protruded from the soaked ashen soil like the roots of a tree turned upside down; one hand seemed to be pointing at the sky with an accusing gesture. Each time I passed that place the protest of those fingers became more expressive of an appeal to God in defiance of those who made the War. Who made the War? I laughed hysterically as the thought passed through my mud-stained mind. But I only laughed mentally, for my box of Stokes gun ammunition left me no breath to spare for an angry guffaw. And the dead were the dead; this was no time to be pitying them or asking silly questions about their outraged lives. Such sights must be taken for granted, I thought, as I gasped and slithered and stumbled with my disconsolate crew. Floating on the surface of the flooded trench was the mask of a human face which had detached itself from the skull.

## V

Plastered with mud and soaked to the skin, the fatigue-party clumped down the steps to the Tunnel. The carrying job was finished; but a stimulating surprise awaited me, for Leake was just back from Battalion H.Q. (somewhere along the Tunnel) and he breezily informed me that I'd been detailed to take command of a hundred bombers in the attack which had been arranged for next morning. 'Twenty-five bombers from each Company; you're to act as reserve for the Cameronians,' he remarked. I stared at him over my mug of reviving but trench-flavoured tea (made with chlorinated water) and asked him to tell me some more. He said: 'Well, they're a bit hazy about it at Headquarters, but the General is frightfully keen on our doing an underground attack along the Tunnel, as well as along the main trench up above. You've got to go and discuss the tactical situation with one of the Company commanders up in the Front Line on our right.' All that I knew about the tactical situation was that if one went along the Tunnel one arrived at a point where a block had been made by blowing it in. On the other side one bumped into the Germans. Above ground there was a barrier and the situation was similar. Bombing along a Tunnel in the dark . . . Had the War Office issued a text book on the subject? . . . I lit my pipe, but failed to enjoy it, probably because the stewed tea had left such a queer taste in my mouth.

Ruminating on the comfortless responsibility imposed on me by this enterprise, I waited until nightfall. Then a superbly cheerful little guide bustled me along a maze of waterlogged ditches until I found myself in a small dug-out with some friendly Scotch officers and a couple of flame-wagging candles. The dug-out felt more like old times than the Hindenburg Tunnel, but the officers made me feel incompetent and uninformed, for they were loquacious about local trench topography which meant nothing to my newly-arrived mind. So I puffed out my Military Cross ribbon, (the dug-out contained two others) nodded my head knowingly, and took an acquiescent share in the discussion of the strategic situation. Details of organization were offered me and I made a few smudgy notes. The Cams didn't think that there was much chance of my party being called on to support them, and they were hoping that the underground attack would be eliminated from operation orders.

I emerged from the desperation jollity of their little den with only a blurred notion of what it was all about. The objective was to clear the trench for 500 yards while other battalions went over the top on our left to attack Fontaine-les-Croiselles. But I was, at the best of times, only an opportunist officer; technical talk in the Army always made me feel mutely inefficient. And now I was floundering home in the dark to organize my command, put something plausible on paper, and take it along to the Adjutant. If only I could consult the Doctor, I thought; for he was back from leave, though I hadn't seen him yet. It seemed to me, in my confused and exhausted condition, that I was at a crisis in my military career; and, as usual, my main fear was that I should make a fool of myself. The idea of making a fool of oneself in that murderous mix-up now appears to me rather a ludicrous one; for I see myself merely as a blundering flustered little beetle; and if someone happens to put his foot on a beetle, it is unjust to accuse the unlucky insect of having made a fool of itself. When I got back to Leake and Rees and Shirley I felt so lost and perplexed that I went straight on to Battalion H.Q.

The Tunnel was a few inches higher than a tall man walking upright; it was fitted with bunks and recessed rooms; in places it was crowded with men of various units, but there were long intervals of unwholesome-smelling solitude. Prying my way along with an electric torch, I glimpsed an assortment of vague shapes, boxes, tins, fragments of broken furniture and frowsy mattresses. It seemed a long way to Headquarters, and the Tunnel was memorable but not fortifying to a fatigued explorer who hadn't slept for more than an hour at a stretch or taken his clothes off since last Tuesday. Once, when I tripped and recovered myself by grabbing the wall, my tentative patch of brightness revealed somebody half hidden under a blanket. Not a very clever spot to be taking a nap, I thought as I stooped to shake him by the shoulder. He refused to wake up, so I gave him a kick. 'God blast you, where's Battalion Headquarters?' My nerves were on edge; and what right had he to be having a good sleep, when I never seemed to get five minutes' rest? . . . Then my beam settled on the livid face of a dead German whose fingers still clutched the blackened gash on his neck . . . Stumbling on, I could only mutter to myself that this was really a bit too thick. (That, however, was an exaggeration; there is nothing remarkable about a dead body in a European War, or a squashed beetle in a cellar.) At Headquarters I found the Adjutant alone, worried and preoccupied with clerical work. He had worked in an office, at accountancy, I believe, before the War; and now most of his fighting was done in writing, though he had served his apprenticeship as a brave and indefatigable platoon commander. He told me that the underground attack had been washed out by a providential counter-order from Division, and asked me to send my organization scheme along as soon as possible. 'Right-O!' I replied, and groped my way back again feeling the reverse of my reply. By a stroke of luck I discovered Ralph Wilmot, sitting by himself in a small recessed room – his dark hair smoothly brushed and his countenance pensive but unperturbed. He might conceivably have been twiddling a liqueur glass in a Piccadilly restaurant. Unfortunately he had no liquid refreshment to offer, but his philosophic way of greeting me was a consolation and in him I confided my dilemma. With an understanding air he assumed his monocle, deliberated for a while, snuffed the candle wick, and wrote out an authoritative looking document headed 'Organization of F. F. Parties'. The gist of it was '15 Bombers (each carrying 5 grenades). 5 Carriers (also act as bayonet men). 1 Full Rank.' There wasn't much in it, he remarked, as he appended 'a little bit of skite about consolidation and defensive flanks'. It certainly looked simple enough when it was done, though I had been at my wits' end about it.

While he was fixing up my future for me I gazed around and thought what a queer refuge I'd found for what might possibly be my final night on earth. Dug-out though it was, the narrow chamber contained a foggy mirror and a clock. The clock wasn't ticking, but its dumb face stared at me, an idiot reminder of real rooms and desirable domesticity. Outside the doorless doorway people were continually passing in both directions with a sound of shuffling feet and mumbling voices. I caught sight of a red-capped Staff Officer, and a party of sappers carrying picks and shovels. The Tunnel was a sort of highway and the night had brought a considerable congestion of traffic. When we'd sent my document along to the Adjutant there was nothing more to be done except sit and wait for operation orders. It was now about ten o'clock.

As evidence of my own soldierly qualities I would like to be able to declare that we eagerly discussed every aspect of the situation as regards next morning's attack. But the truth is that we said nothing at all about it. The thing had to be attempted and there was an end of it (until zero hour). The Brigadier and his Staff (none too bright at map-references) were hoping to satisfy (vicariously) General Whincop (who'd got an unpopular bee in his bonnet about the Rum Ration, and had ordered an impossible raid, two months ago, which had been prevented by a providential thaw and caused numerous deaths in a subsequently sacrificed battalion).

Whincop was hoping to satisfy the Corps Commander, of whom we knew nothing at all, except that he had insulted our Colonel on the Doullens road. The Corps Commander hoped to satisfy the Army Commander, who had as usual informed us that we were 'pursuing a beaten enemy', and who had brought the Cavalry up for a 'break-through'. (It is worth mentioning that the village which was now our Division's objective was still held by the Germans eight months afterwards.) And the Army Commander, I suppose, was in telephonic communication with the Commander-in-Chief, who, with one eye on Marshall Foch, was hoping to satisfy his King and Country. Such being the case, Wilmot and myself were fully justified in leaving the situation to the care of the military caste who were making the most of their Great Opportunity for obtaining medal-ribbons and reputations for leadership; and if I am being caustic and captious about them I can only plead the need for a few minutes' post-war retaliation. Let the Staff write their own books about the Great War, say I. The Infantry were biased against them, and their authentic story will be read with interest.

As for our conversation between ten o'clock and midnight (when my operation orders arrived from the Adjutant) I suppose it was a form of drug, since it was confined to pleasant retrospections of peace. Wilmot was well acquainted with my part of the world and he'd come across many of our local worthies. So we were able to make a little tour of the Kentish

Weald and the Sussex border, as though on a couple of mental bicycles. In imagination we cycled along on a fine summer afternoon, passing certain milestones which will always be inseparable from my life history. Outside Squire Maundle's park gate we shared a distinct picture of his angular attitudes while he addressed his golf ball among the bell-tinklings and baaings of sheep on the sunny slopes above Amblehurst (always followed by a taciturn black retriever). Much has been asserted about the brutalized condition of mind to which soldiers were reduced by life in the Front Line; I do not deny this, but I am inclined to suggest that there was a proportionate amount of simple-minded sentimentality. As far as I was concerned, no topic could be too homely for the trenches.

Thus, while working parties and machine-gunners filed past the door with hollow grumbling voices, our private recess in the Hindenburg Tunnel was precariously infused with evocations of rural England and we challenged our surroundings with remembrances of parish names and farm-houses with friendly faces. A cottage garden was not an easy idea to recover convincingly . . . Bees among yellow wall-flowers on a warm afternoon. The smell of an apple orchard in autumn . . . Such details were beyond our evocation. But they were implied when I mentioned Squire Maundle in his four-wheeled dogcart, rumbling along the Dumbridge Road to attend a County Council Meeting.

'*Secret.* The Bombing Parties of 25 men will rendezvous at 2.30 a.m. to-morrow morning, 16th inst. in shafts near C Coy. H.Q. The greatest care will be taken that each separate Company Party keeps to one side of the Shaft and that the Dump of Bombs be in the trench at the head of these shafts, suitably split. The necessity of keeping absolute silence must be impressed on all men. These parties (under 2nd Lt. Sherston) will come under the orders of O.C. Cameronians at ZERO minus 10. Lt. Dunning and 2 orderlies will act liaison and report to O.C. Cameronians at ZERO minus 5. While the parties are in the shaft they must keep a free passage way clear for runners, etc.'

Such was the document which (had I been less fortunate) would have been my passport to the Stygian shore. In the meantime, with another two hours to sit through, we carried on with our world without end conversation. We were, I think, on the subject of Canterbury Cricket Week when my watch warned me that I must be moving on. As I got up from the table on which we'd been leaning our elbows, a blurred version of my face looked at me from the foggy mirror with an effect of clairvoyance. Hoping that this was an omen of survival, I went along to the rendezvous-shaft and satisfied myself that the Bombing Parties were sitting on the stairs in a bone-chilling draught, with my two subordinate officers in attendance.

Zero hour was 3 a.m. and the prefatory uproar was already rumbling overhead. Having tightened my mud-caked puttees and put my tie straight (there was no rule against wearing a tie in an attack) diffidently I entered the Cameronian H.Q. dug-out, which was up against the foot of the stairs. I was among strangers, and Zero minus 10 wasn't a time for conversational amenities, so I sat self-consciously while the drumming din upstairs was doing its utmost to achieve a reassuring climax. Three o'clock arrived. The tick-tacking telephone-orderly in a corner received a message that the attack had started. They were over the barrier now, and bombing up the trench. The Cameronian Colonel and his Adjutant conversed in the constrained undertones of men who expect disagreeable news. The Colonel was a fine-looking man, but his well-disciplined face was haggard with anxiety. Dunning sat in another corner, serious and respectful, with his natural jollity ready to come to the surface whenever it was called for.

At the end of twenty minutes' tension the Colonel exclaimed abruptly, 'Good God, I wish I knew how they're doing!' . . . And then, as if regretting his manifestation of feeling, 'No harm in having a bit of cake, anyhow.' There was a large home-made cake on the table. I was offered a slice, which I munched with embarrassment. I felt that I had no business to be there at all, let alone helping to make a hole in the Colonel's cake, which was a jolly good one. I couldn't believe that these competent officers were counting on me to be of any use to them if I were required to take an active part in the proceedings upstairs. Then the telephone-orderly announced that communication with Captain Macnair's headquarters had broken down; after that the suspense continued monotonously. I had been sitting there about two and a half hours when it became evident that somebody was descending the steps in a hurry. H.Q. must have kept its cooking utensils on the stairs, for the visitor arrived outside the doorway in a clattering cascade of pots and pans. He was a breathless and dishevelled sergeant, who blurted out an incoherent statement about their having been driven back after advancing a short distance. While the Colonel questioned him in a quiet and controlled voice I rose stiffly to my feet. I don't remember saying anything or receiving any orders, but I felt that the Cameronian officers were sensitive to the delicacy of my situation. There was no question of another slice of home-made cake. Their unuttered comment was, 'Well, old chap, I suppose you're for it now.'

Leaving them to get what satisfaction they could from the sergeant's story, I grinned stupidly at Dunning, popped my helmet on my head, and made for the stairway. It must have been a relief to be doing something definite at last, for without pausing to think I started off with the section of twenty-five who were at the top of the stairs. Sergeant Baldock got them on the move at once, although they were chilled and drowsy after sitting there for over three hours. None of them would have been any the worse for a mouthful of rum at that particular moment. In contrast to the wearisome candlelight of the lower regions, the outdoor world was bright and breezy; animated also by enough noise to remind me that some sort of battle was going on. As we bustled along, the flustered little contingent at my heels revived from its numbness. I had no idea what I was going to do; our destination was in the brain of the stooping Cameronian guide who trotted ahead of me. On the way we picked up a derelict Lewis gun, which I thought might come in handy though there was no ammunition with it. At the risk of being accused of 'taking the wrong half of the conversation' (a favourite phrase of Aunt Evelyn's) I must say that I felt quite confident. (Looking back on that emergency from my arm-chair, I find some difficulty in believing that I was there at all.) For about ten minutes we dodged and stumbled up a narrow winding trench. The sun was shining; large neutral clouds voyaged willingly with the wind; I felt intensely alive and rather out of breath. Suddenly we came into the main trench, and where it was widest we met the Cameronians. I must have picked up a bomb on the way, for I had one in my hand when I started my conversation with young Captain Macnair. Our encounter was more absurd than impressive. Macnair and his exhausted men were obviously going in the wrong direction, and I was an incautious newcomer. Consequently I had the advantage of him while he told me that the Germans were all round them and they'd run out of bombs. Feeling myself to be, for the moment, an epitome of Flintshire infallibility, I assumed an air of jaunty unconcern; tossing my bomb carelessly from left hand to right and back again, I inquired, 'But where *are* the Germans?' – adding 'I can't see any of them.' This effrontery had its effect (though for some reason I find it difficult to describe this scene without disliking my own behaviour). The Cameronian officers looked around them and recovered their composure. Resolved to show them what intrepid reinforcements we were, I assured Macnair that he needn't worry any more and we'd soon put things straight. I then led my party past his, halted them, and went up the trench with Sergeant Baldock – an admirably impassive little man who never ceased to behave like a perfectly trained and confidential man-servant. After climbing over some sort of barricade, we went about fifty yards without meeting anyone. Observing a good many Mills' bombs lying about in little heaps, I sent Baldock back to have them collected and carried further up the trench. Then, with an accelerated heart beat, I went round the corner by myself. Unexpectedly, a small man was there, standing with his back to me, stock still and watchful, a haversack of bombs slung over his left shoulder. I saw that he was a Cameronian corporal; we did not speak. I also carried a bag of bombs; we went round the next bay. There my adventurous ardour experienced a sobering shock.

A fair-haired Scotch private was lying at the side of the trench in a pool of his own blood. His face was grey and serene, and his eyes stared emptily at the sky. A few yards further on the body of a German officer lay crumpled up and still. The wounded Cameronian made me feel angry, and I slung a couple of bombs at our invisible enemies, receiving in reply an egg-bomb, which exploded harmlessly behind me. After that I went bombing busily along, while the corporal (more artful and efficient than I was) dodged in and out of the saps – a precaution which I should have forgotten. Between us we created quite a demonstration of offensiveness, and in this manner arrived at our objective without getting more than a few glimpses of retreating field-grey figures. I had no idea where our objective was, but the corporal informed me that we had reached it, and he seemed to know his business. This, curiously enough, was the first time either of us had spoken since we met.

The whole affair had been so easy that I felt like pushing forward until we bumped into something more definite. But the corporal had a cooler head and he advised discretion. I told him to remain where he was and started to explore a narrow sap on the left side of the trench. (Not that it matters whether it was on the left side or the right, but it appears to be the only detail I can remember; and when all is said and done, the War was mainly a matter of holes and ditches.) What I expected to find along that sap, I can't say. Finding nothing, I stopped to listen. There seemed to be a lull in the noise of the attack along the line. A few machine-guns tapped, spiteful and spasmodic. High up in the fresh blue sky an aeroplane droned and glinted. I thought what a queer state of things it all was, and then decided to take a peep at the surrounding country. This was a mistake which ought to have put an end to my terrestrial adventures, for no sooner had I popped my silly head out of the sap than I felt a stupendous blow in the back between my shoulders. My first notion was that a bomb had hit me from behind, but what had really happened was that I had been sniped from in front. Anyhow my foolhardy attitude toward the Second Battle of the Scarpe had been instantaneously altered for the worse. I leant against the side of the sap and shut my eyes . . . When I reopened them Sergeant Baldock was beside me, discreet and sympathetic, and to my surprise I discovered that I wasn't dead. He helped me back to the trench, gently investigated my wound, put a field-dressing on it, and left me sitting there while he went to bring up some men.

After a short spell of being deflated and sorry for myself, I began to feel rapidly heroical again, but in a slightly different style, since I was now a wounded hero, with my arm in a superfluous sling. All my seventy-five men were now on the scene (minus a few who had been knocked out by our own shells, which were dropping short). I can remember myself talking volubly to a laconic Stokes-gun officer, who had appeared from nowhere with his weapon and a couple of assistants. I felt that I must make one more onslaught before I turned my back on the War and my only idea was to collect all available ammunition and then renew the attack while the Stokes-gun officer put up an enthusiastic barrage. It did not occur to me that anything else was happening on Allenby's Army Front except my own little show. My over-strained nerves had wrought me up to such a pitch of excitement that I was ready for any suicidal exploit. This convulsive energy might have been of some immediate value had there been any objective for it. But there was none; and before I had time to inaugurate anything rash and irrelevant Dunning arrived to relieve me. His air of competent unconcern sobered me down, but I was still inflamed with the offensive spirit and my impetuosity was only snuffed out by a written order from the Cameronian Colonel, who forbade any further advance owing to the attack having failed elsewhere. My ferocity fizzled out then, and I realized that I had a raging thirst. As I was starting my return journey (I must have known then that nothing could stop me till I got to England) the M.O. came sauntering up the trench with the detached demeanour of a gentle botanist. 'Trust him to be up there having a look round,' I thought. Within four hours of leaving it I was back in the Tunnel.

Back at Battalion Headquarters in the Tunnel I received from our Colonel and Adjutant generous congratulations on my supposedly dashing display. In the emergency candlelight of that draughty cellar recess I bade them good-bye with voluble assurances that I should be back in a few weeks; but I was so overstrained and excited that my assurances were noises rather than notions. Probably I should have been equally elated without my wound; but if unwounded, I'd have been still up at the Block with the bombing parties. In the meantime, nothing that happened to me could relieve Battalion H.Q. of its burdens. The Adjutant would go on till he dropped, for he had an inexhaustible sense of duty. I never saw him again; he was killed in the autumn up at Ypres . . . I would like to be able to remember that I smiled grimly and departed reticently. But the 'bombing show' had increased my self-importance, and my exodus from the Front Line was a garrulous one. A German bullet had passed through me leaving a neat hole near my right shoulder-blade and this patriotic perforation had made a different man of me. I now looked at the War, which had been a monstrous tyrant, with liberated eyes. For the time being I had regained my right to call myself a private individual.

The first stage of my return journey took me to the Advanced Dressing Station at Henin. My servant went with me, carrying my haversack. He was a quiet clumsy middle-aged man who always did his best and never complained. While we picked our way along the broken ground of Henin Hill I continued talkative, halting now and again to recover breath and take a last stare at the blighted slope where yesterday I had stumbled to and fro with my working party.

The sky was now overcast and the landscape grey and derelict. The activities of the attack had subsided, and we seemed to be walking in a waste land where dead men had been left out in the rain after being killed for no apparent purpose. Here and there, figures could be seen moving toward the Dressing Station, some of them carrying stretchers.

It was the mid-day stagnation which usually followed an early morning attack. The Dressing Station was a small underground place crowded with groaning wounded. Two doctors were doing what they could for men who had paid a heavy price for their freedom. My egocentricity diminished among all that agony. I remember listening to an emotional padre who was painfully aware that he could do nothing except stand about and feel sympathetic. The consolations of the Church of England weren't much in demand at an Advance Dressing Station. I was there myself merely to go through the formality of being labelled 'walking wounded'. I was told to go on to a place called 'B. Echelon', which meant another three miles of muddy walking. Beat to the world, I reached B. Echelon, and found our Quartermaster in a tent with several officers newly arrived from the Base and one or two back from leave. Stimulated by a few gulps of whisky and water, I renewed my volubility and talked nineteen to the dozen until the kind Quartermaster put me into the mess-cart which carried me to a crossroad where I waited for a motor bus. There, after a long wait, I shook hands with my servant, and the handshake seemed to epitomize my good-bye to the Second Battalion. I thanked him for looking after me so well; but one couldn't wish a man luck when he was going back to the Hindenburg Trench. It may be objected that my attitude toward the Western Front was too intimate; but this was a question of two human beings, one of whom was getting out of it comfortably while the other went back to take his chance in the world's worst war ... In the bus, wedged among 'walking wounded', I was aware that I had talked quite enough. For an hour and a half we bumped and swayed along ruined roads till we came to the Casualty Clearing Station at Warlencourt. It was seven o'clock and all I got that night was a cup of Bovril and an anti-tetanus injection.

The place was overcrowded with bad cases and I had to wait until after midnight for a bed. I remember sitting in a chair listening to the rain pelting on the roof of the tent and the wailing of a wintry wind. I was too exhausted to sleep; my head had lost control of its thoughts, which continued to re-echo my good-bye garrulities; the injection had made me feel chilly and queer, and my wound began to be painful. But I was able to feel sorry for 'the poor old Battalion' (which was being relieved that night) and to be thankful for my own lucky escape.

What I'd been through was nothing compared with the sort of thing that many soldiers endured over and over again; nevertheless I condoled with myself on having had no end of a bad time.

Next afternoon a train (with 500 men and 35 officers on board) conveyed me to a Base Hospital. My memories of that train are strange and rather terrible, for it carried a cargo of men in whose minds the horrors they had escaped from were still vitalized and violent. Many of us still had the caked mud of the war zone on our boots and clothes, and every bandaged man was accompanied by his battle experience. Although many of them talked lightly and even facetiously about it, there was an aggregation of enormities in the atmosphere of that train. I overheard some slightly wounded officers who were excitedly remembering their adventures up at Wancourt, where they'd been bombed out of a trench in the dark. Their jargoning voices mingled with the rumble and throb of the train as it journeyed – so safely and sedately – through the environing gloom. The Front Line was behind us; but it could lay its hand on our hearts, though its bludgeoning reality diminished with every mile. It was as if we were pursued by the Arras Battle which had now become a huge and horrible idea. We might be boastful or sagely reconstructive about our experience, in accordance with our different characters. But our minds were still out of breath and our inmost thoughts in disorderly retreat from bellowing darkness and men dying out in shell-holes under the desolation of returning daylight. We were the survivors; few among us would ever tell the truth to our friends and relations in England. We were carrying something in our heads which belonged to us alone, and to those we had left behind us in the battle. There were dying men, too, on board that Red Cross train, men dying for their country in comparative comfort.

We reached our destination after midnight, and the next day I was able to write in my diary: 'I am still feeling war-like and quite prepared to go back to the Battalion in a few weeks; I am told that my wound will be healed in a fortnight. The doctor here says I am a lucky man as the bullet missed my jugular vein and spine by a fraction of an inch. I know it would be better for me not to go back to England, where I should probably be landed for at least three months and then have all the hell of returning again in July or August.' But in spite of my self-defensive scribble I was in London on Friday evening, and by no means sorry to be carried through the crowd of patriotic spectators at Charing Cross Station. My stretcher was popped into an ambulance which took me to a big hospital at Denmark Hill. At Charing Cross a woman handed me a bunch of flowers and a leaflet by the Bishop of London who earnestly advised me to lead a clean life and attend Holy Communion.

# PART NINE
## HOSPITAL AND CONVALESCENCE

### I

The first few days were like lying in a boat. Drifting, drifting, I watched the high sunlit windows or the firelight that flickered and glowed on the ceiling when the ward was falling asleep. Outside the hospital a late spring was invading the home-service world. Trees were misty green and sometimes I could hear a blackbird singing. Even the screech and rumble of electric trams was a friendly sound; trams meant safety; the troops in the trenches thought about trams with affection. With an exquisite sense of languor and release I lifted my hand to touch the narcissi by my bed. They were symbols of an immaculate spirit – creatures whose faces knew nothing of War's demented language.

For a week, perhaps, I could dream that for me the War was over, because I'd got a neat hole through me and the nurse with her spongings forbade me to have a bath. But I soon emerged from my mental immunity; I began to think; and my thoughts warned me that my second time out in France had altered my outlook (if such a confused condition of mind could be called an outlook). I began to feel that it was my privilege to be bitter about my war experiences; and my attitude toward civilians implied that they couldn't understand and that it was no earthly use trying to explain things to them. Visitors were, of course, benevolent and respectful; my wound was adequate evidence that I'd 'been in the thick of it', and I allowed myself to hint at heroism and its attendant horrors. But as might have been expected my behaviour varied with my various visitors; or rather it would have done so had my visitors been more various. My inconsistencies might become tedious if tabulated collectively, so I will confine myself to the following imaginary instances.

*Some Senior Officer under whom I'd served:* Modest, politely subordinate, strongly imbued with the 'spirit of the Regiment' and quite ready to go out again. 'Awfully nice of you to come and see me, sir.' Feeling that I ought to jump out of bed and salute, and that it would be appropriate and pleasant to introduce him to 'some of my people' (preferably of impeccable social status). Willingness to discuss active service technicalities and revive memories of shared front-line experience.

*Middle-aged or elderly Male Civilian:* Tendency (in response to sympathetic gratitude for services rendered to King and Country) to assume haggard facial aspect of one who had 'been through hell'. Inclination to wish that my wound was a bit worse than it actually was, and have nurses hovering round with discreet reminders that my strength mustn't be overtaxed. Inability to reveal anything crudely horrifying to civilian sensibilities. 'Oh yes, I'll be out there again by the autumn.' (Grimly wan reply to suggestions that I was now honourably qualified for a home-service job.) Secret antagonism to all uncomplimentary references to the German Army.

*Charming Sister of Brother Officer:* Jocular, talkative, debonair, and diffidently heroic. Wishful to be wearing all possible medal-ribbons on pyjama jacket. Able to furnish a bright account of her brother (if still at the front) and suppressing all unpalatable facts about the War. 'Jolly decent of you to blow in and see me.'

*Hunting Friend (a few years above Military Service Age):* Deprecatory about sufferings endured at the front. Tersely desirous of hearing all about last season's sport. 'By Jingo, that must have been a nailing good gallop!' Jokes about the Germans, as if throwing bombs at them was a tolerable substitute for fox-hunting. A good deal of guffawing (mitigated by remembrance that I'd got a bullet hole through my lung). Optimistic anticipations of next season's Opening Meet and an early termination of hostilities on all fronts.

Nevertheless my supposed reactions to any one of these

hypothetical vistors could only be temporary. When alone with
my fellow patients I was mainly disposed toward self-pitying
estrangement from everyone except the troops in the Front Line.
(Casualties didn't count as tragic unless dead or badly maimed.)

When Aunt Evelyn came up to London to see me I felt properly
touched by her reticent emotion; embitterment against civilians
couldn't be applied to her. But after she had gone I resented her
gentle assumption that I had done enough and could now accept a
safe job. I wasn't going to be messed about like that, I told myself.
Yet I knew that the War was unescapable. Sooner or later I should
be sent back to the Front Line, which was the only place where I
could be any use. A cushy wound wasn't enough to keep me out
of it.

I couldn't be free from the War; even this hospital ward was full
of it, and every day the oppression increased. Outwardly it was a
pleasant place to be lazy in. Morning sunshine slanted through
the tall windows, brightening the grey-green walls and the forty
beds. Daffodils and tulips made spots of colour under three red-
draped lamps which hung from the ceiling. Some officers lay
humped in bed, smoking and reading newspapers; others loafed
about in dressing-gowns, going to and from the washing room
where they scraped the bristles from their contented faces. A
raucous gramophone continually ground out popular tunes. In
the morning it was rag-time – *Everybody's Doing it* and *At the
Fox-Trot Ball*. (*Somewhere a Voice is calling, God send you back
to me*, and such-like sentimental songs were reserved for the
evening hours.) Before midday no one had enough energy to
begin talking war shop, but after that I could always hear scraps
of conversation from around the two fireplaces. My eyes were
reading one of Lamb's *Essays*, but my mind was continually
distracted by such phrases as 'Barrage lifted at the first objective',
'shelled us with heavy stuff', 'couldn't raise enough decent
N.C.O.s', 'first wave got held up by machine-guns', and 'bombed
them out of a sap'.

There were no serious cases in the ward, only flesh wounds and
sick. These were the lucky ones, already washed clean of squalor

and misery and strain. They were lifting their faces to the sunlight, warming their legs by the fire; but there wasn't much to talk about except the War.

In the evenings they played cards at a table opposite my bed; the blinds were drawn, the electric light was on, and a huge fire glowed on walls and ceiling. Glancing irritably up from my book I criticized the faces of the card-players and those who stood watching the game. There was a lean airman in a grey dressing-gown, his narrow whimsical face puffing a cigarette below a turban-like bandage; he'd been brought down by the Germans behind Arras and had spent three days in a bombarded dug-out with Prussians, until our men drove them back and rescued him. The Prussians hadn't treated him badly, he said. His partner was a swarthy Canadian with a low beetling forehead, sneering wide-set eyes, fleshy cheeks, and a loose heavy mouth. I couldn't like that man, especially when he was boasting how he 'did in some prisoners'. Along the ward they were still talking about 'counter-attacked from the redoubt', 'permanent rank of captain', 'never drew any allowances for six weeks', 'failed to get through their wire' . . . I was beginning to feel the need for escape from such reminders. My brain was screwed up tight, and when people came to see me I answered their questions excitedly and said things I hadn't intended to say.

From the munition factory across the road, machinery throbbed and droned and crashed like the treading of giants; the noise got on my nerves. I was being worried by bad dreams. More than once I wasn't sure whether I was awake or asleep; the ward was half shadow and half sinking firelight, and the beds were quiet with huddled sleepers. Shapes of mutilated soldiers came crawling across the floor; the floor seemed to be littered with fragments of mangled flesh. Faces glared upward; hands clutched at neck or belly; a livid grinning face with bristly moustache peered at me above the edge of my bed; his hands clawed at the sheets. Some were like the dummy figures used to deceive snipers; others were alive and looked at me reproachfully, as though envying me the warm safety of life which they'd longed for when they shivered in the gloomy dawn, waiting for the whistles to blow and the bombardment to lift . . . A young English private in battle equipment pulled himself painfully toward me and fumbled in his tunic for a letter; as he reached forward to give it to me his head lolled sideways and he collapsed; there was a hole in his jaw and the blood spread across his white face like ink spilt on blotting paper . . .

Violently awake, I saw the ward without its phantoms. The sleepers were snoring and a nurse in grey and scarlet was coming silently along to make up the fire.

## II

Although I have stated that after my first few days in hospital I 'began to think', I cannot claim that my thoughts were clear or consistent. I did, however, become definitely critical and inquiring about the War. While feeling that my infantry experience justified this, it did not occur to me that I was by no means fully informed on the subject. In fact I generalized intuitively, and was not unlike a young man who suddenly loses his belief in religion and stands up to tell the Universal Being that He doesn't exist, adding that if He does, He treats the world very unjustly. I shall have more to say later on about my antagonism to the World War; in the meantime it queered my criticisms of it by continually reminding me that the Adjutant had written to me to tell me that my name had been 'sent in for another decoration'. I could find no fault with this hopeful notion, and when I was allowed out of hospital for the first time my vanity did not forget how nice its tunic would look with one of those (still uncommon) little silver rosettes on the M.C. ribbon, which signified a Bar; or, better still, a red and blue D.S.O.

It was May 2nd and warm weather; no one appeared to be annoyed about the War, so why should I worry? Sitting on the top of a bus, I glanced at the editorial paragraphs of the *Unconservative Weekly*. The omniscience of this ably written journal had become the basis of my provocative views on world affairs. I agreed with every word in it and was thus comfortably enabled to disagree with the bellicose patriotism of the *Morning Post*. The only trouble was that an article in the *Unconservative Weekly* was for me a sort of divine revelation. It told me what I'd never known but now needed to believe, and its ratiocinations and political pronouncements passed out of my head as quickly as they entered it. While I read I concurred; but if I'd been asked to restate the arguments I should have contented myself with saying 'It's what I've always felt myself, though I couldn't exactly put it into words.'

The Archbishop of Canterbury was easier to deal with. Smiling sardonically, I imbibed his 'Message to the Nation about the War and the Gospel'. 'Occasions may arise', he wrote, 'when exceptional obligations are laid upon us. Such an emergency having now arisen, the security of the nation's food supply may largely depend upon the labour which can be devoted to the land. This being so, we are, I think, following the guidance given in the Gospel if in such a case we make a temporary departure from our rule. I have no hesitation in saying that in the need which these weeks present, men and women may with a clear conscience do field-work on Sundays.' Remembering the intense bombardment in front of Arras on Easter Sunday, I wondered whether the Archbishop had given the sanction of the Gospel for that little bit of Sabbath field-work. Unconscious that he was, presumably, pained by the War and its barbarities, I glared morosely in the direction of Lambeth Palace and muttered, 'Silly old fossil!' Soon afterwards I got off the bus at Piccadilly Circus and went into the restaurant where I had arranged to meet Julian Durley.

With Durley I reverted automatically to my active-service self. The war which we discussed was restricted to the doings of the Flintshire Fusiliers. Old So-and-so had been wounded; poor old Somebody had been killed in the Bullecourt show; old Somebody Else was still commanding B Company. Old jokes and grotesquely amusing trench incidents were re-enacted. The Western Front was the same treacherous blundering tragi-comedy which the mentality of the Army had agreed to regard as something between a crude bit of fun and an excuse for a good grumble. I suppose that the truth of the matter was that we were remaining loyal to the realities of our war experience, keeping our separate psychological secrets to ourselves, and avoiding what Durley called 'his dangerous tendency to become serious'. His face, however, retained the haunted unhappy look which it had acquired since the Delville Wood attack last autumn, and his speaking voice was still a hoarse whisper.

When I was ordering a bottle of hock we laughed because the waiter told us that the price had been reduced since 1914, as it was now an unpopular wine. The hock had its happy effect, and soon we were agreeing that the Front Line was the only place where one could get away from the War. Durley had been making a forlorn attempt to enter the Flying Corps, and had succeeded in being re-examined medically. The examination had started hopefully, as Durley had confined himself to nods and headshakings in reply to questions. But when conversation became inevitable the doctor had very soon asked angrily, 'Why the hell don't you stop that whispering?' The verdict had been against his fractured thyroid cartilage; though, as Durley remarked, it didn't seem to him to make much difference whether you shouted or whispered when you were up in an aeroplane. 'You'll have to take some sort of office job,' I said. But he replied that he hated the idea, and then illogically advised me to stay in England as long as I could. I asserted that I was going out again as soon as I could get passed for General Service, and called for the bill as though I were thereby settling my destiny conclusively. I emerged from the restaurant without having uttered a single anti-war sentiment.

When Durley had disappeared into his aimless unattached existence, I sat in Hyde Park for an hour before going back to the hospital. What with the sunshine and the effect of the hock, I felt rather drowsy, and the columns of the *Unconservative Weekly* seemed less stimulating than usual.

On the way back to Denmark Hill I diverted my mind by observing the names on shops and business premises. I was rewarded by Pledge (pawnbroker), Money (solicitor), and Stone (builder). There was also an undertaker named Bernard Shaw. But perhaps the most significant name was Fudge (printing works). What use, I thought, were printed words against a war like this? Durley represented the only reality which I could visualize with any conviction. People who told the truth were likely to be imprisoned, and lies were at a premium . . . All my energy had evaporated and it was a relief to be back in bed. After all, I thought, it's only sixteen days since I left the Second Battalion, so I've still got a right to feel moderately unwell. How luxurious it felt, to be lying there, after a cup of strong tea, with daylight diminishing, and a vague gratitude for being alive at the end of a fine day in late spring. Anyhow the War had taught me to be thankful for a roof over my head at night . . .

Lying awake after the lights were out in the ward, it is possible that I also thought about the Second Battalion. Someone (it must have been Dunning) had sent me some details of the show they'd been in on April 23rd. The attack had been at the place where I'd left them. A little ground had been gained and lost, and then the Germans had retreated a few hundred yards. Four officers had been killed and nine wounded. About forty other ranks killed, including several of the best N.C.O.s. It had been an episode typical of uncountable others, some of which now fill their few pages in Regimental Histories. Such stories look straightforward enough in print, twelve years later; but their reality remains hidden; even in the minds of old soldiers the harsh horror mellows and recedes.

Of this particular local attack the Second Battalion Doctor afterwards wrote, 'The occasion was but one of many when a Company or Battalion was sacrificed on a limited objective to a plan of attack ordered by Division or some higher Command with no more knowledge of the ground than might be got from a map of moderate scale.' But for me (as I lay awake and wondered whether I'd have been killed if I'd been there) April 23rd was a blurred picture of people bombing one another up and down ditches; of a Company stumbling across open ground and getting mown down by machine-guns; of the Doctor out in the dark with his stretcher-bearers, getting in the wounded; and of an exhausted Battalion staggering back to rest-billets to be congratulated by a genial exculpatory Major-General, who explained that the attack had been ordered by the Corps Commander. I could visualize the Major-General all right, though I wasn't aware that he was 'blaming it on the Corps Commander'. And I knew for certain that Ralph Wilmot was now minus one of his arms, so my anti-war bitterness was enabled to concentrate itself on the fact that he wouldn't be able to play the piano again. Finally, it can safely be assumed that my entire human organism felt ultra-thankful to be falling asleep in an English hospital. Altruism is an episodic and debatable quality; the instinct for self-preservation always got the last words when an infantryman was lying awake with his thoughts.

With an apology for my persistent specifyings of chronology, I must relate that on May 9th I was moved on to a Railway Terminus Hotel which had been commandeered for the accom-modation of convalescent officers. My longing to get away from London made me intolerant of the Great Central Hotel, which was being directed by a mind more military than therapeutic. The Commandant was a non-combatant Brigadier-General, and the convalescents grumbled a good deal about his methods, although they could usually get leave to go out in the evenings. Many of them were waiting to be invalided out of the Army, and the daily routine orders contained incongruous elements. We were required to attend lectures on, among other things, Trench Warfare. At my first lecture I was astonished to see several officers on crutches, with legs amputated, and at least one man had lost that necessary faculty for trench warfare, his eyesight. They appeared to be accepting the absurd situation stoically; they were allowed to smoke. The Staff Officer who was drawing diagrams on a black-board was obviously desirous of imparting information about the lesson which had been learnt from the Battle of Neuve Chapelle or some equally obsolete engagement. But I noticed several faces in the audience which showed signs of tortured nerves, and it was unlikely that their efficiency was improved by the lecturer who concluded by reminding us of the paramount importance of obtaining offensive ascendancy in no-man's-land.

In the afternoon I had an interview with the doctor who was empowered to decide how soon I went to the country. One of the men with whom I shared a room had warned me that this uniformed doctor was a queer customer. 'The blighter seems to take a positive pleasure in tormenting people,' he remarked, adding, 'He'll probably tell you that you'll have to stay here till you're passed fit for duty.' But I had contrived to obtain a letter from the Countess of Somewhere, recommending me for one of the country houses in her Organization; so I felt fairly secure. (At that period of the War people with large houses received convalescent officers as guests.)

The doctor, a youngish man dressed as a temporary Captain, began by behaving quite pleasantly. After he'd examined me and the document which outlined my insignificant medical history, he asked what I proposed to do now. I said that I was hoping to get sent to some place in the country for a few weeks. He replied that I was totally mistaken if I thought any such thing. An expression, which I can only call cruel, overspread his face. 'You'll stay here; and when you leave here, you'll find yourself back at the front in double-quick time. How d'you like that idea?' In order to encourage him, I pretended to be upset by his severity; but he seemed to recognize that I wasn't satisfactory material for his peculiar methods, and I departed without having contested the question of going to the country. I was told afterwards that officers had been known to leave his doctor's room in tears. But it must not be supposed that I regard his behaviour as an example of Army brutality. I prefer to think of him as a man who craved for power over his fellow men. And though his power over the visiting patients was brief and episodic, he must have derived extraordinary (and perhaps sadistic) satisfaction from the spectacle of young officers sobbing and begging not to be sent back to the front.

I never saw the supposedly sadistic doctor again; but I hope that someone gave him a black eye, and that he afterwards satisfied his desire for power over his fellow men in a more public-spirited manner.

Next morning I handed the letter of the Countess to a slightly higher authority, with the result that I only spent three nights in the Great Central Hotel, and late on a fine Saturday afternoon I travelled down to Sussex to stay with Lord and Lady Asterisk.

## III

Nutwood Manor was everything that a wounded officer could wish for. From the first I was conscious of a kindly welcome. It was the most perfect house I'd ever stayed in. Also, to put the matter plainly, it was the first time I'd ever stayed with an Earl. 'Gosh! This is a slice of luck,' I thought. A reassuring man-servant conducted me upstairs. My room was called 'The Clematis Room'; I noticed the name on the door. Leaning my elbows on the window-sill, I gazed down at the yew hedges of a formal garden; woods and meadows lay beyond and below, glorious with green and luminous in evening light; far away stood the Sussex Downs, and it did my heart good to see them. Everything in the pretty room was an antithesis to ugliness and discomfort. Beside the bed there was a bowl of white lilac and a Bible. Opening it at random to try my luck, I put my finger on the following verse from the Psalms: 'The words of his mouth were smoother than butter, but war was in his heart.' Rather an odd coincidence, I thought, that the word 'war' should turn up like that; but the Old Testament's full of fighting . . . While I was changing into my best khaki uniform I could hear quiet feet and murmurous voices moving about the house; doors closed discreetly on people about to dress for dinner. Still almost incredulous at my good fortune I went downstairs, to be greeted by a silver-haired and gracious hostess, and introduced to three other officers, all outwardly healthy and gentlemanly-looking. I was presented to Lord Asterisk, over eighty and crippled with rheumatism, but resolutely holding on to a life which had been devoted to useful public service. Respectfully silent, I listened to his urbane eloquence and felt sufficiently at my ease to do justice to a very good dinner. The port wine went its round; and afterwards, in the drawing-room, I watched Lady Asterisk working at some embroidery while one of the officers played Gluck and Handel on the piano. Nothing could have been more tranquil and harmonious than my first evening at Nutwood Manor. Nevertheless I failed to fall asleep in the Clematis Room. Lying awake didn't matter much at first; there was plenty to ruminate about; the view across the Weald at sunset had revived my memories of 'the good old days when I hunted with the Ringwell'. I had escaped from the exasperating boredom of hospital life, and now for a few weeks I could forget about the War . . . But the War insisted on being remembered, and by 3 a.m. it had become so peremptory that I could almost believe that some of my friends out in France must be waiting to go over the top. One by one, I thought of as many of them as I could remember . . .

I'd overheard Lady Asterisk talking about spiritualism to one of the officers; evidently she was a strong believer in the 'unseen world'. Perhaps it was this which set me wondering whether, by concentrating my mind on, say, young Ormand (who was still with the Second Battalion) I might be able to receive some reciprocal communication. At three o'clock in the morning a sleepless mind can welcome improbabilities and renounce its daylight scepticism. Neither voice nor vision rewarded my expectancy.

But I was rewarded by an intense memory of men whose courage had shown me the power of the human spirit – that spirit which could withstand the utmost assault. Such men had inspired me to be at my best when things were very bad, and they outweighed all the failures. Against the background of the War and its brutal stupidity those men had stood glorified by the thing which sought to destroy them . . .

I went to the window and leant out. The gables of the house began to loom distinct against a clear sky. An owl hooted from the woods; cocks were crowing from distant farms; on the mantelpiece a little clock ticked busily. Oppressed by the comfort of my surroundings, I felt an impulse to dress and go out for a walk. But Arras and the Somme were a long way off; I couldn't walk there and didn't want to; but they beckoned me with their bombardments and the reality of the men who endured them. I wanted to be there again for a few hours, because the trenches really were more interesting than Lady Asterisk's rose-garden. Seen from a distance, the War had a sombre and unforgettable fascination for its bondsmen. I would have liked to go and see what was happening, and perhaps take part in some exciting little exploit. I couldn't gainsay certain intense emotional experiences which I'd lived through in France. But I also wanted to be back at Nutwood Manor for breakfast . . . Returning to my bed I switched on the yellow shaded light. Yes; this was the Clematis Room, and nothing could be less like the dug-out where I'd sat a month ago talking about Sussex with Ralph Wilmot. Through the discurtained window the sky was deep nocturnal blue. I turned out the lamp, and the window became a patch of greyish white, with treetops dark and still in the strange quietude before dawn. I heard the cuckoo a long way off. Then a blackbird went scolding along the garden.

I awoke to a cloudless Sabbath morning. After breakfast Lady Asterisk led me into the garden and talked very kindly for a few minutes.

'I am sure you have had a very trying time at the front,' she said, 'but you must not allow yourself to be worried by unpleasant memories. We want our soldier-guests to forget the War while they are with us.'

I replied, mumbling, that in such surroundings it wouldn't be easy to worry about anything; and then the old Earl came out on to the terrace, pushing the wheeled apparatus which enabled him to walk.

Often during the next three weeks I was able to forget about the War; often I took refuge in the assuasive human happiness which Nutwood Manor's hospitality offered me. But there were times when my mental mechanism was refractory, and I reverted to my resolution to keep the smoke-drifted battle memories true and intense, unmodified by the comforts of convalescence. I wasn't going to be bluffed back into an easy-going tolerant state of mind, I decided, as I opened a daily paper one morning and very deliberately read a despatch from 'War Correspondents' Head-quarters'.

'I have sat with some of our lads, fighting battles over again, and discussing battles to be,' wrote some amiable man who had apparently mistaken the War for a football match between England and Germany. 'One officer – a mere boy – told me how he'd run up against eleven Huns in an advanced post. He killed two with a Mills' bomb ("Grand weapon, the Mills'!" he laughed, his clear eyes gleaming with excitement) wounded another with his revolver, and marched the remainder back to our own lines . . .' I opened one of the illustrated weeklies and soon found an article on 'War Pictures at the Royal Academy'. After a panegyric about 'Forward the Guns!' (a patriotic masterpiece by a lady who had been to the Military Tournament in pre-War days) the following sentence occurred: 'I think I like Mr. Blank's "Con-talmaison" picture best. He almost makes one feel that he must have been there. The Nth Division are going over the second line I expect – the tips of their bayonets give one this impression – and it is a picture which makes one's pulse beat a lot faster . . .'

'The tips of their bayonets give one that impression' . . . Obviously the woman journalist who wrote those words was deriving enjoyment from the War, though she may not have been aware of the fact. I wondered why it was necessary for the Western Front to be 'attractively advertised' by such intolerable twaddle. What *was* this camouflage War which was manufactured by the press to aid the imaginations of people who had never seen the real thing? Many of them probably said that the papers gave them a sane and vigorous view of the overwhelming tragedy. 'Naturally,' they would remark, 'the lads from the front are inclined to be a little morbid about it; one expects that, after all they've been through. Their close contact with the War has diminished their

realization of its spiritual aspects.' Then they would add something about 'the healing of Nations'. Such people needed to have
their noses rubbed in a few rank physical facts, such as what a
company of men smelt like after they'd been in action for a week
. . . The gong rang for luncheon, and Lady Asterisk left off reading
a book by Tagore (whose mystical philosophies had hitherto
seemed to me nebulous and unsatisfying).

It must not be supposed that I was ungrateful for my good luck.
For several days on end I could feel obliviously contented, and in
weaker moments there was an absurd hope that the War might be
over before next autumn. Rambling among woods and meadows,
I could 'take sweet counsel' with the country-side; sitting on a
grassy bank and lifting my face to the sun, I could feel an intensity
of thankfulness such as I'd never known before the War; listening
to the little brook that bubbled out of a copse and across a rushy
field, I could discard my personal relationship with the military
machine and its ant-like armies. On my way home I would pass
old Mr. Jukes leaning on his garden gate, or an ancient labourer
mending gaps in a hedge. I would stop to gaze at the loveliness of
apple-blossom when the sun came out after a shower. And the
protective hospitality of Nutwood Manor was almost bewildering
when compared with an average twenty-four hours in a front-line
trench.

All this was well enough; but there was a limit to my season of
sauntering; the future was a main road where I must fall into step
and do something to earn my 'pay and allowances'. Lady Asterisk
liked to have serious helpful little talks with her officers, and one
evening she encouraged me to discuss my immediate horizon. I
spoke somewhat emotionally, with self-indulgence in making a
fine effect rather than an impartial resolve to face facts. I
suggested that I'd been trying to make up my mind about taking
a job in England, admitting my longing for life and setting against
it the idea of sacrifice and disregard of death. I said that most of
my friends were assuring me that there was no necessity for me to
go out for the third time. While I talked I saw myself as a noble

suffering character whose death in action would be deeply deplored. I saw myself as an afflicted traveller who had entered Lady Asterisk's gates to sit by the fire and rest his weary limbs. I did not complain about the War; it would have been bad form to be bitter about it at Nutwood Manor; my own 'personal problem' was what I was concerned with . . .

We were alone in the library. She listened to me, her silver hair and handsome face bent slightly forward above a piece of fine embroidery. Outwardly emotionless, she symbolized the patrician privileges for whose preservation I had chucked bombs at Germans and carelessly offered myself as a target for a sniper. When I had blurted out my opinion that life was preferable to the Roll of Honour she put aside her reticence like a rich cloak. 'But death is nothing,' she said. 'Life, after all, is only the beginning. And those who are killed in the War – they help us from up there. They are helping us to win.' I couldn't answer that; this 'other world', of which she was so certain, was something I had forgotten about since I was wounded. Expecting no answer, she went on with a sort of inflexible sympathy (almost 'as if my number was already up', as I would have expressed it), 'It isn't as though you were heir to a great name. No; I can't see any definite reason for your keeping out of danger. But, of course, you can only decide a thing like that for yourself.'

I went up to the Clematis Room feeling caddishly estranged and cynical; wondering whether the Germans 'up there' were doing anything definite to impede the offensive operations of the Allied Powers. But Lady Asterisk wasn't hard-hearted. She only wanted me 'to do the right thing' . . . I began to wish that I could talk candidly to someone. There was too much well-behaved acquiescence at Nutwood Manor; and whatever the other officers there thought about the War, they kept it to themselves; they had done their bit for the time being and were conventional and correct, as if the eye of their Colonel was upon them.

Social experience at Nutwood was varied by an occasional visitor. One evening I sat next to the new arrival, a fashionable young woman whose husband (as I afterwards ascertained) was campaigning in the Cameroons. Her manner implied that she was ready to take me into her confidence, intellectually; but my responses were cumbersome and uneasy, for her conversation struck me as containing a good deal of trumped-up intensity. A fine pair of pearls dangled from her ears, and her dark blue eyes goggled emptily while she informed me that she was taking lessons in Italian. She was 'dying to read Dante', and had already started the Canto about Paolo and Francesca; adored D'Annunzio, too, and had been reading *his* Paolo and Francesca (in French). 'Life is so wonderful – so great – and yet we waste it all in this dreadful War!' she exclaimed. Rather incongruously, she then regaled me with some typical gossip from high quarters in the Army. Lunching at the Ritz recently, she had talked to Colonel Repington, who had told her – I really forget what, but it was excessively significant, politically, and showed that there was no need for people to worry about Allenby's failure to advance very far at Arras. Unsusceptible to her outward attractions, I came to the conclusion that she wasn't the stamp of woman for whom I was willing to make the supreme sacrifice.

Lord Asterisk had returned that evening from London, where he'd attended a dinner at the House of Lords. The dinner had been in honour of General Smuts (for whom I must parenthetically testify my admiration). This name made me think of Joe Dottrell, who was fond of relating how, in the Boer War, he had been with a raiding party which had nocturnally surprised and almost captured the Headquarters of General Smuts. I wondered whether the anecdote would interest Lord Asterisk; but (the ladies having left the table) he was embarking on his customary after-dinner oratory, while the young officer guests sipped their port and coffee and occasionally put in a respectful remark. The old fellow was getting very feeble, I thought, as I watched the wreckage of his fine and benevolent face. He sat with his chin on his chest; his brow and nose were still firm and authoritative. Sometimes his voice became weak and querulous, but he appeared to enjoy rolling out his deliberate parliamentary periods. Talking about the War, he surprised me by asserting the futility of waiting for a definite military decision. Although he had been a Colonial Governor, he was 'profoundly convinced of the uselessness of some of our Colonies', which, he said, might just as well be handed over to the Germans. He turned to the most articulate officer at the table. 'I declare to you, my dear fellow' (voice sinking to a mumble), 'I declare to you' (louder), 'have you any predominating awareness' (pause) 'of – *Sierra Leone?*'

As for Belgium, he invoked the evidence of history to support him in his assertion that its 'redemption' by the Allies was merely a manifestation of patriotic obliquity. The inhabitants of Belgium would be just as happy as a German Subject-State. To the vast majority of them their national autonomy meant nothing. While I was trying to remember the exact meaning of the word autonomy, he ended the discussion by remarking, 'But I'm only an old dotard!' and we pretended to laugh, naturally, as if it were quite a good joke. Then he reverted to a favourite subject of his, viz., the ineffectiveness of ecclesiastical administrative bodies. 'Oh what worlds of dreary (mumble) are hidden by the hats of our episcopal dignitaries! I declare to you, my dear fellow, that it is my profound conviction that the preponderance of mankind is entirely – yes, most grievously indifferent to the deliberations of that well-intentioned but obtuse body of men, the Ecclesiastical Commissioners!' Slightly sententious, perhaps; but no one could doubt that he was a dear old chap who had done his level best to leave the world in better order than he'd found it.

There were times when I felt perversely indignant at the 'cushiness' of my convalescent existence. These reactions were mostly caused by the few letters which came to me from the front. One of Joe Dottrell's hastily pencilled notes could make me unreasonably hostile to the cheerful voices of croquet players and inarticulately unfriendly to the elegant student of Italian when she was putting her pearl necklace out in the sun, 'because pearls do adore the sun so!'

It wasn't easy to feel animosity against the pleasant-mannered

neighbours who dropped in to tea. Nibbling cucumber sandwiches, they conceded full military honours to any officer who
had been wounded. They discussed gardening and joked about
domestic difficulties; they talked about war-work and public
affairs; but they appeared to be refusing to recognize the realities
which were implied by a letter from an indomitable quartermaster
in France. 'The Battalion has been hard at it again and had a
rough time, but as usual kept their end up well – much to the joy
of the Staff, who have been round here to-day like flies round a
jam-pot, congratulating the Colonel and all others concerned. I
am sorry to say that the Padre got killed . . . He was up with the
lads in the very front and got sniped in the stomach and died
immediately. I haven't much room for his crowd as a rule, but he
was the finest parson I've ever known, absolutely indifferent to
danger. Young Brock (bombing officer – he said he knew you at
Clitherland) was engaging the Boche single-handed when he was
badly hit in the arm, side, and leg. They amputated his left leg, but
he was too far gone and we buried him to-day. Two other officers
killed and three wounded. Poor Sergeant Blaxton was killed. All
the best get knocked over. . . . The boys are now trying to get to
Amiens to do a bit of courting.' Morosely I regarded the Clematis
Room. What earthly use was it, ordering boxes of kippers to be
sent to people who were all getting done in, while everyone at
home humbugged about with polite platitudes? . . . Birdie
Mansfield wrote from Yorkshire; he had been invalided out of
the Army. 'I'm fed to the teeth with wandering around in mufti
and getting black looks from people who pass remarks to the
effect that it's about time I joined up. Meanwhile I exist on my
provisional pension (3s a day). A few days' touring round these
munition areas would give you food for thought. The average
conversation is about the high cost of beer and the ability to evade
military service by bluffing the Tribunals.'

I looked at another letter. It was from my servant (to whom I'd
sent a photograph of myself and a small gramophone). 'Thank
you very much for the photo, which is like life itself, and the men
in the Company say it is just like him. The gramophone is much

enjoyed by all. I hope you will pardon my neglect in not packing the ground-sheet with your kit.' What could one do about it? Nothing short of stopping the War could alter the inadequacy of kippers and gramophones or sustain my sense of unity with those to whom I sent them.

On the day before I departed from Nutwood Manor I received another letter from Dottrell. It contained bad news about the Second Battalion. Viewed broadmindedly, the attack had been quite a commonplace fragment of the War. It had been a hopeless failure, and with a single exception all officers in action had become casualties. None of the bodies had been brought in. The First and Second Battalions had been quite near one another, and Dottrell had seen Ormand a day or two before the show. 'He looked pretty depressed, though outwardly as jolly as ever.' Dunning had been the first to leave our trench; had shouted 'Cheerio' and been killed at once. Dottrell thanked me for the box of kippers . . .

Lady Asterisk happened to be in the room when I opened the letter. With a sense of self-pitying indignation I blurted out my unpleasant information. Her tired eyes showed that the shock had brought the War close to her, but while I was adding a few details her face became self-defensively serene. 'But they are safe and happy now,' she said. I did not doubt her sincerity, and perhaps they *were* happy now. All the same, I was incapable of accepting the deaths of Ormand and Dunning and the others in that spirit. I wasn't a theosophist. Nevertheless I left Nutwood with gratitude for the kindness I had received there. I had now four weeks in which to formulate my plans for the future.

# PART TEN
# INDEPENDENT ACTION

## I

At daybreak on June 7th the British began the Battle of Messines by exploding nineteen full-sized mines. For me the day was made memorable by the fact that I lunched with the editor of the *Unconservative Weekly* at his club. By the time I entered that imposing edifice our troops had advanced more than two miles on a ten-mile front and a great many Germans had been blown sky-high. To-morrow this news would pervade clubland on a wave of optimism and elderly men would glow with satisfaction.

In the meantime prospects on the Russian Front were none too bright since the Revolution; but a politician called Kerensky ('Waiter, bring me a large glass of light port') appeared to be doing his best for his country and one could only hope that the Russian Army would – humph – stick to its guns and remember its obligations to the Allies and their War Aims.

My luncheon with Mr. Markington was the result of a letter impulsively written from Nutwood Manor. The letter contained a brief outline of my War service and a suggestion that he ought to publish something outspoken so as to let people at home know what the War was really like. I offered to provide such details as I knew from personal experience. The style of my letter was stilted, except for a postscript: 'I'm fed up with all the hanky-panky in the daily papers.' His reply was reticent but friendly, and I went to his club feeling that I was a mouthpiece for the troops in the trenches. However, when the opportunity for altruistic eloquence arrived, I discovered, with relief, that none was expected of me. The editor took most of my horrifying information on trust, and I was quite

content to listen to his own acrimonious comments on contemporary affairs. Markington was a sallow spectacled man with
earnest uncompromising eyes and a stretched sort of mouth
which looked as if it had ceased to find human follies funny. The
panorama of public affairs had always offered him copious
occasions for dissent; the Boer War had been bad enough, but this
one had provided almost too much provocation for his embitterment. In spite of all this he wasn't an alarming man to have lunch
with; relaxing into ordinary humanity, he could enjoy broad
humour, and our conversation took an unexpected turn when he
encouraged me to tell him a few army anecdotes which might be
censored if I were to print them. I felt quite fond of Markington
when he threw himself back into his chair in a paroxysm of
amusement. Most of his talk, however, dealt with more serious
subjects, and he made me feel that the world was in an even worse
condition than my simple mind had suspected. When I questioned
him about the probable duration of the War he shrugged his
shoulders. The most likely conclusion that he could foresee was a
gradual disintegration and collapse of all the armies. After the
War, he said, conditions in all countries would be appalling, and
Europe would take fifty years to recover. With regard to what I
suggested in my letter, he explained that if he were to print
veracious accounts of infantry experience his paper would be
suppressed as prejudicial to recruiting. The censorship officials
were always watching for a plausible excuse for banning it, and
they had already prohibited its foreign circulation. 'The soldiers
are not allowed to express their point of view. In war-time the
word patriotism means suppression of truth,' he remarked, eyeing
a small chunk of Stilton cheese on his plate as if it were incapable
of agreeing with any but ultra-Conservative opinions. 'Quite a
number of middle-aged members of this club have been to the
front,' he continued. 'After a dinner at G.H.Q. and a motor drive
in the direction of the trenches, they can talk and write in support
of the War with complete confidence in themselves. Five years ago
they were probably saying that modern civilization had made a
European War unthinkable. But their principles are purchasable.

Once they've been invited to visit G.H.Q. they never look back. Their own self-importance is all that matters to them. And any lie is a good lie as long as it stimulates unreasoning hatred of the enemy.'

He listened with gloomy satisfaction to my rather vague remarks about incompetent Staff work. I told him that our Second Battalion had been almost wiped out ten days ago because the Divisional General had ordered an impossible attack on a local objective. The phrase 'local objective' sounded good, and made me feel that I knew a hell of a lot about it . . .

On our way to the smoking-room we passed a blandly Victorian bust of Richard Cobden, which caused Markington to regret that the man himself wasn't above ground to give the present Government a bit of his mind. Ignorant about Cobden's career, I gazed fixedly at his marble whiskers, nodded gravely, and inwardly resolved to look up a few facts about him. 'If Cobden were alive now,' said Markington, 'the *Morning Post* would be anathematizing him as a white-livered defeatist! You ought to read his speeches on International Arbitration – not a very popular subject in these days!'

I was comfortably impressed by my surroundings, for the club was the Mecca of the Liberal Party. From a corner of the smoking-room I observed various eminent-looking individuals who were sipping coffee and puffing cigars, and I felt that I was practically in the purlieus of public life. Markington pointed out a few Liberal politicians whose names I knew, and one conspicuous group included a couple of novelists whose reputations were so colossal that I could scarcely believe that I was treading the same carpet as they were. I gazed at them with gratitude; apart from their eminence, they had provided me with a great deal of enjoyment, and I would have liked to tell them so. For Markington, however, such celebrities were an everyday occurrence, and he was more interested in my own sensations while on active service. A single specimen of my eloquence will be enough. 'As a matter of fact I'm almost sure that the War doesn't seem nearly such a bloody rotten show when one's out there as it does when one's back in England. You see as soon as one gets across the Channel one sort of feels as if it's no good worrying any more – you know what I mean – like being part of the Machine again, with nothing to be done except take one's chance. After that one can't bother about anything except the Battalion one's with. Of course, there's a hell of a lot of physical discomfort to be put up with, and the unpleasant sights seem to get worse every year; but apart from being shelled and so on, I must say I've often felt extraordinarily happy even in the trenches. Out there it's just one thing after another, and one soon forgets the bad times; it's probably something to do with being in the open air so much and getting such a lot of exercise ... It's only when one gets away from it that one begins to realize how stupid and wasteful it all is. What I feel now is that if it's got to go on there ought to be a jolly sound reason for it, and I can't help thinking that the troops are being done in the eye by the people in control.' I qualified these temperate remarks by explaining that I was only telling him how it had affected me personally; I had been comparatively lucky, and could now see the War as it affected infantry soldiers who were having an infinitely worse time than I'd ever had – particularly the privates.

When I inquired whether any peace negotiations were being attempted, Markington said that England had been asked by the new Russian Government, in April, to state definitely her War Aims and to publish the secret treaties made between England and Russia early in the War. We had refused to state our terms or publish the treaties. 'How damned rotten of us!' I exclaimed, and I am afraid that my instinctive reaction was a savage desire to hit (was it Mr. Lloyd George?) very hard on the nose. Markington was bitter against the military caste in all countries. He said that all the administrative departments in Whitehall were trying to get the better of one another, which resulted in muddle and waste on an unprecedented scale. He told me that I should find the same sort of things described in Tolstoy's *War and Peace*, adding that if once the common soldier became articulate the War couldn't last a month. Soon afterwards he sighed and said he must be getting back to the office; he had his article to write and the paper went to press that evening. When we parted in Pall Mall he told me to keep in touch with him and not worry about the War more than I could help, and I mumbled something about it having been frightfully interesting to meet him.

As I walked away from Markington my mind was clamorous with confused ideas and phrases. It seemed as if, until to-day, I had been viewing the War through the loop-hole of a trench parapet. Now I felt so much 'in the know' that I wanted to stop strangers in the street and ask them whether they realized that we ought to state our War Aims. People ought to be warned that there was (as I would have expressed it) some dirty work going on behind their backs. I remembered how sceptical old Lord Asterisk had been about the redemption of 'gallant little Belgium' by the Allies. And now Markington had gloomily informed me that our Aims were essentially acquisitive, what we were fighting for was the Mesopotamian Oil Wells. A jolly fine swindle it would have been for me, if I'd been killed in April for an Oil Well! But I soon forgot that I'd been unaware of the existence of the Oil Wells before Markington mentioned them, and I conveniently assimilated them as part of my evidential repertoire.

Readers of my pedestrian tale are perhaps wondering how soon I shall be returning to the temperate influence of Aunt Evelyn. In her latest letter she announced that a Zeppelin had dropped a bomb on an orchard about six miles away; there had also been an explosion at the Powder Mills at Dumbridge, but no one had been hurt. Nevertheless Butley was too buzzing and leisurely a background for my mercurial state of mind; so I stayed in London for another fortnight, and during that period my mental inquietude achieved some sort of climax. In fact I can safely say that my aggregated exasperations came to a head; and, naturally enough, the head was my own. The prime cause of this psychological thunderstorm was my talk with Markington, who was unaware of his ignitionary effect until I called on him in his editorial room on the Monday after our first meeting. Ostensibly I went to ask his advice; in reality, to release the indignant emotions which his editorial utterances had unwittingly brought to the surface of my consciousness. It was a case of direct inspiration; I had, so to speak, received the call, and the editor of the *Unconservative Weekly* seemed the most likely man to put me on the shortest road to martyrdom. It really felt very fine, and as long as I was alone my feelings carried me along on a torrent of prophetic phrases. But when I was inside Markington's office (he sitting with fingers pressed together and regarding me with alertly mournful curiosity) my internal eloquence dried up and I began abruptly. 'I say, I've been thinking it all over, and I've made up my mind that I ought to do something about it.' He pushed his spectacles up on to his forehead and leant back in his chair. 'You want to do something?' 'About the War, I mean. I just can't sit still and do nothing. You said the other day that you couldn't print anything really outspoken, but I don't see why I shouldn't make some sort of statement – about how we ought to publish our War Aims and all that and the troops not knowing what they're fighting about. It might do quite a lot of good, mightn't it?' He got up and went to the window. A secretarial typewriter tick-tacked in the next room. While he stood with his back to me I could see the tiny traffic creeping to and fro on Charing Cross Bridge and a barge going down the river in the sunshine. My heart was beating violently. I knew that I couldn't turn back now. Those few moments seemed to last a long time; I was conscious of the stream of life going on its way, happy and untroubled, while I had just blurted out something which alienated me from its acceptance of a fine day in the third June of the Great War. Returning to his chair, he said, 'I suppose you've realized what the results of such an action would be, as regards yourself?' I replied that I didn't care two damns what they did to me as long as I got the thing off my chest. He laughed, looking at me with a gleam of his essential kindness. 'As far as I am aware, you'd be the first soldier to take such a step, which would, of course, be welcomed by the extreme pacifists. Your service at the front would differentiate you from the conscientious objectors. But you must on no account make this gesture – a very fine one if you are really in earnest about it – unless you can carry it through effectively. Such an action would require to be carefully thought out, and for the present I advise you to be extremely cautious in what you say and do.' His words caused me an uncomfortable feeling that perhaps I was only making a fool of myself; but this was soon mitigated by a glowing sense of martyrdom. I saw myself 'attired with sudden brightness, like a man inspired', and while Markington continued his counsels of prudence my resolve strengthened toward its ultimate obstinacy. After further reflection he said that the best man for me to consult was Thornton Tyrrell. 'You know him by name, I suppose?' I was compelled to admit that I didn't. Markington handed me *Who's Who* and began to write a letter while I made myself acquainted with the details of Tyrrell's biographical abridgement, which indicated that he was a pretty tough proposition. To put it plainly he was an eminent mathematician, philosopher, and physicist. As a mathematician I've never advanced much beyond 'six from four you can't, six from fourteen leaves eight'; and I knew no more about the functions of a physicist than a cat in a kitchen. 'What sort of a man is he to meet?' I asked dubiously. Markington licked and closed the envelope of his rapidly written letter. 'Tyrrell is the most uncompromising character I know. An extraordinary brain, of course. But you needn't be alarmed by that; you'll find him perfectly easy to get on with. A talk with him ought to clarify your ideas. I've explained your position quite briefly. But, as I said before, I hope you won't be too impetuous.'

I put the letter in my pocket, thanked him warmly, and went soberly down the stairs and along the quiet side-street into the Strand. While I was debating whether I ought to buy and try to read one of Tyrrell's books before going to see him, I almost bumped into a beefy Major-General. It was lunch-time and he was turning in at the Savoy Hotel entrance. Rather grudgingly, I saluted. As I went on my way, I wondered what the War Office would say if it knew what I was up to.

## II

Early in the afternoon I left the letter at Tyrrell's address in Bloomsbury. He telegraphed that he could see me in the evening, and punctually at the appointed hour I returned to the quiet square. My memory is not equal to the effort of reconstructing my exact sensations, but it can safely be assumed that I felt excited, important, and rather nervous. I was shown into an austere-looking room where Tyrrell was sitting with a reading lamp at his elbow. My first impression was that he looked exactly like a philosopher. He was small, clean-shaven, with longish grey hair brushed neatly above a fine forehead. He had a long upper lip, a powerful ironic mouth, and large earnest eyes. I observed that the book which he put aside was called *The Conquest of Bread* by Kropotkin, and I wondered what on earth it could be about. He put me at my ease by lighting a large pipe, saying as he did so, 'Well, I gather from Markington's letter that you've been experiencing a change of heart about the War.' He asked for details of my career in the Army, and soon I was rambling on in my naturally inconsequent style. Tyrrell said very little, his object being to size me up. Having got my mind warmed up, I began to give him a few of my notions about the larger aspects of the War. But he interrupted my 'and after what Markington told me the other day, I must say', with, 'Never mind about what Markington told you. It amounts to this, doesn't it – that you have ceased to believe what you are told about the objects for which you supposed yourself to be fighting?' I replied that it did boil down to something like that, and it seemed to me a bloody shame, the troops getting killed all the time while people at home humbugged themselves into believing that everyone in the trenches enjoyed it. Tyrrell poured me out a second cup of tea and suggested that I should write out a short personal statement based on my conviction that the War was being unnecessarily prolonged by the refusal of the Allies to publish their war aims. When I had done this we could discuss the next step to be taken. 'Naturally I should help you in every way possible,' he said. 'I have always regarded all wars as acts of criminal folly, and my hatred of this one has often made life seem almost unendurable. But hatred makes one vital, and without it one loses energy. "Keep vital" is a more important axiom than "love your neighbour". This act of yours, if you stick to it, will probably land you in prison. Don't let that discourage you. You will be more alive in prison than you would be in the trenches.' Mistaking this last remark for a joke, I laughed, rather half-heartedly. 'No; I mean that seriously,' he said. 'By thinking independently and acting fearlessly on your moral convictions you are serving the world better than you would do by marching with the unthinking majority who are suffering and dying at the front because they believe what they have been told to believe. Now that you have lost your faith in what you enlisted for, I am certain that you should go on and let the consequences take care of themselves. Of course your action would be welcomed by people like myself who are violently opposed to the War. We should print and circulate as many copies of your statement as possible . . . But I hadn't intended to speak as definitely as this. You must decide by your own feeling and not by what anyone else says.' I promised to send him my statement when it was written and walked home with my head full of exalted and disorderly thoughts. I had taken a strong liking for Tyrrell, who probably smiled rather grimly while he was reading a few more pages of Kropotkin's *Conquest of Bread* before going upstairs to his philosophic slumbers.

Although Tyrrell had told me that my statement needn't be more than 200 words long, it took me several days to formulate. At first I felt that I had so much to say that I didn't know where to begin. But after several verbose failures it seemed as though the essence of my manifesto could be stated in a single sentence: 'I say this War ought to stop.' During the struggle to put my unfusilierish opinions into some sort of shape, my confidence often diminished. But there was no relaxation of my inmost resolve, since I was in the throes of a species of conversation which made the prospect of persecution stimulating and almost enjoyable. No; my loss of confidence was in the same category as my diffidence when first confronted by a Vickers Machine-gun and its Instructor. While he reeled off the names of its numerous component parts, I used to despair of ever being able to remember them or understand their workings. 'And unless I know all about the Vickers Gun I'll never get sent out to the front,' I used to think. Now, sitting late at night in an expensive but dismal bedroom in Jermyn Street, I internally exclaimed, 'I'll never be able to write out a decent statement and the whole blasted protest will be a washout! Tyrrell thinks I'm quite brainy, but when he reads this stuff he'll realize what a dud I am.'

What could I do if Tyrrell decided to discourage my candidature for a court martial? Chuck up the whole idea and go out again and get myself killed as quick as possible? 'Yes,' I thought, working myself up into a tantrum, 'I'd get killed just to show them all I don't care a damn.' (I didn't stop to specify the identity of 'them all'; such details could be dispensed with when one had lost one's temper with the Great War.) But common sense warned me that getting sent back was a slow business, and getting killed on purpose an irrelevant gesture for a platoon commander. One couldn't choose one's own conditions out in France . . . Tyrrell had talked about 'serving the world by thinking independently'. I must hang on to that idea and remember the men for whom I believed myself to be interceding. I tried to think internationally; the poor old Boches must be hating it just as much as we did; but I couldn't propel my sympathy as far as the Balkan States, Turks, Italians, and all the rest of them; and somehow or other the French were just the French and too busy fighting and selling things to the troops to need my intervention. So I got back to thinking about 'all the good chaps who'd been killed with the First and Second Battalions since I left them' . . . Ormand, dying miserably out in a shell-hole . . . I remembered his exact tone of voice when saying that if his children ever asked what he did in the Great War, his answer would be, 'No bullet ever went quick enough to catch me'; and how he used to sing 'Rock of ages cleft for me, let me hide myself in thee,' when we were being badly shelled. I thought of the typical Flintshire Fusilier at his best, and the vast anonymity of courage and cheerfulness which he represented as he sat in a front-line trench cleaning his mess-tin. How could one connect him with the gross profiteer whom I'd overheard in a railway carriage remarking to an equally repulsive companion that if the War lasted another eighteen months he'd be able to retire from business? . . . How could I co-ordinate such diversion of human behaviour, or believe that heroism was its own reward? Something must be put on paper, however, and I re-scrutinized the rough notes I'd been making: *Fighting men are victims of conspiracy among (a) politicians; (b) military caste; (c) people who are making money out of the War.* Under this I had scribbled, *Also personal effort to dissociate myself from intolerant prejudice and conventional complacence of those willing to watch sacrifices of others while they sit safely at home.* This was followed by an indignant afterthought. *I believe that by taking this action I am helping to destroy the system of deception, etc., which prevents people from facing the truth and demanding some guarantee that the torture of humanity shall not be prolonged unnecessarily through the arrogance and incompetence of . . .* Here it broke off, and I wondered how many c's there were in 'unnecessarily'. *I am not a conscientious objector. I am a solider who believes he is acting on behalf of soldiers.* How inflated and unconvincing it all looked! If I wasn't careful I should be yelling like some crank on a barrel in Hyde Park. Well, there was nothing for it but to begin all over again. I couldn't ask Tyrrell to give me a few hints. He'd insisted that I must be independent-minded, and had since written to remind me that I must decide my course of action for myself and not be prompted by anything he'd said to me.

Sitting there with my elbows on the table I stared at the dingy red wallpaper in an unseeing effort at mental concentration. If I stared hard enough and straight enough, it seemed, I should see through the wall. Truth would be revealed, and my brain would become articulate. *I am making this statement as an act of wilful defiance of military authority because I believe that the War is being deliberately prolonged by those who have the power to end it.* That would be all right as a kick-off, anyhow. So I continued my superhuman cogitations. Around me was London with its darkened streets; and far away was the War, going on with wave on wave of gunfire, devouring its victims, and unable to blunder forward either to Paris or the Rhine. The air-raids were becoming serious, too. Looking out of the window at the searchlights, I thought how ridiculous it would be if a bomb dropped on me while I was writing out my statement.

## III

Exactly a week after our first conversation I showed the statement to Tyrrell. He was satisfied with it as a whole and helped me to clarify a few minor crudities of expression. Nothing now remained but to wait until my leave had expired and then hurl the explosive document at the Commanding Officer at Clither-land (an event which I didn't permit myself to contemplate clearly). For the present the poor man only knew that I'd applied for an instructorship with a Cadet Battalion at Cambridge. He wrote that he would be sorry to lose me and congratulated me on what he was generous enough to describe as my splendid work at the front. In the meantime Tyrrell was considering the question of obtaining publicity for my protest. He introduced me to some of his colleagues on the 'Stop the War Committee' and the 'No Conscription Fellowship'. Among them was an intellectual conscientious objector (lately released after a successful hunger-strike). Also a genial veteran Socialist (recognizable by his red tie and soft grey hat) who grasped my hand with rugged good wishes. One and all, they welcomed me to the Anti-War Move-ment, but I couldn't quite believe that I had been assimilated. The reason for this feeling was their antipathy to everyone in a uniform. I was still wearing mine, and somehow I was unable to dislike being a Flintshire Fusilier. This little psychological dilemma now seems almost too delicate to be divulged. In their eyes, I suppose, there was no credit attached to the fact of having been at the front; but for me it had been a supremely important experience. I am obliged to admit that if these anti-war enthusiasts hadn't happened to be likeable I might have secretly despised them. Any man who had been on active service had an unfair advantage over those who hadn't. And the man who had really endured the War at its worst was everlastingly differentiated from everyone except his fellow soldiers.

Tyrrell (a great man and to be thought of as 'in a class by himself') took me up to Hampstead one hot afternoon to interview a member of Parliament who was 'interested in my case'. Walking alongside of the philosopher I felt as if we were a pair of conspirators. His austere scientific intellect was far beyond my reach, but he helped me by his sense of humour, which he had contrived, rather grimly, to retain, in spite of the exasperating spectacle of European civilization trying to commit suicide. The M.P. promised to raise the question of my statement in the House of Commons as soon as I had sent it to the Colonel at Clitherland, so I began to feel that I was getting on grandly. But except for the few occasions when I saw Tyrrell, I was existing in a world of my own (in which I tried to keep my courage up to protest-pitch). From the visible world I sought evidence which could aggravate my quarrel with acquiescent patriotism. Evidences of civilian callousness and complacency were plentiful, for the thriftless licence of war-time behaviour was an unavoidable spectacle, especially in the Savoy Hotel Grill Room which I visited more than once in my anxiety to reassure myself of the existence of bloated profiteers and uniformed jacks in office. Watching the guzzlers in the Savoy (and conveniently overlooking the fact that some of them were officers on leave) I nourished my righteous hatred of them, anathematizing their appetites with the intolerance of youth which made me unable to realize that comfort-loving people are obliged to avoid self-knowledge – especially when there is a war on. But I still believe that in 1917 the idle, empty-headed, and frivolous ingredients of Society were having a tolerably good time, while the officious were being made self-important by nicely graded degrees of uniformed or un-uniformed war-emergency authority. For middle-aged persons who faced the War bleakly, life had become unbearable unless they persuaded themselves that the slaughter was worth while. Tyrrell was comprehensively severe on everyone except inflexible pacifists. He said that the people who tried to resolve the discords of the War into what they called 'a higher harmony' were merely enabling themselves to contemplate the massacre of the young men with an easy conscience. 'By Jingo, I suppose you're right!' I exclaimed, wishing that I were able to express my ideas with such comprehensive clarity.

Supervising a platoon of Cadet Officers at Cambridge would have been a snug alternative to 'general service abroad' (provided that I could have bluffed the cadets into believing that I knew something about soldiering). I was going there to be interviewed by the Colonel and clinch my illusory appointment; but I was only doing this because I considered it needful for what I called 'strengthening my position'. I hadn't looked ahead much, but when I did so it was with an eye to safeguarding myself against 'what people would say'.

When I remarked to Tyrrell that 'people couldn't say I did it so as to avoid going back to France if I had been given a job in England', he pulled me up short.

'What people say doesn't matter. Your own belief in what you are doing is the only thing that counts.' Knowing that he was right, I felt abashed; but I couldn't help regretting that my second decoration had failed to materialize. It did not occur to me that a bar to one's Military Cross was a somewhat inadequate accretion to one's qualifications for affirming that the War was being deliberately prolonged by those who had the power to end it. Except for a bullet-hole in my second best tunic, all that I'd got for my little adventure in April consisted of a gilt-edged card on which the Divisional General had inscribed his congratulations and thanks. This document was locally referred to as 'one of Whincop's Bread Cards', and since it couldn't be sewn on to my tunic I did my best to feel that it was better than nothing.

Anyhow, on a glaring hot morning I started to catch a train to Cambridge. I was intending to stay a night there for it would be nice to have a quiet look round and perhaps go up to Grantchester in a canoe. Admittedly, next month was bound to be ghastly; but it was no good worrying about that . . . Had I enough money on me? Probably not; so I decided to stop and change a cheque at my bank in Old Broad Street. Changing a cheque was always a comforting performance. 'Queer thing, having private means,' I thought. 'They just hand you out the money as if it was a present from the Bank Manager.' It was funny, too, to think that I was still drawing my Army pay. But it was the wrong moment for such humdrum cogitations, for when my taxi stopped in that narrow thoroughfare, Old Broad Street, the people on the pavement were standing still, staring up at the hot white sky. Loud bangings had begun in the near neighbourhood, and it was obvious that an air-raid was in full swing. This event could not be ignored; but I needed money and wished to catch my train, so I decided to disregard it. The crashings continued, and while I was handing my cheque to the cashier a crowd of women clerks came wildly down a winding stairway with vociferations of not unnatural alarm. Despite this commotion the cashier handed me five one-pound notes with the stoical politeness of a man who had made up his mind to go down with the ship. Probably he felt as I did – more indignant than afraid; there seemed no sense in the idea of being blown to bits in one's own bank. I emerged from the building with an air of soldierly unconcern; my taxi-driver, like the cashier, was commendably calm, although another stupendous crash sounded as though very near Old Broad Street (as indeed it was). 'I suppose we may as well go on to the station,' I remarked, adding, 'it seems a bit steep that one can't even cash a cheque in comfort!' The man grinned and drove on. It was impossible to deny that the War was being brought home to me. At Liverpool Street there had occurred what, under normal conditions, would be described as an appalling catastrophe. Bombs had been dropped on the station and one of them had hit the front carriage of the noon express to Cambridge. Horrified travellers were hurrying away. The hands of the clock indicated 11.50; but railway time had been interrupted; for once in its career, the imperative clock was a passive spectator. While I stood wondering what to do, a luggage trolley was trundled past me; on it lay an elderly man, shabbily dressed, and apparently dead. The sight of blood caused me to feel quite queer. This sort of danger seemed to demand a quality of courage dissimilar to front-line fortitude. In a trench one was acclimatized to the notion of being exterminated and there was a sense of organized retaliation. But here one was helpless; an invisible enemy sent destruction spinning down from a fine weather sky; poor old men bought a railway ticket and were trundled away again dead on a barrow; wounded women lay about in the station groaning. And one's train didn't start . . . Nobody could say for certain when it *would* start, a phlegmatic porter informed me; so I migrated to St. Pancras and made the journey to Cambridge in a train which halted good-naturedly at every station. Gazing at sleepy green landscapes, I found difficulty in connecting them (by the railway line) with the air-raid which (I was afterwards told) had played hell with Paternoster Avenue. 'It wouldn't be such a bad life,' I thought, 'if one were a station-master on a branch line in Bedfordshire.' There was something attractive, too, in the idea of being a commercial traveller, creeping about the country and doing business in drowsy market towns and snug cathedral cities. If only I could wake up and find myself living among the parsons and squires of Trollope's Barsetshire, jogging easily from Christmas to Christmas, and hunting three days a week with the Duke of Omnium's Hounds . . .

The elms were so leafy and the lanes invited me to such rural remoteness that every time the train slowed up I longed to get out and start on an indefinite walking tour – away into the delusive Sabbath of summer – away from air-raids and inexorable moral responsibilities and the ever-increasing output of munitions.

But here was Cambridge, looking contented enough in the afternoon sunshine, as though the Long Vacation were on. The Colleges appeared to have forgotten their copious contributions to the Roll of Honour. The streets were empty, for the Cadets were out on their afternoon parades – probbly learning how to take compass-bearings, or pretending to shoot at an enemy who was supposedly advancing from a wood nine hundred yards away. I knew all about that type of training. 'Half-right; haystack; three fingers left of haystack; copse; nine hundred; AT THE COPSE, ten rounds rapid, FIRE!' There wasn't going to be any musketry-exercise instructing for me, however. I was only 'going through the motions' of applying for a job with the Cadet Battalion. The orderly room was on the ground floor of a college. In happier times it had been a library (the books were still there) and the Colonel had been a History Don with a keen interest in the Territorials. Playing the part of respectful young applicant for instructorship in the Arts of War, I found myself doing it so convincingly that the existence of my 'statement' became, for the moment, an improbability. 'Have you any specialist knowledge?' inquired the Colonel. I told him that I'd been Battalion Intelligence Officer for a time (suppressing the fact that I'd voluntarily relinquished that status after three days of inability to supply the necessary eye-wash reports). 'Ah, that's excellent. We find the majority of men very weak in map-reading,' he replied, adding, 'our main object, of course, is to instil first-rate morale. It isn't always easy to impress on these new army men what we mean by the tradition of the pre-War regimental officer . . . Well, I'm sure you'll do very good work. You'll be joining us in two or three weeks, I think? Good-bye till then.' He shook my hand rather as if I'd won a History Scholarship, and I walked out of the college feeling that it was a poor sort of joke on him. But my absence as an instructor was all to the good as far as he was concerned, and I was inclined to think that I was better at saying the War ought to stop than at teaching cadets how to carry it on. Sitting in King's Chapel I tried to recover my conviction of the nobility of my enterprise and to believe that the pen which wrote my statement had 'dropped from an angel's wing'. I also reminded myself that Cambridge had dismissed Tyrrell from his lectureship because he disbelieved in the War. 'Intolerant old blighters!' I inwardly exclaimed. 'One can't possibly side with people like that. All they care about is keeping up with the other college in the casualty lists.' Thus refortified, I went down to the river and hired a canoe.

## IV

Back at Butley, I had fully a fortnight in which to take life easily before tackling 'wilful defiance of military authority'. I was, of course, compelled to lead a double life, and the longer it lasted the less I liked it. I am unable to say for certain how far I was successful in making Aunt Evelyn believe that my mind was free from anxiety. But I know that it wasn't easy to sustain the evangelistic individuality which I'd worked myself up to in London. Outwardly those last days of June progressed with nostalgic serenity. I say nostalgic, because in my weaker moods I longed for the peace of mind which could have allowed me to enjoy having tea out in the garden on fine afternoons. But it was no use trying to dope my disquiet with Trollope's novels or any of my favourite books. The purgatory I'd let myself in for always came between me and the pages; there was no escape for me now. Walking restlessly about the garden at night I was oppressed by the midsummer silence and found no comfort in the twinkling lights along the Weald. At one end of the garden three poplars tapered against the stars; they seemed like sentries guarding a prisoner. Across the uncut orchard grass, Aunt Evelyn's white beehives glimmered in the moonlight like bones. The hives were empty, for the bees had been wiped out by the Isle of Wight disease. But it was no good moping about the garden. I ought to be indoors improving my mind, I thought, for I had returned to Butley resolved to read for dear life – circumstances having made it imperative that I should accumulate as much solid information as I could. But sedulous study only served to open up the limitless prairies of my ignorance, and my attention was apt to wander away from what I was reading. If I could have been candid with myself I should have confessed that a fortnight was inadequate for the completion of my education as an intellectual pacifist. Reading the last few numbers of Markington's weekly was all very well as a tonic for disagreeing with organized public opinion, but even if I learnt a whole article off by heart I should only have built a little hut on the edge of the prairie. 'I must have all the arguments at my fingers' ends,' I had thought when I left London. The arguments, perhaps, were epitomized in Tyrrell's volume of lectures ('given to me by the author', as I had written on the flyleaf). Nevertheless those lectures on political philosophy, though clear and vigorous in style, were too advanced for my elementary requirements. They were, I read on the first page, 'inspired by a view of the springs of action which has been suggested by the War. And all of them are informed by the hope of seeing such political institutions established in Europe as shall make men averse from war – a hope which I firmly believe to be realizable, though not without a great and fundamental reconstruction of economic and social life.' From the first I realized that this was a book whose meanings could only be mastered by dint of copious underlining. *What integrates an individual life is a consistent creative purpose or unconscious direction.* I underlined that, and then looked up 'integrate' in the dictionary. Of course, it meant the opposite to *disintegrate*, which was what the optimists of the press said would soon happen to the Central Powers of Europe. Soon afterwards I came to the conclusion that much time would be saved if I underlined the sentences which *didn't* need underlining. The truth was that there were too many ideas in the book. I was forced to admit that nothing in Tyrrell's lectures could be used for backing up my point of view when I was being interrogated by the Colonel at Clitherland . . . The thought of Clitherland was unspeakably painful. I had a vague hope that I could get myself arrested without going there. It would be so much easier if I could get my case dealt with by strangers.

Aunt Evelyn did her best to brighten the part of my double life which included her, but at meal times I was often morose and monosyllabic. Humanly speaking, it would have been a relief to confide in her. As a practical proposition, however, it was impossible. I coudn't allow my protest to become a domestic controversy, and it was obviously kinder to keep my aunt in the dark about it until she received the inevitable shock. I remember one particular evening when the suspense was growing acute. At dinner Aunt Evelyn, in her efforts to create cheerful conversation, began by asking me to tell her more about Nutwood Manor. It was, she surmised, a very well-arranged house, and the garden must have been almost perfection. 'Did azaleas grow well there?' Undeterred by my gloomily affirmative answer, she urged me to supply further information about the Asterisks and their friends. She had always heard that old Lord Asterisk was such a fine man, and must have had a most interesting life, although, now she came to think of it, he'd been a bit of a Radical and had supported Gladstone's Home Rule Bill. She then interrupted herself by exclaiming: 'Naughty, naughty, naughty!' But this rebuke was aimed at one of the cats who was sharpening his claws on the leather seat of one of the Chippendale chairs. Having thrown my napkin at the cat, I admitted that Lord Asterisk was a dear old chap, though unlikely to live much longer. Aunt Evelyn expressed concern about his infirmity, supplementing it with her perennial 'Don't eat so fast, dear; you're simply bolting it down. You'll ruin your digestion.' She pressed me to have some more chicken, thereby causing me to refuse, although I should have had some more if she'd kept quiet about it. She now tried the topic of my job at Cambridge. What sort of rooms should I live in? Perhaps I should have rooms in one of the colleges which would be very nice for me – much nicer than those horrid huts at Clitherland. Grumpily I agreed that Cambridge was preferable to Clitherland. A bowl of strawberries, perhaps the best ones we'd had that summer, created a diversion. Aunt Evelyn regretted the unavoidable absence of cream, which enabled me to assure her that some of the blighters I'd seen in London restaurants weren't denying themselves much; and I went off into a diatribe against profiteers and officials who gorged at the Ritz and the Savoy while the poorer classes stood for hours in queues outside food shops.

Much relieved at being able to agree with me about something, Aunt Evelyn almost overdid her indignant ejaculations, adding that it was a positive scandal – the disgracefully immoral way most of the young women were behaving while doing war-work. This animation subsided when we got up from the table. In the drawing-room she lit the fire 'as the night felt a bit chilly and a fire would make the room more cheerful'. Probably she was hoping to spend a cosy evening with me; but I made a bad beginning, for the lid fell off the coffee-pot and cracked one of the little blue and yellow cups, and when Aunt Evelyn suggested that we might play one of our old games of cribbage or halma, I said I didn't feel like that sort of thing. Somehow I couldn't get myself to behave affectionately toward her, and she had irritated me by making uncomplimentary remarks about Markington's paper, a copy of which was lying on the table. (She said it was written by people who were mad with their own self-importance and she couldn't understand how I could read such a paper.) Picking it up I went grumpily upstairs and spent the next ten minutes trying to teach Popsy the parrot how to say 'Stop the War'. But he only put his head down to be scratched, and afterwards obliged me with his well-known rendering of Aunt Evelyn calling the cat. On her way up to bed she came in (with a glass of milk) and told me that she was sure I wasn't feeling well. Wouldn't it be a good thing if I were to go to the seaside for a few days' golf? But this suggestion only provided me with further evidence that it was no earthly use expecting her to share my views about the War. Games of golf indeed! I glowered at the glass of milk and had half a mind to throw it out of the window. Afterwards I decided that I might as well drink it, and did so.

Late on a sultry afternoon, when returning from a mutinous-minded walk, I stopped to sit in Butley Churchyard. From Butley Hill one looks across a narrow winding valley, and that afternoon the woods and orchards suddenly made me feel almost as fond of them as I'd been when I was in France. While I was resting on a flat-topped old tombstone I recovered something approximate to peace of mind. Gazing at my immediate surroundings, I felt that 'joining the great majority' was a homely – almost a comforting – idea. Here death differed from extinction in modern warfare. I ascertained from the nearest headstone that *Thomas Welfare, of this Parish, had died on October 20th*, 1843, *aged* 72. *'Respected by all who knew him.'* Also Sarah, wife of the above. *'Not changed but glorified.'* Such facts were resignedly acceptable. They were in harmony with the simple annals of this quiet corner of Kent. One could speculate serenely upon the homespun mortality of such worthies, whose lives had 'taken place' with the orderly and inevitable progression of a Sunday service. They made the past seem pleasantly prosy in contrast with the monstrous emergencies of to-day. And Butley Church, with its big-buttressed square tower, was protectively permanent. One could visualize it there for the last 599 years, measuring out the unambitious local chronology with its bells, while English history unrolled itself along the horizon with coronations and rebellions and stubbornly disputed charters and covenants. Beyond all that, the 'foreign parts' of the world widened incredibility toward regions reported by travellers' tales. And so outward to the windy universe of astronomers and theologians. Looking up at the battlemented tower, I improvised a clear picture of some morning – was it in the seventeenth century? Men in steeple-crowned hats were surveying a rudimentary-looking landscape with anxious faces, for trouble was afoot and there was talk of the King's enemies. But the insurgence always passed by. It had never been more than a rumour for Butley, whether it was Richard of Gloucester or Charles the First who happened to be losing his kingdom. It was difficult to imagine that Butley had contributed many soldiers for the Civil Wars, or even for Marlborough and Wellington, or that the village carpenter of those days had lost both his sons in Flanders. Between the church door and the lych gate the plump yews were catching the rays of evening. Along that path the coffined generations had paced with sober church-going faces. There they had stood in circumspect groups to exchange local gossip and discuss the uncertainly reported events of the outside world. They were a long way off now, I thought – their names undecipherable on tilted headstones or humbly oblivioned beneath green mounds. For the few who could afford a permanent memorial, their remoteness from posterity became less as the names became more legible, until one arrived at those who had watched the old timbered inn by the churchyard being burnt to the ground – was it forty years ago? I remembered Captain Huxtable telling me that the catastrophe was supposed to have been started by the flaring up of a pot of glue which a journeyman joiner had left on a fire while he went to the tap-room for a mug of beer. The burning of the old Bull Inn had been quite a big event for the neighbourhood; but it wouldn't be thought much of in these days; and my mind reverted to the demolished churches along the Western Front, and the sunlit inferno of the first day of the Somme Battle. There wouldn't be much Gray's Elegy atmosphere if Butley were in the Fourth Army area!

Gazing across at the old rifle butts – now a grassy indentation on the hillside half a mile away – I remembered the volunteers whose torchlight march-past had made such a glowing impression on my nursery-window mind, in the good old days before the Boer War. Twenty years ago there had been an almost national significance in the fact of a few Butley men doing target practice on summer evenings.

Meanwhile my meditations had dispelled my heavy-heartedness, and as I went home I recovered something of the exultation I'd felt when first forming my resolution. I knew that no right-minded Butley man could take it upon himself to affirm that a European war was being needlessly prolonged by those who had the power to end it. They would tap their foreheads and sympathetically assume that I'd seen more of the fighting than was good for me. But I felt the desire to suffer, and once again I had a glimpse of something beyond and above my present troubles – as though I could, by cutting myself off from my previous existence, gain some new spiritual freedom and live as I had never lived before.

'They can all go to blazes,' I thought, as I went home by the field path. 'I know I'm right and I'm going to do it,' was the rhythm of my mental monologue. If all that senseless slaughter had got to go on, it shouldn't be through any fault of mine. 'It won't be any fault of mine,' I muttered.

A shaggy farm horse was sitting in the corner of a field with his front legs tucked under him; munching placidly, he watched me climb the stile into the old green lane with its high thorn hedges.

## V

Sunshade in one hand and prayer-book in the other, Aunt Evelyn was just starting for morning service at Butley. 'I really must ask Captain Huxtable to tea before you go away. He looked a little hurt when he inquired after you last Sunday,' she remarked. So it was settled that she would ask him to tea when they came out of church. 'I really can't think why you haven't been over to see him,' she added, dropping her gloves and then deciding not to wear them after all, for the weather was hot and since she had given up the pony cart she always walked to church. She put up her pink sunshade and I walked with her to the front gate. The two cats accompanied us, and were even willing to follow her up the road, though they'd been warned over and over again that the road was dangerous. Aunt Evelyn was still inclined to regard all motorists as reckless and obnoxious intruders. The roads were barely safe for human beings, let alone cats, she exclaimed as she hurried away. The church bells could also be heard across the fields, and very peaceful they sounded.

July was now a week old. I had overstayed my leave several days and was waiting until I heard from the Depot. My mental condition was a mixture of procrastination and suspense, but the suspense was beginning to get the upper hand of the procrastination, since it was just possible that the Adjutant at Clitherland was assuming that I'd gone straight to Cambridge.

Next morning the conundrum was solved by a telegram, *Report how situated*. There was nothing for it but to obey the terse instructions, so I composed a letter (brief, courteous, and regretful) to the Colonel, enclosing a typewritten copy of my statement, apologizing for the trouble I was causing him, and promising to return as soon as I heard from him. I also sent a copy to Dottrell, with a letter in which I hoped that my action would not be entirely disapproved of by the First Battalion. Who else was there, I wondered, feeling rather rattled and confused. There was Durley, of course, and Cromlech also – fancy my forgetting him! I could rely on Durley to be sensible and sympathetic; and David was in a convalescent hospital in the Isle of Wight, so there was no likelihood of his exerting himself with efforts to dissuade me. I didn't want anyone to begin interfering on my behalf. At least I hoped that I didn't; though there were weak moments later on when I wished they would. I read my statement through once more (though I could have recited it only too easily) in a desperate effort to calculate its effect on the Colonel. '*I am making this statement as an act of wilful defiance of military authority, because I believe that the War is being deliberately prolonged by those who have the power to end it. I am a soldier, convinced that I am acting on behalf of soldiers. I believe that this War, upon which I entered as a war of defence and liberation, has now become a war of aggression and conquest. I believe that the purposes for which I and my fellow soldiers entered upon this War should have been so clearly stated as to have made it impossible to change them, and that, had this been done, the objects which actuated us would now be attainable by negotiation. I have seen and endured the sufferings of the troops, and I can no longer be a party to prolong the sufferings for ends which I believe to be evil and unjust. I am not protesting against the conduct of the War, but against the political errors and insincerities for which the fighting men are being sacrificed. On behalf of those who are suffering now I make this protest against the deception which is being practised on them; also I believe that I may help to destroy the callous complacency with which the majority of those at home regard the continuance of agonies which they do not share, and which they have not sufficient imagination to realize.*' It certainly sounds a bit pompous, I thought, and God only knows what the Colonel will think of it.

Thus ended a most miserable morning's work. After lunch I walked down the hill to the pillar-box and posted my letters with a feeling of stupefied finality. I then realized that I had a headache and Captain Huxtable was coming to tea. Lying on my bed with the window curtains drawn, I compared the prospect of being in a prison cell with the prosy serenity of this buzzing summer afternoon. I could hear the cooing of the white pigeons and the soft clatter of their wings as they fluttered down to the little bird-bath on the lawn. My sense of the life-learned house and the garden enveloped me as though all the summers I had ever known were returning in a single thought. I had felt the same a year ago, but going back to the War next day hadn't been as bad as this.

Theoretically, to-day's tea-party would have made excellent material for a domestic day-dream when I was at the front. I was safely wounded after doing well enough to be congratulated by Captain Huxtable. The fact that the fighting men were still being sacrificed needn't affect the contentment of the tea-party. But everything was blighted by those letters which were reposing in the local pillar-box, and it was with some difficulty that I pulled myself together when I heard a vigorous ring of the front-door bell, followed by the firm tread of the Captain on the polished wood floor of the drawing-room, and the volubility of Aunt Evelyn's conversational opening alternating with the crisp and cheery baritone of her visitor. Captain Huxtable was an essentially cheerful character ('waggish' was Aunt Evelyn's favourite word for him) and that afternoon he was in his most jovial mood. He greeted me with a reference to Mahomet and the Mountain, though I felt more like a funeral than a mountain, and the little man himself looked by no means like Mahomet, for he was wearing brown corduroy breeches and a white linen jacket, and his face was red and jolly after the exertion of bicycling. His subsequent conversation was, for me, strongly flavoured with unconscious irony. Ever since I had joined the Flintshire Fusiliers our meetings always set his mind alight with memories of his 'old corps', as he called it; I made him, he said, feel half his age.

Naturally, he was enthusiastic about anything connected with the fine record of the Flintshires in this particular war, and when Aunt Evelyn said, 'Do show Captain Huxtable the card you got from your General,' he screwed his monocle into his eye and inspected the gilt-edged trophy with intense and deliberate satisfaction. I asked him to keep it as a souvenir of his having got me into the Regiment – (bitterly aware that I should soon be getting myself out of it pretty effectively!). After saying that I couldn't have given him anything which he'd value more highly, he suggested that I might do worse than adopt the Army as a permanent career (forgetting that I was nearly ten years too old for such an idea to be feasible). But no doubt I was glad to be going to the Depot for a few days, so as to have a good crack with some of my old comrades, and when I got to Cambridge I must make myself known to a promising young chap (a grandson of his cousin, Archdeacon Crocket) who was training with the Cadet Battalion. After a digression around this year's fruit crop, conversation turned to the Archbishop of Canterbury's message to the nation about Air Raid Reprisals. In Captain Huxtable's opinion the Church couldn't be too militant, and Aunt Evelyn thoroughly agreed with him. With forced facetiousness I described my own air-raid experience. 'The cashier in the bank was as cool as a cucumber,' I remarked. There were cucumber sandwiches on the table, but the implications of the word 'cashier' were stronger, since for me it was part of the price of martyrdom, while for the Captain it epitomized an outer darkness of dishonour. But the word went past him, innocent of its military meaning, and he referred to the increasing severity of the German air-raids as 'all that one can expect from that gang of ruffians'. But there it was, and we'd got to go through with it; nothing could be worse than a patched-up peace; and Aunt Evelyn 'could see no sign of a change of heart in the German nation'.

The Captain was delighted to see in to-day's *Times* that another of those cranky pacifist meetings had been broken up by some Colonial troops; and he added that he'd like to have the job of dealing with a 'Stop the War' meeting in Butley. To him a conscientious objector was the antithesis of an officer and a gentleman, and no other point of view would have been possible for him. The Army was the framework of his family tradition; his maternal grandfather had been a Scotch baronet with a distinguished military career in India – a fact which was piously embodied in the Memorial Tablet to his mother in Butley Church. As for his father – 'old Captain Huxtable' – (whom I could hazily remember, white-whiskered and formidable) he had been a regular roaring martinet of the gouty old school of retired officers, and his irascibilities were still legendary in our neighbourhood. He used to knock his coachman's hat off and stamp on it. 'The young Captain', as he was called in former days, had profited by these paroxysms, and where the parent would have bellowed 'God damn and blast it all' at his bailiff, the son permitted himself nothing more sulphurous than 'con-found', and would have thought twice before telling even the most red-hot Socialist to go to the devil.

Walking round the garden after tea – Aunt Evelyn drawing his attention to her delphiniums and he waggishly affirming their inferiority to his own – I wondered whether I had exaggerated the 'callous complacency' of those at home. What could elderly people do except try and make the best of their inability to sit in a trench and be bombarded? How could they be blamed for refusing to recognize their ignoble elements in the War except those which they attributed to our enemies?

Aunt Evelyn's delphinium spires were blue against the distant blue of the Weald and the shadows of the Irish yews were lengthening across the lawn . . . Out in France the convoys of wounded and gassed were being carried into the Field Hospitals, and up in the Line the slaughter went on because no one knew how to stop it. 'Men are beginning to ask for what they are fighting,' Dottrell had written in his last letter. Could I be blamed for being one of those at home who were also asking that question? Must the War go on in order that colonels might become brigadiers and brigadiers get Divisions, while contractors and manufacturers enriched themselves, and people in high places ate and drank well and bandied official information and organized entertainments for the wounded? Some such questions I may have asked myself, but I was unable to include Captain Huxtable and Aunt Evelyn in the indictment.

## VI

I had to wait until Thursday before a second Clitherland telegram put me out of my misery. Delivered early in the afternoon and containing only two words, *Report immediately*, it was obviously a telegram which did not need to be read twice. But the new variety of suspense which it created was an improvement on what I'd been enduring, because I could end it for certain by reporting at Clitherland within twenty-four hours. All considerations connected with my protest were now knocked on the head. It no longer mattered whether I was right or whether I was wrong, whether my action was public spirited or whether it was preposterous. My mind was insensible to everything but the abhorrent fact that I was in for an appalling show, with zero hour fixed for to-morrow when I arrived at the Depot.

In the meantime I must pack my bag and catch the five-something train to town. Automatically I began to pack in my usual vacillating but orderly manner; then I remembered that it would make no difference if I forgot all the things I needed most. By this time to-morrow I shall be under arrest, I thought, gloomily rejecting my automatic pistol, water bottle, and whistle, and rummaging in a drawer for some khaki socks and handkerchiefs. A glimpse of my rather distracted-looking face in the glass warned me that I must pull myself together by to-morrow. I must walk into the Orderly Room neat and self-possessed and normal. Anyhow the parlourmaid had given my tunic buttons and belt a good rub up, and now Aunt Evelyn was rapping on the door to say that tea was ready and the taxi would be here in half an hour. She took my abrupt departure quite as a matter of course, but it was only at the last moment that she remembered to give me the bundle of white pigeons' feathers which she had collected from the lawn, knowing how I always like some for pipe-cleaners. She also reminded me that I was forgetting to take my golf clubs; but I shouldn't get any time for golf, I said, plumping myself into the taxi, for there wasn't too much time to catch the train.

The five-something train from Baldock Wood was a slow affair; one had to change at Dumbridge and wait forty minutes. I remember this because I have seldom felt more dejected than I did when I walked out of Dumbridge Station and looked over the fence of the County Cricket Ground. The afternoon was desolately fine and the ground, with its pavilion and enclosures, looked blighted and forsaken. Here, in pre-eminently happier times, I had played in many a club match and had attentively watched the varying fortunes of the Kent Eleven; but now no one had even troubled to wind up the pavilion clock.

Back in the station I searched the bookstall for something to distract my thoughts. The result was a small red volume which is still in my possession. It is called *The Morals of Rousseau*, and contains, naturally enough, extracts from that celebrated author. Rousseau was new to me and I cannot claim that his morals were any help to me on that particular journey or during the ensuing days when I carried him about in my pocket. But while pacing the station platform I remembered a certain couplet, and I mention this couplet because, for the next ten days or so, I couldn't get it out of my head. There was no apparent relevancy in the quotation (which I afterwards found to be from Cowper). It merely persisted in saying:

> *I shall not ask Jean Jacques Rousseau*
> *If birds confabulate or no.*

London enveloped my loneliness. I spent what was presumably my last night of liberty in the bustling dreariness of one of those huge hotels where no one ever seems to be staying more than a single night. I had hoped for a talk with Tyrrell, but he was out of town. My situation was, I felt, far too serious for theatre going – in fact I regarded myself as already more or less under arrest; I was going to Clitherland under my own escort, so to speak. So it may be assumed that I spent that evening alone with J.J. Rousseau.

Next morning – but it will suffice if I say that next morning (although papers announced *Great Russian Success in Galicia*) I had no reason to feel any happier than I had done the night before. I am beginning to feel that a man can write too much about his own feelings, even when 'what he felt like' is the nucleus of his narrative. Nevertheless I cannot avoid a short summary of my sensations while on the way to Liverpool. I began by shutting my eyes and refusing to think at all; but this effort didn't last long. I tried looking out of the window; but the sunlit fields only made me long to be a munching cow. I remembered my first journey to Clitherland in May 1915. I had been nervous then – diffident about my ability to learn how to be an officer. Getting out to the Front had been an ambition rather than an obligation, and I had aimed at nothing more than to become a passably efficient second-lieutenant. Pleasantly conscious of my new uniform and anxious to do it credit, I had felt (as most of us did in those days) as if I were beginning a fresh and untarnished existence. Probably I had travelled by this very train. My instant mental transition from that moment to this (all intervening experience excluded) caused me a sort of vertigo. Alone in that first-class compartment, I shut my eyes and asked myself out loud what this thing was which I was doing; and my mutinous act suddenly seemed outrageous and incredible. For a few minutes I completely lost my nerve. But the express train was carrying me along; I couldn't stop it, any more than I could cancel my statement. And when the train pulled up at Liverpool I was merely a harassed automaton whose movements were being manipulated by a typewritten manifesto. To put it plainly, I felt 'like nothing on earth' while I was being bumped and jolted out to the Camp in a ramshackle taxi.

It was about three o'clock when the taxi passed the gates of Brotherhood's Explosive Works and drew up outside the officers' quarters at Clitherland. The sky was cloudless and the lines of huts had an air of ominous inactivity. Nobody seemed to be about, for at that hour the troops were out on the training field. A bored sentry was the only witness to my arrival, and for him there was nothing remarkable in a second-lieutenant telling a taxi-man to dump his luggage down outside the officers' mess. For me, however, there now seemed something almost surreptitious about my return. It was as though I'd come skulking back to see how much damage had been caused by that egregious projectile, my protest. But the camp was exactly as it would have been if I'd returned as a dutiful young officer. It was I who was desolate and distracted; and it would have been no consolation to me if I could have realized that, in my mind, the familiar scene was having a momentary and ghastly existence which would never be repeated.

For a few moments I stared wildly at the huts, conscious (though my brain was blank) that there was some sort of climax in my stupefied recognition of reality. One final wrench, and all my obedient associations with Clitherland would be shattered.

It is probable that I put my tie straight and adjusted my belt-buckle to its central position between the tunic buttons. There was only one thing to be done after that. I walked into the Orderly Room, halted in front of a table, and saluted dizzily.

After the glaring sunlight, the room seemed almost dark. When I raised my eyes it was not the Colonel who was sitting at the table, but Major Macartney. At another table, ostensibly busy with Army forms and papers, was the Deputy-Assistant-Adjutant (a good friend of mine who had lost a leg at Gallipoli). I stood there, incapable of expectation. Then, to my astonishment, the Major rose, leant across the table, and shook hands with me.

'How are you, Sherston? I'm glad to see you back again.' His deep voice had its usual kindly tone, but his manner betrayed acute embarrassment. No one could have been less glad to see me back again than he was. But he at once picked up his cap and asked me to come with him to his room, which was only a few steps away. Silently we entered the hut, our feet clumping along the boards of the passage. Speechless and respectful, I accepted the chair which he offered me. There we were, in the comfortless little room which had been his local habitation for the past twenty-seven months. There we were; and the unfortunate Major hadn't a ghost of an idea what to say.

He was a man of great delicacy of feeling. I have seldom known as fine a gentleman. For him the interview must have been as agonizing as it was for me. I wanted to make things easier for him; but what could I say? And what could he do for me, except, perhaps, offer me a cigar? He did so. I can honestly say that I have never refused a cigar with anything like so much regret. To have accepted it would have been a sign of surrender. It would have meant that the Major and myself could have puffed our cigars and debated – with all requisite seriousness, of course – the best way of extricating me from my dilemma. How blissful that would have been! For my indiscretion might positively have been 'laughed off' (as a temporary aberration brought on, perhaps, by an overdose of solitude after coming out of hospital). No such agreeable solution being possible, the Major began by explaining that the Colonel was away on leave. 'He is deeply concerned about you, and fully prepared to overlook the' – here he hesitated – 'the paper which you sent him. He has asked me to urge you most earnestly to – er – dismiss the whole matter from your mind.' Nothing could have been more earnest than the way he looked at me when he stopped speaking. I replied that I was deeply grateful but I couldn't change my mind. In the ensuing silence I felt that I was committing a breach, not so much of discipline as of decorum.

The disappointed Major made a renewed effort. 'But, Sherston, isn't it *possible* for you to reconsider your – er – ultimatum?' This was the first time I'd heard it called an ultimatum, and the locution epitomized the Major's inability to find words to fit the situation. I embarked on a floundering explanation of my mental attitude with regard to the War; but I couldn't make it sound convincing, and at the back of my mind was a misgiving that I must seem to him rather crazy. To be telling the acting-Colonel of my regimental Training Depot that I had come to the conclusion that England ought to make peace with Germany – was this altogether in focus with rightmindedness? No; it was useless to expect him to take me seriously as an ultimatumist. So I gazed fixedly at the floor and said, 'Hadn't you better have me put under arrest at once?' – thereby causing poor Major Macartney additional discomfort. My remark recoiled on me, almost as if I'd uttered something unmentionable. 'I'd rather die than do such a thing!' he exclaimed. He was a reticent man, and that was his way of expressing his feeling about those whom he had watched, month after month, going out to the trenches, as he would have gone himself had he been a younger man.

At this point it was obviously his duty to remonstrate with me severely and to assert his authority. But what fulminations could be effective against one whose only object was to be put under arrest? . . . 'As long as he doesn't really think I'm dotty!' I thought. But he showed no symptom of that, as far as I was aware; and he was a man who made one feel that he trusted one's integrity, however much he might disagree with one's opinions.

No solution having been arrived at for the present, he now suggested – in confidential tones which somehow implied sympathetic understanding of my predicament – that I should go to the Exchange Hotel in Liverpool and there await further instructions. I gladly acquiesced, and we emerged from the hut a little less funereally than we had entered it. My taxi-man was still waiting, for in my bewilderment I had forgotten to pay him. Once more the Major grasped my hand, and if I did not thank him for his kindness it was because my gratitude was too great. So I trundled unexpectedly back to Liverpool; and although, in all likelihood, my troubles were only just starting, an immense load had been lifted from my mind. At the Exchange Hotel (which was quiet and rarely frequented by the Clitherland officers) I thoroughly enjoyed my tea, for I'd eaten nothing since breakfast. After that I lit my pipe and thought how nice it was not to be under arrest. I had got over the worst part of the show, and now there was nothing to be done except stick to my statement and wait for the M.P. to read it out in the House of Commons.

## VII

For the next three days I hung about the Exchange Hotel in a state
of mind which need not be described. I saw no one I knew except
a couple of Clitherland subalterns who happened to be dining in
the Hotel. They cheerily enquired when I was coming out to the
Camp. Evidently they were inquisitive about me, without
suspecting anything extraordinary, so I inferred that Orderly
Room had been keeping my strange behaviour secret. On Tuesday
my one-legged friend, the Deputy-Assistant-Adjutant, came to see
me. We managed to avoid mentioning everything connected with
my 'present situation', and he regaled me with the gossip of the
Camp as though nothing were wrong. But when he was departing
he handed me an official document which instructed me to
proceed to Crewe next day for a Special Medical Board. A railway
warrant was enclosed with it.

Here was a chance of turning aside from the road to court-
martialdom, and it would be inaccurate were I to say that I never
gave the question two thoughts. Roughly speaking, two thoughts
were exactly what I did give to it. One thought urged that I might
just as well chuck the whole business and admit that my gesture
had been futile. The other one reminded me that this was an
inevitable conjuncture in my progress, and that such temptations
must be resisted inflexibly. Not that I ever admitted the possibility
of my accepting the invitation to Crewe; but I did become
conscious that acceptance would be much pleasanter than refusal.
Submission being impossible, I called in pride and obstinacy to
aid me, throttled my warm feelings toward my well-wishers at
Clitherland Camp and burnt my boats by tearing up both railway
warrant and Medical Board instructions.

On Wednesday I tried to feel glad that I was cutting the Medical
Board, and applied my mind to Palgrave's *Golden Treasury of
Songs and Lyrics*. I was learning by heart as many poems as
possible, my idea being that they would be a help to me in prison,
where, I imagined, no books would be allowed. I suppose I ought
to try and get used to giving up tobacco, I thought, but I went on

smoking just the same (the alternative being to smoke as many pipes as I could while I'd got the chance).

On Thursday morning I received an encouraging letter from the M.P. who urged me to keep my spirits up and was hoping to raise the question of my statement in the House next week. Early in the afternoon the Colonel called to see me. He found me learning Keats's *Ode to a Nightingale*. 'I cannot see what flowers are at my feet, Nor what soft . . .' What soft was it, I wondered, re-opening the book. But here was the Colonel, apparently unincensed, shaking my hand, and sitting down opposite me, though already looking fussed and perplexed. He wasn't a lively-minded man at the best of times, and he didn't pretend to understand the motives which had actuated me. But with patient common-sense arguments, he did his best to persuade me to stop wanting to stop the War. Fortified by the M.P.'s letter in my pocket, I managed to remain respectfully obdurate, while expressing my real regret for the trouble I was causing him. What appeared to worry him most was the fact that I'd cut the Medical Board. 'Do you realize, Sherston, that it had been specially arranged for you and that an R.A.M.C. Colonel came all the way from London for it?' he ejaculated ruefully, wiping the perspiration from his forehead. The poor man, whose existence was dominated by documentary instructions from 'higher quarters', had probably been blamed for my non-appearance; and to disregard such an order was, to one with his habit of mind, like a reversal of the order of nature. As the interview dragged itself along, I began to feel quite optimistic about the progress I was making. The Colonel's stuttering arguments in support of 'crushing Prussian militarism' were those of a middle-aged civilian; and as the overworked superintendent of a reinforcement manufactory, he had never had time to ask himself why North Welshmen were being shipped across to France to be gassed, machine-gunned, and high explosived by Germans. It was absolutely impossible, he asserted, for the War to end until it ended – well, until it ended as it ought to end. Did I think it right that so many men should have been sacrificed for no purpose? 'And surely it stands to reason, Sherston, that you must be wrong when you set your own opinion against the practically unanimous feeling of the whole British Empire.' There was no answer I could make to that, so I remained silent, and waited for the British Empire idea to blow over. In conclusion he said, 'Well, I've done all I can for you. I told Mersey Defences that you missed your Board through a misunderstanding of the instructions, but I'm afraid the affair will soon go beyond my control. I beg you to try and reconsider your refusal by to-morrow, and to let us know at once if you do.'

He looked at me almost irately, and departed without another word. When his bulky figure had vanished I felt that my isolation was perceptibly increasing. All I needed to do was to wait until the affair had got beyond his control. I wished I could have a talk with Tyrrell. But even he wasn't infallible, for in all our discussions about my plan of campaign he had never foreseen that my senior officers would treat me with this kindly tolerance which was so difficult to endure.

During the next two days my mind groped and worried around the same purgatorial limbo so incessantly that the whole business began to seem unreal and distorted. Sometimes the wording of my thoughts became incoherent and even nonsensical. At other times I saw everything with the haggard clarity of insomnia.

So on Saturday afternoon I decided that I really must go and get some fresh air, and I took the electric train to Formby. How much longer would this ghastly show go on, I wondered, as the train pulled up at Clitherland Station. All I wanted now was that the thing should be taken out of my own control, as well as the Colonel's. I didn't care how they treated me as long as I wasn't forced to argue about it any more. At Formby I avoided the Golf Course (remembering, with a gleam of woeful humour, how Aunt Evelyn had urged me to bring my 'golf sticks', as she called them). Wandering along the sand dunes I felt outlawed, bitter, and baited. I wanted something to smash and trample on, and in a paroxysm of exasperation I performed the time-honoured gesture of shaking my clenched fists at the sky. Feeling no better for that, I ripped the M.C. ribbon off my tunic and threw it into the mouth of the Mersey. Weighted with significance though this action was, it would have felt more conclusive had the ribbon been heavier. As it was, the poor little thing fell weakly on to the water and floated away as though aware of its own futility. One of my point-to-point cups would have served my purpose more satisfyingly, and they'd meant much the same to me as my Military Cross.

Watching a big boat which was steaming along the horizon, I realized that protesting against the prolongation of the War was about as much use as shouting at the people on board that ship.

Next morning I was sitting in the hotel smoking-room in a state of stubborn apathy. I had got just about to the end of my tether. Since it was Sunday and my eighth day in Liverpool I might have chosen this moment for reviewing the past week, though I had nothing to congratulate myself on except the fact that I'd survived seven days without hauling down my flag. It is possible that I meditated some desperate counter-attack which might compel the authorities to treat me harshly, but I had no idea how to do it. 'Damn it all, I've half a mind to go to church,' I thought, although as far as I could see there was more real religion to be found in the *Golden Treasury* than in a church which only approved of military-aged men when they were in khaki. Sitting in a sacred edifice wouldn't help me, I decided. And then I was taken completely by surprise; for there was David Cromlech, knobby-faced and gawky as ever, advancing across the room. His arrival brought instantaneous relief, which I expressed by exclaiming: 'Thank God you've come!'

He sat down without saying anything. He, too, was pleased to see me, but retained that air of anxious concern with which his eyes had first encountered mine. As usual he looked as if he'd slept in his uniform. Something had snapped inside me and I felt rather silly and hysterical. 'David, you've got an enormous black smudge on your forehead,' I remarked. Obediently he moistened his handkerchief with his tongue and proceeded to rub the smudge off, tentatively following my instructions as to its whereabouts.

During this operation his face was vacant and childish, suggesting an earlier time when his nurse had performed a similar service for him. 'How on earth did you manage to roll up from the Isle of Wight like this?' I inquired. He smiled in a knowing way. Already he was beginning to look less as though he were visiting an invalid; but I'd been so much locked up with my own thoughts lately that for the next few minutes I talked nineteen to the dozen, telling him what a hellish time I'd had, how terribly kind the depot officers had been to me, and so on. 'When I started this anti-war stunt I never dreamt it would be such a long job, getting myself run in for a court martial,' I concluded, laughing with somewhat hollow gaiety.

In the meantime David sat moody and silent, his face twitching nervously and his fingers twiddling one of his tunic buttons. 'Look here, George,' he said, abruptly, scrutinizing the button as though he'd never seen such a thing before, 'I've come to tell you that you've got to drop this anti-war business.' This was a new idea, for I wasn't yet beyond my sense of relief at seeing him. 'But I can't drop it,' I exclaimed. 'Don't you realize that I'm a man with a message? I thought you'd come to see me through the court martial as "prisoner's friend".' We then settled down to an earnest discussion about the 'political errors and insincerities for which the fighting men were being sacrificed'. He did most of the talking, while I disagreed defensively. But even if our conversation could be reported in full, I am afraid that the verdict of posterity would be against us. We agreed that the world had gone mad; but neither of us could see beyond his own experience, and we weren't life-learned enough to share the patient selfless stoicism through which men of maturer age were acquiring anonymous glory. Neither of us had the haziest idea of what the politicians were really up to (though it is possible that the politicians were only feeling their way and trusting in providence and the output of munitions to solve their problems). Nevertheless we argued as though the secret confabulations of Cabinet Ministers in various countries were as clear as daylight to us, and our assumption was that they were all wrong, while we, who had been in the trenches, were far-seeing and infallible. But when I said that the War ought to be stopped and it was my duty to do my little bit to stop it, David replied that the War was bound to go on till one side or the other collapsed, and the Pacifists were only meddling with what they didn't understand. 'At any rate Thornton Tyrrell's a jolly fine man and knows a bloody sight more about everything than you do,' I exclaimed. 'Tyrrell's only a doctrinaire,' replied David, 'though I grant you he's a courageous one.' Before I had time to ask what the hell he knew about doctrinaires, he continued, 'No one except people who've been in the real fighting have any right to interfere about the War; and even they can't get anything done about it. All they can do is to remain loyal to one another. And you know perfectly well that most of the conscientious objectors are nothing but skrimshankers.' I retorted that I knew nothing of the sort, and mentioned a young doctor who'd played Rugby Football for Scotland and was now in prison although he could have been doing hospital work if he'd wanted to. David then announced that he'd been doing a bit of wire-pulling on my behalf and that I should soon find that my Pacifist M.P. wouldn't do me as much good as I expected. This put my back up. David had no right to come butting in about my private affairs. 'If you've really been trying to persuade the authorities not to do anything nasty to me,' I remarked, 'that's about the hopefullest thing I've heard. Go on doing it and exercise your usual tact, and you'll get me two years' hard labour for certain, and with any luck they'll decide to shoot me as a sort of deserter.' He looked so aggrieved at this that I relented and suggested that we'd better have some lunch. But David was always an absent-minded eater, and on this occasion he prodded disapprovingly at his food and then bolted it down as if it were medicine.

A couple of hours later we were wandering aimlessly along the shore at Formby, and still jabbering for all we were worth. I refused to accept his well-meaning assertion that no one at the Front would understand my point of view and that they would only say that I'd got cold feet. 'And even if they do say that,' I argued, 'the main point is that by backing out of my statement I shall be betraying my real convictions and the people who are supporting me. Isn't that worse cowardice than being thought cold-footed by officers who refuse to think about anything except the gentlemanly traditions of the Regiment? I'm not doing it for fun, am I? Can't you understand that this is the most difficult thing I've ever done in my life? I'm not going to be talked out of it just when I'm forcing them to make a martyr of me.' 'They won't make a martyr of you,' he replied. 'How do you know that?' I asked. He said that the Colonel at Clitherland had told him to tell me that if I continued to refuse to be 'medically-boarded' they would shut me up in a lunatic asylum for the rest of the War. Nothing would induce them to court martial me. It had all been arranged with some big bug at the War Office in the last day or two. 'Why didn't you tell me before?' I asked. 'I kept it as a last resort because I was afraid it might upset you,' he replied, tracing a pattern on the sand with his stick. 'I wouldn't believe this from anyone but you. Will you swear on the Bible that you're telling the truth?' He swore on an imaginary Bible that nothing would induce them to court martial me and that I should be treated as insane. 'All right, then, I'll give way.' As soon as the words were out of my mouth I sat down on an old wooden breakwater.

So that was the end of my grand gesture. I ought to have known that the blighters would do me down somehow, I thought, scowling heavily at the sea. It was appropriate that I should behave in a glumly dignified manner, but already I was aware that an enormous load had been lifted from my mind. In the train David was discreetly silent. He got out at Clitherland. 'Then I'll tell Orderly Room they can fix up a Board for you to-morrow,' he remarked, unable to conceal his elation. 'You can tell them anything you bloody well please!' I answered ungratefully. But as soon as I was alone I sat back and closed my eyes with a sense of exquisite relief. I was unaware that David had, probably, saved me from being sent to prison by telling me a very successful lie. No doubt I should have done the same for him if our positions had been reversed.

It was obvious that the less I said to the Medical Board the better. All the necessary explanations of my mental condition were contributed by David, who had been detailed to give evidence on my behalf. He had a long interview with the doctors while I waited in an ante-room. Listening to their muffled mumblings, I felt several years younger than I'd done two days before. I was now an irresponsible person again, absolved from any obligation to intervene in world affairs. In fact the present performance seemed rather ludicrous, and when David emerged, solemn and concerned, to usher me in, I entered the 'Bird Room' assuring myself that I should not ask Jean Jacques Rousseau if birds confabulated or no. The Medical Board consisted of a Colonel, a Major, and a Captain. The Captain was a civilian in uniform, and a professional neurologist. The others were elderly Regular Army doctors, and I am inclined to think that their acquaintance with Army Forms exceeded their knowledge of neurology.

While David fidgeted about the ante-room I was replying respectfully to the stereotyped questions of the Colonel, who seemed slightly suspicious and much mystified by my attitude to the War. Was it on religious grounds that I objected to fighting, he inquired. 'No, sir; not particularly,' I replied. 'Fighting on religious grounds' sounded like some sort of a joke about the Crusades. 'Do you consider yourself qualified to decide when the War should stop?' was his next question. Realizing that he was only trying to make me talk rubbish, I evaded him by admitting that I hadn't thought about my qualifications, which wasn't true. 'But your friend tells us that you were very good at bombing. Don't you still dislike the Germans?' I have forgotten how I answered that conundrum. It didn't matter what I said to him, as long as I behaved politely. While the interrogations continued, I felt that sooner or later I simply must repeat that couplet out loud – 'if birds confabulate or no'. Probably it would be the best thing I could do, for it would prove conclusively and comfortably that I was a harmless lunatic. Once I caught the neurologist's eye, which signalled sympathetic understanding, I thought. Anyhow, the Colonel (having demonstrated his senior rank by asking me an adequate number of questions) willingly allowed the Captain to suggest that they couldn't do better than send me to Slateford Hospital. So it was decided that I was suffering from shell-shock. The Colonel then remarked to the Major that he supposed there was nothing more to be done now. I repeated the couplet under my breath. 'Did you say anything?' asked the Colonel, frowning slightly. I disclaimed having said anything and was permitted to rejoin David.

When we were walking back to my hotel I overheard myself whistling cheerfully, and commented on the fact. 'Honestly, David, I don't believe I've whistled for about six weeks!' I gazed up at the blue sky, grateful because, at that moment, it seemed as though I had finished with the War.

Next morning I went to Edinburgh. David, who had been detailed to act as my escort, missed the train and arrived at Slateford War Hospital several hours later than I did. And with my arrival at Slateford War Hospital this volume can conveniently be concluded.